Nurture That Is Christian

*Developmental Perspectives
on Christian Education*

A
BRIDGEPOINT
BOOK

BridgePoint,
the academic
imprint of
Victor Books, is
your connection
for the best in
serious reading
that integrates
the passion of
the heart with
the scholarship
of the mind.

Nurture That Is Christian

Developmental Perspectives on Christian Education

edited by

James C. Wilhoit & John M. Dettoni

A
BRIDGEPOINT
BOOK

Acknowledgments

We are both grateful to the able work of three assistants: Amber Hudson, Christine Yu, and Bill Kerschbaum. These Wheaton College students, working at various points in the process, carefully checked references and documentation for each article.

Scripture taken from the *Holy Bible, New International Version*®. Copyright © 1973, 1978, 1984 by International Bible Society. Used by permission of Zondervan Publishing House. All rights reserved.

Editors: Jane Vogel/Robert N. Hosack
Designer: Andrea Boven

Library of Congress Cataloging-in-Publication Data

Nurture that is Christian / James C. Wilhoit & John M. Dettoni, editors.
    p.   cm.
Includes bibliographical references.
ISBN: 1-56476-268-8
1. Christian education — Psychology. 2. Developmental psychology.
I. Wilhoit, Jim. II. Dettoni, John.
BV1464.N87   1995
268'.01'9 — dc20   95-36641
                                            CIP

BridgePoint is the academic imprint of Victor Books.

© 1995 by Victor Books/SP Publications, Inc.
All rights reserved. Printed in the United States of America.

1 2 3 4 5 6 7 8 9 10 Printing/Year 99 98 97 96 95

Contents

90323

Foreword
Ted Ward

As a field of academic study, Christian education has gradually come to accept developmentalism as its theoretical base. As the intellectual quality of literature and research in the field has increased, the importance of a sound theoretical base has increased. Judging by the surging mainstream of academic literature in the field of Christian education, the choice has settled on one variation or another of developmentalism, largely because of the compatibility and consistency between its presuppositions and the essential foundations for the field in Christian theology.

Biblical studies and Christian theology set criteria for the conceptual and methodological shape of the field. Christian educators can pick and choose among the contending educational theories, but in order to be responsible to both the academic rubrics and the theological tenets, the choice of theory must be in harmony with the rudiments of Christian values and ideation. For example, *operant conditioning,* with its roots in behaviorism and mechanistic philosophy, can hardly be considered an acceptable base of educational theory for nontherapeutic education of normal learners. Its presuppositions about the nature of humankind and its legitimization of imposed will cannot be reconciled with the scriptural base of Christianity. Developmentalism passes this test rather well, especially if Christian definitions and supernatural components of the person are recognized alongside the inherent naturalism from which developmentalism springs.

UNDERSTANDING LEARNING: THREE MAJOR OPTIONS

Presuppositions about the nature of learning exist explicitly or implicitly in every plan for teaching. Understanding of the theory of education brings these more clearly to the educator's attention. How one views learning has much to do with curricular designs and the choices of educational procedures. Although the literature on teaching and learning suggests many detailed variations, three different basic views of learning lie at the bottom of things:

Learning as Acquisition of Knowledge
Among the most ancient and revered of all views of learning is the belief that to learn is to gain knowledge. The simplicity and evident truth of that little idea have driven the educational processes of the world for centuries. The image of the human mind is that of a storage compartment. The function is that of acquiring, sorting, labeling, and storing for precise and prompt retrieval; forgetting results from leaks in the storage system or from poor labeling systems and misfiling. The task of teaching, then, is to organize and present information in a logical and memorable form.

Learning as Acquisition of Responses
A nineteenth-century contribution of the emerging field of psychology and its stepchild, professional education, was the notion that what really defines learning is the process of connecting certain responses to certain stimuli. When presented with a given task, the mind responds in a given way; this connection is accepted as evidence of learning. The task of teaching becomes a matter of conditioning learners to respond in specific "correct" ways to specific tasks or questions.

Learning as Construction of Knowledge

In recent years the study of human perception and the function of the human brain has led in the direction of the expanded understanding of learning. The learner is now seen in terms of discovering, building, and reorganizing. The learning process is not just a matter of input and filing or mechanical connections; it is better described as a matter of the learner's building of unique images of truth (more precisely, building one's grasp of truth), as a matter of construction and discovery. The learner always looks at the outer world through a filter system: worldview, cognitive orientation, and affective coloration. The learner makes meaning of new interactions and new experiences, weaving new material and old into insightful reorganizations. The perceptual grasp of anything new is always constructed of bits and pieces of previous experience and understandings. Thus teaching is helping learners process the meanings of new experiences and deepened awareness within deliberate nurture of the connections between old and new. Such teaching facilitates the learner's own constructive capabilities of seeking insightful meanings.

Beyond the basic choice among these three views of learning, the educator must adopt or form a view of how learning relates to the whole of human life and experience. Questions that must be answered range widely: Why do some people learn more than others or more easily than others? Why are motivations so different among people? What are talents, and why do they seem unique and individualistic? Granting that there are individual differences of great importance, is human commonality of similar or greater importance? Is learning more an individual function or a social function?

Beyond these questions, which Christian educators share with other educators, are unique questions that arise out of concern for spiritual development: In what ways does spiritual development depend on a base of knowledge? Does spiritual development depend in any way on mental development? In what ways does spiritual development differ from or go beyond other manifestations of the human development process? What is the function and task of education in the matter of spiritual development? What roles can educators, parents, and other members of the Christian community play which will contribute to spiritual development?

CRITERIA FOR THEORY IN CHRISTIAN EDUCATION

Theory provides guidance for the practical processes of human endeavor. In education, theory provides a basis for judgment about what is appropriate and inappropriate for learning. The Bible is not a book of scientific theory. Its purposes are quite different: The Bible is God's major means of revealing the being and the activities of God as creator, sustainer, and redeemer of the universe. It provides the authoritative means for human beings to know God. But it presumes that God's created universe will be studied in its own terms and that the findings from evidences in any and all particulars in that universe will be understood in light of the creational presuppositions and godly values revealed in the Bible.

Thus, for the Christian, sound theory is especially important. In the discovering and organizing of truth about the nature of the human being as learner, for example, theory is the expression of the structure, the principles, the patterns, and the nature of things. Indeed, this use of *nature* expresses the gift of the Creator that enables human beings to name, understand, and communicate with one another about the way things are — a gift of the I AM (Ex. 3:14).

The Christian criteria for theory demand that all inferences about the nature of things be drawn with careful respect for the natural evidences. Further, the interpretative function within theory-building must be thoughtfully informed by data about God's purposes and values as revealed in the Bible. The failure to develop theory that is faithful to revealed evidence and consistent with the attributes, motives, and intentions of God is ultimately idolatrous. Whether in the derivation of theory from research evidences or in the application of theory to educational practice, the Christian must recognize that he or she walks on holy ground. These matters of research and intellectual inquiry are as intimately related to truth as the very fingerprints of God in His wondrous creation. The neglect of truth is an insult to God.

Rudiments for Educational Theory That Is Christian

Education, for the Christian, is grounded in God's mandates to parents and to the church, the community of faith. The task of facilitating spiritual development is more apparent in biblical mandates than is the general task of helping people learn. Thus the Christian educator must start from a somewhat different vantage point in the selection and refinement of theory. Theory for Christian education must not simply explain and inform cognitive learning processes; it must be comprehensive enough to deal with the unity of personhood, ranging from physical attributes to the spiritual uniqueness of humankind.

Reflections of the Creation

Development is part of the creation story. As God, by His Word, brought the universe into being, He set into place the processes by which this creation would bear testimony to its Creator. Thus God put in place elaborate processes of continuous change, maturing, and re-creating. Life itself is represented by birth, development, and death, all in interlocking cycles.

Only the underlying structure, the patterns of development, and the cycles remain constant; all else changes. The creation is not static; it is dynamic. The earth, the astronomical universe, and the atomic elements which underlie it all are in constant process of change. Nothing stands still.

Life is best described in motion. Change and movement are fundamental to the God-given nature of life itself. Not all change is godly change, of course, but the evidence in both the *natural revelation* (God's universe, comprehended scientifically) and the *special revelation* (God's Word, comprehended theologically through faith) points toward God's intentions as the source and explanation of the unfolding, developmental, stage-by-stage nature of things. The very pattern of the Bible shows God revealing Himself in ever more specific and intimate details. The picture in Scripture is in stages, a virtual developmental model of conceptual communication. Thus Christians can recognize this same activity of God in the sequence, stages, and patterns of human development. God's internal consistency can rightly be celebrated in the developmental view of human life.

Every developing person is capable of communion with God because of the created characteristic of God's own "breath" within, signifying a spiritual essence within the flesh and blood. In addition, in all the other attributes of humanness, God's hand is revealed in the unfolding developmental processes. Thus, human development can be interpreted as a reflection of the image of God (Gen. 1:27).

Emphasis on Spiritual Development
For the Christian educator the calling is *to facilitate spiritual development* and whatever other matters of learning and development are supportive of that end.

Christianity is a religion of the book. God has chosen to communicate with humankind most explicitly in this book. God's people are expected to read and thus become intimately involved with God's revelation. It is far too easy, therefore, for Christians to think of the maturing of spirituality as a matter of reading and cognitive acquisition.

In much of Christian education, schooling imagery and cognitive motives tend to overwhelm the Bible's own emphasis on experience, acting upon truth, and the more celebrative, commemorative, and emotional qualities of God's involvement with humankind—especially as revealed in the life, death, and resurrection of Jesus Christ. The sad habit of "keeping school" in the church seems to be blindly rooted in the assumption that schools have better answers to the questions of educational strategy and logistics.

In recent years developmental theory has provided some respite from this delimiting habit. Developmental theory is being accepted not only because it suggests a more humane and interactive way of understanding teaching and learning in the cognitive sense, but it seems to offer a better way to understand spiritual development, as well.

POPULARIZING DEVELOPMENTALISM

Although developmental theory is not new, its popularity within Christian education has been accentuated within the past twenty years. Two circumstances seem to account for the timing.

First, Christian education as a field of practical ministry has been concerned very little with matters of theory, especially theory that does not derive directly from theology and ecclesiastical matters. It has been a highly traditional field, feeding itself by eating away at its own roots. But with the emergence of social science over the last hundred years, the field of Christian education has found it more difficult to maintain its aloofness from the disciplined study of human characteristics. One by one, leaders within religious education have come to see the value in paying attention to "outside" data. A long chain of scholars represents this long and arduous campaign to bring a developmental perspective to religious education and to integrate theological and scientific understandings: Bushnell, Coe, Havighurst, LeBar, Richards, and Wilhoit, to name a few.

Second, as the research of Lawrence Kohlberg burst upon the scene in the late 1960s and early 1970s, religious educators of all sorts took notice. Many saw, or tried to see, in Kohlberg's view of the nature and formation of human conscience a glimpse of the development of faith and spirituality. Kohlberg was clearly taking a developmental view of something much closer to the spiritual categories than had the typical cognitive researcher. The prospects for useful developmentalism were eagerly sought.

As with any popular movement, people tried to read into the excitement whatever they chose. Some saw in Kohlberg's work a sort of master paradigm for the understanding of faith development; James Fowler has suggested an example of such a paradigm. Others have fallen into a widely yawning trap as they searched for spiritual gold among the artifacts of a highly cognitive model. Others thought they saw both poor methodology and exaggerated interpretations. But the parade of Kohlberg's followers grew longer, and suddenly far more Christian educators were taking research seriously. The impetus for innovation often emerges from strange sources.

When enthusiasm is based on an incomplete understanding, reactions can turn sour very quickly. After news of Kohlberg's apparent suicide, a quick chill fell across the particulars of "the Kohlberg model." But the corner was already turned; never again will it be academically respectable to deny the importance of social science in the understanding of faith and spirituality. The concepts and models are still emerging. Certain matters are becoming clearer. No one has the picture altogether fully formed as yet, but the future of theory for Christian education seems sure to be an informed synthesis of theological rudiments and scientific evidences.

A Model for Inquiry:
Toward a Theory of Spiritual Ecology

Perhaps the most important characteristic of developmental theory is its capability of relating widely to the whole range of human attributes. In effect, developmentalism is a *meta-theory* that explains the connections, similarities, and contrasts among particular developmental theories, each of which explains components of the whole. The acceptability and utility of developmental theories derive largely from their relatedness to one another and their compatible fit within the larger picture. As a meta-theory, developmentalism suggests new possibilities: not only can we see moral development and faith development through this filter, but we can imagine more precisely how *spiritual development* might look if it were to come more clearly into focus.

Arising from the study of biology, the concept of ecology has provided a significant set of presuppositions about the creation. Referring to the more theoretical use of the term, rather than its popular use as political activism to save an owl or a whale or "to clean up the environment," *ecology* refers to the interdependence of each component in the creation with respect to each other component. The basic presupposition is that everything functions within an integrated whole — no individual component or system exists without reference to what exists around it. By extension, the concept suggests that any organism or system within the universe is internally interrelated — every part is joined together in such a way as to affect each other for mutual better or worse.

As human behavior has been intensively studied throughout this century, more and more evidences about the nature of the human being, individually and in social relationships, have been accumulating. There are many ways to organize these findings, of course, and any list is sure to slight some categories and exaggerate others. The following list is flawed in this respect, but it does constitute a useful taxonomy:

Physical Development

In which the human body is studied from conception to death, revealing the unfolding in a sequenced pattern of the genetically grounded components of the person's physical reality.

Intellectual Development

In which the development of the mind is assessed through all sorts of mental measurements and technologically instrumented studies of the brain and the nervous system. Matters range widely from physical characteristics of the neural processes clear across to the outcomes of a spelling test in the third grade.

Emotional Development

In which the human emotions emerge and develop through self-discipline and responses to social interactions. This category encompasses many of the most distinctively human of all attributes: the capacities for empathy, perspectivism, emotional response, and profound long-lasting psychosocial effects of emotional experiences.

Social Development

In which a human is traced through the stages of interaction with other persons, revealing patterns which are remarkably common across cultures and across widely diverse human groups. The models and paradigms which emerge from this field of research show remarkable structural similarities to other aspects of human development.

Moral Development

In which the cognitive aspects of moral choice are seen as a subset of intellectual developmental patterns. Perhaps more will be discovered about the emergence and formation of the unique human characteristics that are summarized in the general term "conscience." The remarkable human capacity to make judgments of right and wrong is clearly more than just the intellectual accumulation of rules. Kohlberg opened this window of inquiry, but he did not until later in life recognize the closely related issue of connections between moral judgment and moral behavior.

Conclusion

These five human developmental domains raise sound key issues. How do each of these empirical aspects of the person relate to each other? How does development in one aspect or characteristic relate to the others? To what extent are these aspects related to the ecological whole of a human life?

Most important, how does each relate to the nonempirical phenomenon, *spiritual development?* A developmental perspective invites the educator to see each human life as a unique person emerging through common aspects that can be observed, measured, and evaluated, yet in essence a human soul, a soul with spiritual reality at core, alive through God's redemptive grace or else spiritually dead in sin, unregenerate (Eph. 2:1).

This model suggests questions about how the five empirical aspects may each serve as input and output functions to and from the spiritual core. Classical Christian education has no difficulty in seeing how intellectually grasped matters may serve as input and output to spiritual development, but is there not similar value to be ascribed to each of the empirical aspects?

ENCOURAGEMENT AND WARNING

Christian education is rapidly developing into a knowledge-using and knowledge-generating discipline. As the quality of our questions matures and the unity of faith and learning is more fully appropriated, we will have need to learn the arts of gentle and orderly change. Those who lead, shape, and inform Christian education carry a stewardship of the highest sort. We report to the people of the church—the community of faith in Jesus Christ. Vast change will be needed as we take biblical truth and scientific evidence more seriously. But we dare not become arrogant in the process. We cannot force change. Our Lord did not. He wept over Jerusalem even as He held Himself accountable to the Father.

Developmental emphasis in the practice of Christian education and an intellectual and philosophical grasp of developmental strategies, concepts, and modes of inquiry promise a significant period of increasing knowledge. We should strive toward this end. But there are dangers. We can readily fall into fads, especially if the special insights of this or that person become over-dramatized. Human understanding, even at its best, always is incomplete and flawed. We seek knowledge and understanding, but our posture and stance should demonstrate humility and commitment to one another as colleagues in a community of learning and faith.

Knowledge can be used as a power tool. We should not do this. Knowledge can be used to intimidate people. We should not do this. Knowledge can become an end in itself—to be worshiped as those who have been blessed with insights admire themselves in a mirror. We must not do this. We must acknowledge that wisdom begins with knowledge and leads us to the fear of the Lord (Job 28:28), and to ongoing development of the whole person in Christ (Eph. 4:15-16).

FOR FURTHER READING

Bjorklund, D.F. (1988). *Children's thinking: Developmental function and individual differences.* Pacific Grove, CA: Brooks/Cole.

Bronfenbrenner, U. (1979). *The ecology of human development.* Cambridge, MA: Harvard University Press.

Coles, R. (1987). *The moral life of children.* New York: The Atlantic Monthly Press.

Coles, R. (1990). *The spiritual life of children.* Boston: Houghton Mifflin.

Dykstra, C. (1981). *Vision and character.* New York: Paulist Press.

Kagan, J., & Lamb, S. (1990). *The emergence of morality in young children.* Chicago: The University of Chicago Press.

1

Introduction

John M. Dettoni and James C. Wilhoit

Every generation of Christians finds itself wrestling with the issue of how best to pass on the faith to the coming generation of Christians. It is a question that is answered implicitly by all sincere Christian parents as they seek to nurture their children, but it is also a question that has perennially attracted the best theological minds of the church. For example, Augustine, Aquinas, Luther, Calvin, Wesley, and Barth all wrestled with the issue of how we best nurture Christians.

The issue of nurturing Christians is perennial because it is so central to who we are as a people. Jesus Himself was a teacher, and in His commission for the church He commanded us to be a community committed to teaching (Matt. 28:19-20). Teaching and learning are an integral part of our identity as Christians. We believe that we are required to learn and to grow in our faith. But we also wrestle time and again with these issues because we teach in very different historical, social, cultural, and geographic settings.

The model of parents teaching their children as found in Deuteronomy 6:1-9 is a fit model for an agrarian culture of the early part of Jewish history. The peripatetic discipleship model of Jesus in the Gospels was fit for Jesus' day. But we cannot assume that the particulars of these models are automatically applicable to us in the postindustrial world, East and/or West. This is not to say that Deuteronomy 6 and Jesus' models of teaching are without value for us. We need, rather, to examine these models carefully, recognize the principles inherent within them, and apply them to our own situations.

Embedded in both the command of Moses in Deuteronomy 6 and in the disciple-making of Jesus is an inherent recognition of a number of developmental considerations. The Lord's command to Israel through Moses, and Jesus' own teaching, are replete with what we now term *developmental teaching*. These developmental considerations are the basis of this volume. It is our hope and desire that readers will be enlightened to be effective teachers for spiritual nurture, development, and discipleship of the followers of Christ.

CONTEMPORARY CHALLENGES FOR CHRISTIAN EDUCATION

The perennial question of how we can best nurture Christians continues in each generation, including our own. This is a volume by North Americans, written primarily by and to Christian educators working in that environment. We find ourselves with a unique set of issues today.

Information Explosion

First, knowledge acquisition by students has become relatively easy. In the nineteenth century, pupils in one-room schoolhouses in rural Illinois were issued at the beginning of the year a small tablet of paper, which would have to serve them for all their writing needs. Much of their writing and practice were done on a slate so that paper could be conserved. These schools were limited in the books that were available and were without libraries that are now standard in our public schools. Students in our schools and church education programs today have a whole range of technologies at their disposal, from the seemingly simple availability of adequate paper to interactive video, virtual reality, and information superhighways, which makes the acquisition of large amounts of knowledge a less daunting task than a hundred years ago. We live in an era where dissemination of knowledge, or at least of information, can be done with relative ease. Although information is easily attained, however, it may have little effect upon one's actual beliefs or behavior.

Qualified Teachers

Second, the annals of the American Sunday School Union provide a fascinating glimpse into the struggles of the nineteenth-century Sunday School movement in the United States. One of the major struggles these early educational pioneers wrestled with as they set up Sunday Schools was finding teachers with the necessary skills and abilities for classroom teaching. Even when the minimum requirements were defined as being literate, being a genuine Christian, and having a heartfelt interest in teaching children, the ranks could not always be filled. Because of these limitations on the part of the teaching staff, the American Sunday School Union and other curriculum organizations began to develop educational materials which later were dubbed as "teacher proof." The teacher became a record keeper and material purveyor but unfortunately was not seen as one of the most crucial variables affecting students' learning. Today the situation is different in some North American churches. One can find teachers who are highly skilled and independent thinkers, who have a deep desire to be disciples of Christ, and who are genuinely interested in teaching their students. In such a setting one is able to employ approaches to education that acknowledge and value the teacher's own life experiences, study, and disciplined Christian reflection on life.

The Role of Media

Third, we live in a generation in which electronic media play an incredible role in influencing and shaping the values of our society. This means that any supposed moral and spiritual hegemony composed of family, church, school, and "the press" has ended. Any number of competing philosophies can be presented to Christian learners, many of which openly challenge Christian assumptions. It also means that Christian educators have an opportunity to use marvelous tools for learning that can be more holistic than traditional teaching approaches.

Destructive Societal Forces

Fourth, certain trends in our society seem to wage an all-out assault on the individual. Corporations spend billions of dollars annually on advertising that implicitly tells us that we are inferior and lack certain qualities unless we buy the product that is being hawked. The glamour of life-choices that ultimately prove self-destructive are paraded before us daily in far more seductive and appealing ways than for former generations. The disruptions in family life seem to have taken an unusual toll upon our children, and it is imperative that Christian education programs take into account the traumas that now are experienced by so many of our children.

Global Village

Fifth, we live in a "global village." What happens in Ukraine, Bosnia, Somalia, Vietnam, Bolivia, or any other place in the world is quickly relayed to the rest of the world. In no other time in history has almost everyone in the world been in potential contact with everyone else. We cannot escape from the world unless we turn into hermits or go into a cloistered monastery. All of the social, political, economic, and catastrophic events of the world are potentially at our fingertips twenty-four hours a day. People are becoming more and more aware of the multicultural differences and similarities of those far distant from themselves. Teachers within the church can ill afford not to bring the world into focus in their teaching. Christians today cannot live isolated from the social, economic, and political events that occur in Washington, D.C., Moscow, Ho Chi Minh City, and all other capitals of this world's countries. The events of today scream for meaning in a world that seems to have lost its moorings and is adrift in an endless universe.

ALTERNATIVE CHRISTIAN EDUCATION

With this set of issues, many Christian educators after World War II began to look for alternative ways of conceiving Christian education. The most viable answers came from two very different groups during this time period. First, a group of educators who had been influenced by neo-orthodoxy began by asserting the need to return to a true biblical faith and an appropriate focus on the real-life struggles of people. James Smart's influential book, *The Teaching Ministry of the Church,* calls for a solid biblical foundation for our teaching, but one which recognizes the reality of each learner's situation and the common struggles we all face (1954). The very human and biblical face of these writers resonated with many Christian educators.

In a different theological tradition, writers such as Lois LeBar, in *Education That Is Christian,* and Clarence Benson, in *A Popular History of Christian Education,* held that it was not enough for education to have a decided biblical content, but it also must be done in a biblical way (Benson, 1943; LeBar, 1958). These writers were deeply impressed that most of Jesus' teaching was begun by a question from the audience, and that it was not abstract theological discussion but a very concrete and God-centered answer to a real-world question. These neo-orthodox and evangelical writers began calling for a new way of conceiving Christian education. The major premises that emerged in their writings were that Christian education should be marked by:

- *An emphasis on learning in community.* Christians are not to be solitary creatures. By learning in community we begin to learn how to live in community. Also, the community provides one of the best learning environments as people with similar struggles and stories can come alongside and point us to the hope that lies in Christ.

- *Knowledge seen as a means to an end.* The goal of our instruction, as St. Paul reminds us, is love from a pure heart (1 Tim. 1:5). We seek to nurture Christlikeness and true discipleship, not merely the ability to recall Bible trivia.

- *As much emphasis on how we think about our faith as on what we know.* All the educators mentioned above were a bit discouraged by the heavy emphasis upon right answers that seemed to mark so many Sunday

Schools. In contrast, they emphasize that we need to teach people who can think Christianly about contemporary issues and will develop ways of thinking that will allow them to stand up against the cultural and societal currents that will inevitably flow against them. More especially, people need to become followers of Christ, being transformed into His likeness more and more.

● *An articulated assurance that God can be known and that our theological tradition possesses an appropriate understanding of God and His work in the world.* All these writers were influenced by John Dewey's idea that knowledge is best understood when it can be used as a tool for doing things. However, they are concerned that Dewey was too relativistic in his outlook. They affirm both that truth can be known with certainty and that every believer's understanding of God and the Scriptures can be enhanced and refined. They seek to affirm the historical creeds by saying, "Yes, God can be known in a normative fashion, but we all see through a glass darkly, and our personal theologies always stand in need of reformulation." This is a dramatic insight and allows them to propose that teaching in even the most conservative churches need not be simply a transmission of the truth from the mind of the teacher to the mind of the student but can be a genuine invitation for the learners to come and better live out the truth of the Gospel message personally.

● *A view of the student as a dynamic organism and not a machine or passive lump of clay to be easily shaped by external forces.* These writers all affirm the dignity of persons and acknowledged our complexity. They call for teachers to respect our diversity and to treat us as individuals who are actively seeking to make meaning out of life rather than as passive bystanders who are uninterested in questions of meaning and purpose.

- *A perspective of learning as being holistic.* In the early twentieth century there had been quite a fascination with seeing religious education as being the acquisition of highly organized religious knowledge, but these authors had seen how ineffective that was in actually changing persons' lives. Instead they argue for the need for a rich and diverse Christian education that involves the whole person, not just the cognitive and spiritual.

Implicit in these writings is the notion that Christian education is not merely Sunday School or Bible study. Christian education is rightly conceived as the intentional process of helping a person to be formed in Christ, nurtured in Him through Scripture by the Holy Spirit and the human teacher, and encouraged to continual development into a maturing disciple of Christ. All Christian parents, Christian teachers, and pastors, regardless of their subtitles, are Christian educators. All who serve and minister in the church are Christian educators of some sort. Although this concept is implicit, many church leaders have viewed Christian education as something that "real pastors" do not do. Hence, directors of Christian education or pastoral assistants in Christian education, children's directors, and youth ministry became the loci for Christian education on the local church level. Real pastors preached and went to meetings. Christian educators taught children and youth. All this is changing as church leaders and laity in general recognize the all-encompassing need for spiritual formation, nurture, and discipleship throughout the church's varied programs. Everything from the worship service to bowling can be seen through the grid of helping or hindering the development and maturation of people in Christ.

THE RISING INTEREST IN DEVELOPMENTAL PSYCHOLOGY

In the early 1950s many of the major presuppositions of a progressive approach to Christian education had been established in both the evangelical and mainline Protestant camps. The major tenets, as enumerated above, grew out of a thoughtful synthesis of progressive education and biblical reflections. The prominent writers of the 1950s and early 1960s in Christian education drew largely from theological and practical sources as they constructed their theory. A number of these writers in the 1960s began to turn to the social sciences as a way of refining their Christian education theory, but most of these attempts were not very successful. A classic example of these is Robert Boehlke's work, *Learning Theories and Christian Education* (1962). In this work he identifies four major schools of learning theories and seeks to identify their implications for Christian education. The work has become a classic because of his careful scholarship and theological reflections, but it also represents the difficulty of using secular learning theory as a source of shaping and influencing Christian education. First, most of these theories were simply too parsimonious to provide the generalizable answers that are needed in a practical field like Christian education. The questions they successfully answered were so narrow and so specialized that they provided very little guidance for classroom teachers. Also, as Boehlke found, some of the theories presupposed very different views of human nature than orthodox Christian educators are comfortable with (e.g., the mechanistic view of humankind presupposed by certain behaviorist theories).

Boehlke's work stands as the best of a number of attempts to bolster this progressive Christian education by turning to learning theory. Perhaps one of the most recent authors to do this was Lawrence O. Richards, who, in *A Theology of Christian Education,* sought to integrate a social learning theory with Christian education (1975). He is not as explicit in his integration as Boehlke, but Richards seeks to enrich this same basic pattern of education from the perspective of social learning. In doing so he picks up one strain found in the LeBar-Smart paradigm: a strong emphasis on community. However, social learning theory does not do adequate justice to a number of the tenets of this approach.

Over the last twenty years a number of Christian educators have begun to turn to the area of developmental psychology and have found fruitful correlations between the general findings of this area of study and effective discipleship and nurturing in the church. We must acknowledge that Christian educators first had an ideological identification with the progressive paradigm and have found that certain major tenets in developmental psychology are very supportive of this paradigm (see Foreword).

At times, Christian educators have erred in seeing the field of human development as a kind of monolithic endorsement of their outlook. In fact, the field is quite diverse and includes persons that believe they are giving very different answers to the same questions about human learning, growth, and development. We see this volume as a way of helping Christian educators become more intentional in their use of a developmental perspective that is integrated with one's theology as well as with the art of teaching. Often we have been content simply to make a raid on the social sciences and find those things which support our presuppositions. Likewise, we have not taken sufficient time to allow the social sciences to challenge and refine some of our educational practices and theories.

THE CONNECTIONS BETWEEN THE BIBLE AND DEVELOPMENTAL PSYCHOLOGY

In this volume we contend that contemporary developmental psychology offers numerous useful insights into the practice of the teaching ministry of the church. We find that it is a field of study that has enriched our theory and challenged our practice. We do not claim that this is the only appropriate place outside of Scripture to ground one's theory, but we would argue that it is supported by biblical and theological reflection, is useful, and has served the discipline well. We see at least four significant points of connection between developmentalism and Christianity.

Continuous Maturation

First, a developmental approach to education asserts that one of the most salient features of the human is that we are creatures who are in a continuous maturation process. We view human beings as active participants in their own development rather than as persons who are merely unfolding according to a predetermined genetic pattern, or are merely living out the scripts imposed on them by a prior generation or contemporary society, or are merely a bundle of conditioned reflexes. Developmentalism asserts the value of individuals and their decisions and that our interactions with other persons influence our development and destiny. We see an initial correlation between developmentalism and Scripture in that both use similar words. Both the Scriptures and the writers in developmentalism are fond of words like *growth* and *maturity.* This is no mere coincidence. The writers of Scripture could have chosen words like *molding:* "people are just wet clay — they need to be molded"; *shaping:* "we need to shape these children into perfect little Christians"; *insight:* "when the Spirit gives you the insight, then you will understand." We are so used to the language of growth and maturity found in the New Testament that we forget that many secular systems of education and other religions offer very different views of what it means to learn.

In the New Testament we are admonished to grow in the grace and knowledge of the Lord Jesus Christ (2 Peter 3:18), and His own early years are summarized in Luke 2:52 by saying that "Jesus grew in wisdom and stature, and in the favor of God and men." The fundamental assertion of all of this is that Christians do not emerge from the spiritual experience of being born again as full and complete Christians but as childlike Christians, who, like human children, have all the potential for growing into complete and mature adults but need to be nurtured and guided. The implications of this are staggering, and we oftentimes do not honor this commitment to the lifelong growth of Christians enough.

Some evangelical writers have been concerned that this emphasis on growth and development leads to an implicit compromise of the faith. They indicate that the language of the Bible is really that of crisis and not a kind of continuous growth. We concur with writers like Donald Bloesch that indeed liberal theologians have emphasized growth and underplayed crisis (1978, pp. 109–114), but we do not see the two as being in an irreconcilable tension. Many of the developmentalists write about the necessity of crises of various types to promote or foster development. We affirm the New Testament's use of the metaphor of growth and the Reformers' commitment to the idea of the Christian life as a process of growth rather than instantaneous maturity through illumination or other intervention. Many Christians have begun their new life in Christ through a crisis event, but many others had a gradual conversion experience. The issue is not crisis versus noncrisis but being regenerated, which is a work of the Holy Spirit. Along with regeneration is the continued development or maturation of a person into increasing Christlikeness.

Organism vs. Machine

Second, an important assumption to the biblical writers is that the person is an organism, not a mere machine. In the opening chapters of Genesis we read of the creation of human and animal life. People are seen as distinct from animals because we were created in the image of God and are therefore image-bearers of God. Our responsibilities are to be good stewards and care for all of God's creation. While the Bible addresses issues of psychology, it does not propose a formal psychology. One can see in the rich images used to describe human thought and decision-making that the biblical writers view persons as being marvelously complex and dynamic beings. Words like *heart, mind, kidneys,* and *loins* describe some of the influences upon human conduct and belief.

One writer described his view of Christian education by saying it was "the modification of student behavior as it affects his religious life" (J.M. Lee in Burgess, 1975, p. 128). This is not a developmental approach but sees the person as a relatively passive being who has certain behavioral deficits that simply need to be modified. Consider a Christian college that ran an ad describing itself as a "character factory." The idea here seems to be that the students arrive as raw material and are shaped and molded in a highly efficient educational factory environment in a uniform way according to rigid specifications. The ad makes it clear that this college does not accentuate the notion of individual differences or varied backgrounds of its students, nor that students grow and develop over time. Instead it suggests that its "one size fits all" curriculum is the most efficient way of shaping students' character. The emphasis in such an institution is not developmental but rather sees students as uniform and pliable.

Motivation

Third, Scripture places a significant emphasis on the motivation for one's actions. In the Sermon on the Mount, Jesus made it very clear that His true disciples were those who served others and gave public obedience to His commandments out of genuine love for God and love for neighbor. Jesus expressed deep concern that some very religious people of His day were doing their good works merely to fulfill the Law's requirement, attract attention, or receive positive comments. A well-known mark of Jesus' teaching was an emphasis on the motivation and the importance of proper motivation in performing religious practices.

Developmentalism helps us to understand human learning and action by making a distinction between the content of our thinking (i.e., what we think) and the process of our thinking (i.e., the reasons we give for doing something). At many points, developmentalism supports the truth of Jesus that we are changed most deeply not merely by learning certain phrases but by having our deep structures of thinking altered. (See Matt. 15:11-19 and Rom. 14:17-18.)

Developmental Differences and Holistic Development

Fourth, in Scripture we find an implicit recognition of developmental differences. It comes in what we might call a recognition of the need for instruction to be age appropriate, meaning that we do not ask children to complete tasks that require them to read and write before they have developed the ability to do these. For example, Paul, in 1 Corinthians 13:11, describes changes in himself by saying that when he was a child he thought like a child, and now that he is an adult he has put away his childish ways. And Hebrews 6:1 states, "Therefore let us leave the elementary teachings about Christ and go on to maturity." Scripture also emphasizes holistic spiritual development; that is, what we now term cognitive, moral, spiritual, social, emotional, and physical development. Luke 2:42, 52 speaks of Jesus growing in all areas of His life and in His relationship with God and human beings. The biblical writers have an implicit understanding that people differ in terms of their abilities to understand and relate to themselves, other people, ideas, and God, which is not related simply to age or amount of knowledge.

INTRODUCTION

KEY DEVELOPMENTAL PERSPECTIVES ON LEARNING

Developmentalism provides us with perspectives or viewpoints through which we can view the experiences and actions we call learning. There are a number of such perspectives that enable us to perceive how developmentalism views the world of the learner and the teacher.

Perspective One

Growth and development of persons in all areas of their lives come primarily from inner processes. No one can grow another person. Growth comes from within, not from external causes. To be sure, external, environmental factors either help or hinder development, but actual development occurs when human beings choose actively to engage their mental processes with various stimuli of their environment. Without some external stimuli, there would be no growth. But without the internal processing of those stimuli there is absolutely no growth. Stimuli without internal processing is useless, evidenced by the large amount of teaching versus the small amount of actual learning that occurs in our churches and schools. In order for learning and therefore development to occur, active engagement of learners with the stimuli must occur. This engagement is an inner process; that is, the making of meaning for oneself of the data of one's experiences. Apart from that engagement there is no true learning. A person may memorize something for later regurgitation at a test, but this has not produced development unless the learner has internally restructured his or her mind to adapt the new data to already existing ways of thinking, processing data, and responding to externals.

Perspective Two

Internal processes and operations cause growth, development, and learning. These processes are God-given, and it is by them that people make sense of reality for themselves. The internal processes are internal functions of the persons through which meaning is attributed to their experiences with people, animal and vegetable kingdoms, data, and ideas; that is, their entire environments. Development and learning occur based on the developmental stages of the persons attempting to learn. Development is tainted by sin but redeemed by Christ and encouraged by the great divine Teacher-Encourager, the Holy Spirit, working in and through human teachers.

Perspective Three

Environment contributes to growth and development, but does not cause them to occur. Teachers — that is, intentional informal and formal teachers such as parents, pastors, peers, and professors — all influence learning and development. Yet none of them actually causes learning to occur. Likewise, the environment, consisting of the geographic and socio-historic-cultural milieu, influences learning through the stimuli that it provides. Thus, all the human and nonhuman elements provide stimuli for learners to process. Meaning, change, growth, development, and therefore learning occur only because learners actively engage themselves with those stimuli and make various adaptations to what they already know, do, and are.

Perspective Four

Development is an inner change of how one processes experiences. Development is the internal change from a simple to more complex processing ability. These changes occur because people find that the old way of processing their experiences no longer satisfies: something is lacking. They recognize their thinking is less than complete. They begin slowly to recognize the need for deeper, more complex functioning with regard to their environment. Answers that appeared simple and straightforward become simplistic. They search for new perspectives, new ways to understand issues, questions, thinking, and ultimately meaning. They change their basic categories of thinking from less complex to more complex, from less developed to more developed. When this happens, learning occurs.

Perhaps a simple analogy would help. What causes a bean seed to sprout and to grow into a fruitful bean plant? Is it the ground in which it is planted? Is it the sun and water? Is it fertilizer? Is it the cultivation by the gardener? No! None of these. These all enable or hinder the growth processes. So from where is the growth? The growth is from within the bean seed.

The seed exists in order to grow. But it will not grow in its seed packet; it must be planted and nurtured. The bean seed is changed in the growth process from a relatively simple seed to a complex plant. So with humans. We are all made to grow.

Our growth is influenced by our environments. Strong, nurturing, supportive environments will help us to grow more quickly, limited only by our inherited genetic makeup. Less helpful environments will hinder growth and development, much as a seed will find it difficult to grow in a crack on the concrete sidewalk. Surprisingly, seeds do grow in cracks in the concrete, as evidenced by several weeds on our front walks. But concrete sidewalks are not where anyone would plant bean seeds with the hope of eating beans in sixty days. No, we plant seeds where they will most likely grow and we continue to nurture them. So it is with human beings.

People will develop regardless of their environment, but it is the responsibility of teachers to make that environment as conducive to growth and development as possible. As we grow, we change our internal process of making meaning out of our experiences. We operate categories of thinking that are increasingly complex. Teachers of various sorts work with the God-given processes that are within each person to facilitate growth and development.

Developmental Assumptions

Every science has its own set of assumptions upon which it builds its theory and from which it views the realities that surround it. Developmentalism has its own set of assumptions that form the basic premises of that approach to the teaching-learning processes. There are at least eleven basic, identifiable assumptions inherent in developmentalism. These are as follow:

Assumption One
Human beings are more similar than they are dissimilar. This means that the "human family" is more alike than not. All humans share the same basic developmental makeup. Therefore certain basic, structural ways of learning are similar to all people. While learning styles may differ from person to person and

from culture to culture, the structural or principle means by which learning styles affect learning is the same for all people. That is, all people must interact with their environment, transact with people, and adapt to their experiences with environment, people, ideas, and their own thoughts.

Assumption Two

Human beings will be only human. Human learning is of a different kind than animals. We cannot treat other normal human learners as we would treat rats, pigeons, mice, or one of our pets. We train animals; we help people to learn, grow, and develop. Our teaching must be commensurate with our view of humanity as higher than animals and of a different order than animals. We understand how to teach by the study of how people learn, grow, and develop, not primarily through research on training animals.

Assumption Three

Human beings are made to grow. It is of the very nature inherent in all people that they develop from less to more mature people. Those who do not grow have some sort of disease. Given a modicum of nurture, normal people will continue to mature. A teacher's role is not to make learners develop; rather, it is to work with their growth processes in order to help them to grow and develop into increasingly more mature people.

Assumption Four

Growth may be uneven. People will develop in all areas of their lives, though not necessarily to the most mature, and in the moral and spiritual/faith domains not necessarily with the best of content for their development. The issue is, to what level or internal structures of maturity will learners develop and with what content will they build these developmental structures?

Assumption Five

Patterns of development are in the nature of the person. A study of humans will demonstrate how people learn. It is the responsibility of the researcher to carefully describe human learning processes, and it is the responsibility of the human teacher to work with those processes to facilitate learning most effectively. To help people learn, we must study the nature of human development and work with those God-given parameters.

Assumption Six

Patterns of development cannot be significantly altered. Since basic patterns are established in the nature of being human, teachers cannot dramatically modify those patterns by external influences. Therefore, teachers cannot teach something that is developmentally above the learners, no matter how much the teachers attempt to "get them to learn it." No amount of teaching of five-year-olds will produce children capable of abstract theological thought. Forcing people to learn something that they cannot understand might cause them to memorize the material, but memorization does not mean they understand what has been placed into memory. Instead, teachers need to work with those basic patterns of development rather than contrary to them.

Assumption Seven

Human beings are integrated wholes. The whole person must be considered in teaching-learning processes. Teachers court learning disasters if they neglect the whole person and teach only to the mind or soul. Humans are not disembodied spirits or bodiless minds. People are composed of six domains: physical, cognitive, social, affective, moral, and spiritual/faith. All of these are integrated within the person, who is enmeshed in his/her socio-cultural-historic-geographic environment. All effective teaching ultimately teaches the whole person.

Assumption Eight

External environment either enables or hinders development. It does not control it. What and how teachers teach will effect learning, but their teaching is not the only element that affects the learning process. One of the major roles of teachers is to be learning facilitators, not learning hinderers. Environment is extremely important because it is the raw material that provides stimuli to and for learners. Learners, however, can and often do ignore their environmental stimuli, misunderstand it or, on the other hand, benefit from it as stimuli to mature. Learners choose which of these three responses they will make and, in so doing, they control their own learning. Teachers bring to the attention of the learners numerous data, examples, experiences, and concepts that will be encouragements for learners to grow and develop into maturing individuals.

Assumption Nine

Development is a basic change in the internal categories of making meaning for oneself out of one's experiences. To learn is to develop, to lose limitations; it is not just adding new skills. New skills are not evidence of development. Development is evidenced when learners relate to data, experiences, and people in structurally different ways. Developmental learning is a basic inner change in how people process their responses to ideas, other persons, and events. As development occurs, the limitations of less mature perspectives are replaced by more and more mature ones. By so doing, one continually reduces the errors of understanding that come from immature internal structures of meaning. Instead, one has increasingly more adequate internal categories or internal structures of meaning with which to handle various complex stimuli.

Assumption Ten

Development and learning can be thwarted or stalemated. Not everyone will continue to develop to what he or she was created to be. People often do not want to move from their state of equilibrium because it causes too much discomfort. Likewise, environment can play a thwarting role by not providing sufficient nurture and support to encourage growth. Ultimately, in our social context, people generally choose their environment just as we choose which TV program we watch, what magazines we read, and to what in general we will pay attention. Even a primitive person in a jungle chooses the stimuli to which he or she will attend.

BASIC ELEMENTS OF CHRISTIAN DEVELOPMENTALISM

When we look at developmentalism from within a Christian, biblical framework, we can see several basic elements that suggest themselves as foundational to our understanding of being both human and Christian. These elements are as follows.

The Reality of God

God is! That was the message that the Lord God told Moses at the burning bush (Ex. 3:14). The Christian teacher begins with God and moves from Him to creation, to people who are made in God's image (Gen. 1:26-27). We recognize the Triune God, revealed as Father and planner, as Son who is Redeemer and Lord, as Holy Spirit who is helper, encourager, and teacher.

The Reality of Scripture

Scripture is from God and is the special source of God's revelation of Himself to all people. Humanity can study the natural world and discover in it some of the secrets of creation. The natural world points beyond itself to the God of creation, revealing enough of God for humanity to be able to recognize that we are not alone on the earth, yet not enough of God to help us to know Him personally (Rom. 1:18-30). Human beings need God's self-revelation as found in Scripture. Without that special revelation, all humanity would continue to dwell in darkness (Isa. 9:2).

The Reality of Environmental Influences

Humans live in a geographic, social, cultural, and historical milieu that contains many influences, some good, some bad, others neutral. These all impact us to one degree or other. Within our environment we find significant influences of certain types of people, for example, parents, other primary caregivers, peers, professors and teachers, pastors, relatives, and community. These cannot be discarded or minimized in their influence. We cannot separate environment from development of the individual, but we must be sure not to attribute to environment more than its fair share of influence.

The Reality of Sin's Influence on
Both the Individual and Environment

Sin seeks to frustrate all of God's will for the world, including development into all that we have been created to be. Ultimately sin is the root of social and environmental evil that hinders positive contributions from environmental stimuli. Sin also is personal evil that causes us to choose against God. All humans sin because they are fallen creatures. But Satan, deceiving us, tries to cause us to sin even more, making us even more sons and daughters of hell. Part of sin's curse is to thwart our natural interest in God and to continually darken our minds and cause alienation and separation from God's will. This is especially the case in the domains of moral and faith development.

Secular developmentalists do not recognize sin's poisonous effects on human development. Nevertheless, they seek to be good scientists who accurately describe human growth and development. While they do not take God, sin, redemption, and sanctification into their thinking, they have still found that they have to deal with less-than-complete maturing in the vast majority of people whom they study. This less-than-complete development is explainable by a biblical-theological understanding of the root sinfulness of human nature.

Christian developmentalists realize sin's pervasiveness and look for ways to overcome sin's effects on both the teacher and the learner. The Holy Spirit's power becomes crucial in the teaching-learning process as the sole means by which sin can be defeated and effective learning can occur.

The Reality of Personal Responsibility to Develop
The people of Israel tried to convince Ezekiel, and therefore the Lord, that they were not responsible for their sins. They quoted the proverb, "The fathers eat sour grapes, and the children's teeth are set on edge" (Ezek. 18:2). Ezekiel's response was that each person was responsible for his or her sin. They could no longer try to pass the blame back to their parents. So in human development, each person is responsible to keep himself or herself developing. No one can blame the social structures, cultural norms, or lack of sufficient stimulation for lack of development. The environment is full of stimuli, just as it is full of the revelation of the character of God (see Rom. 1:18-20; Ps. 19:1-4). It is the perversity of human sin that keeps us from growing, either through sin's action in our environment and/or in our own lives.

The Reality of Cognitive, Moral, and Spiritual Values
Based on the Nature of God

These values are revealed in five major structures that are foundational to the world of all humans: wisdom, righteousness/ justice, mercy, truth, and love (see Prov. 3:13, 19-20; Isa. 45:18-25; and Rom. 3:25-26; 5:8). These five values characterize the very nature of God Himself and are reflected, though as through a veil, in nature. They are plainly seen in Christ and are revealed to us in Scripture. These five values are the building blocks of our rational, social, emotional, moral, and spiritual universe. They are the basic, deep structures on which human relationships are built and are the attributes of the very divine character itself.

God has constructed the nonphysical universe with these five structures, and humans have the responsibility as scientists to investigate the meaning of those structures in order to be enlightened about the nonempirical world in which we live. We also have the responsibility to discover how these structures or categories of development enable us to develop from less to more mature people in Christ.

The Reality of Discernible, Describable,
and Measurable Stages of Development

Developmental stages are empirically described and are open to refinement as behavioral science becomes more precise in its ability to discern and describe human realities. Though creation is God's action, structures of creation can be discerned by behavioral scientists who scrutinize the created structures of human development. One does not have to be a Christian in order to describe accurately creation's structures. The reason that this reality is part of a Christian perspective is that the ground for description is the orderliness of our human universe. Such orderliness exists because God has not created chaos but sustains order and structure.

The Reality of the Positive Value of Human Life

Human life is valuable because it is created in the image of the Triune God. Volumes have been written on the *imago dei*. At this point all that we need to say is that humanity bears within its very nature something of God's image. At the least, this means a sense of self-reflective thinking, moral judgment and justice, right and wrong, *agape* love, community, and communication. The image of God has been marred by sin, redeemed by Christ's atonement for sin, and is being restored by the indwelling Holy Spirit. All people are bearers of the image of God. All people have and do sin and are in rebellion against God. All Christians are called to urge others to become reconciled to God and to allow the Holy Spirit to restore that original divine image. Christian teachers work with the Spirit of God to do this through their teaching developmentally.

The Reality of the Contributions of Christian Theology

These contributions are especially pertinent in the areas of moral and faith development. For example, Kohlberg (see chapter 3) identified justice as the end of moral development. His view of justice is ultimately defined as everyone being treated as equal. This is far from a biblical perspective. Biblically, justice is the very nature of God's being. God is just and what God does is always just, but He does not treat all persons the same. Biblical justice is far more akin to relational responsibility than it is to mere equality. If God treated us all with equal justice according to what we deserved, we would all be condemned. Instead, God has tempered His divine attribute of justice with His steadfast love, with *agape.* Thus *agape*, not justice, becomes the final stage of moral development, and a truly moral individual is one who acts lovingly toward one's neighbor, not only justly.

In the domain of faith development (see chapter 4), Christian theology asserts that the content of faith is even more important than the development of "internal faithing structures." More mature faith structures that are non-Christian are ultimately worthless. Content and structure must fit into a whole that establishes a person's well-being for eternity and not just for a time. It is worth nothing to have a mature faith development structure if the referent to faith is not both valid and true. Better to be less developed and whole than more developed and spiritually sick. Of course, the goal should be for a mature faith that has a valid, true referent. Then one is both mature and whole.

INTRODUCTION

The Reality of the Interface between
Theological Reflection with Empirical Observations

Developmentalism does not exist in a theological/philosophical vacuum. Although empirical developmentalism can adequately describe what is, philosophical and theological reflection are necessary in order to make meaning out of empirical observations. Behavioral science must turn to the more ultimate issue: to ask questions about the meaning and value of these observations. These can be asked only from within a metaphysical and ontological framework, not an empirical one. One's philosophical and theological systems will determine the meaning of the empirical observations. Kohlberg is a good example of a developmentalist who turned to philosophy to explain his findings and to ground them in a philosophical framework other than empiricism. Christian developmentalists see creation as a reflection of the Creator. They look for direction of meaning from Scripture.

USING THIS BOOK

As you read the following chapters, you will discover for yourself the power of the contributions of many behavioral scientists for our understanding of the teaching-learning processes. In some cases, the behavioral scientists will not totally agree with each other. You may decide that some of their constructs are so simple as to lack power or so complex that they fail to illuminate. Nevertheless, each of these scientists of human behavior has made, and many continue to make, major contributions for us who are called to help people to know Christ and to make Him known. The behavioral scientists all seek to describe how people learn, grow, develop, and mature. Certainly this is the goal of all Scripture, too. We must learn from those who spend their lives studying human learning. But we must also not take everything they have to say as "gospel." So read critically, using your analytical faculties to discern what is a contribution to our understanding of the teaching and learning processes of helping persons to grow up in Christ in all areas of their lives. Biblical and theological reflection must be the means to ascertain truth and meaning from empirical data.

This book is divided into three major sections, plus this introductory chapter and a final chapter. Section 1 features brief introductions to major contemporary developmentalists. Authors of these chapters have sought to provide basic information regarding major developmentalists.

The second section looks at developmentalism from the perspective of age-groups. These chapters are integrative in that the authors seek to draw together a number of developmental findings as they pertain to particular age-groups. The final chapter in this section looks at the family from a developmental perspective.

The third section is an attempt to apply theory and age-related developmental findings to various practices of teaching within the church and Christian school. Authors here seek to point to the implications of developmentalism for particular teaching methods and teacher actions. These teacher activities are based solidly on the research referenced in the introductory chapter and sections 1 and 2.

The final chapter seeks to answer the question of what characterizes a developmental teacher. Is it technique or is it more? Should we ask what a developmental teacher *does* or what a developmental teacher *is?* Is it practice or being that makes the difference in being a developmental teacher?

FOR FURTHER READING

Downs, P. (1994). *Teaching for spiritual growth: An introduction to Christian education.* Grand Rapids: Zondervan.

Habermas, R. and Issler, K. (1992). *Teaching for reconciliation.* Grand Rapids: Baker.

LeBar L. and Plueddemann, J. (1995). *Education that is Christian.* Wheaton, IL: Victor Books.

Loder, J.E. (1989). *The transforming moment.* Colorado Springs: Helmers & Howard.

Piaget, J. *Structuralism* (1968). New York: Harper Colophon Books.

Steele, L.L. (1990). *On the way: A practical theology of Christian formation.* Grand Rapids: Baker.

Wilhoit, J.C. (1991, 2nd ed.). *Christian education and the search for meaning.* Grand Rapids: Baker.

Wolterstorff, N. (1980). *Educating for responsible action.* Grand Rapids: Eerdmans.

Section 1

Major Contemporary Developmentalists

2

The Power of Piaget

James E. Plueddemann

Growing up is both difficult and exciting, exhilarating and frustrating. The task of Christian education is to help people grow to become all God intends of them. Piaget does not tell us all there is to know about how people grow up, but he does provide valuable insights for the Christian educator.

The pendulum of Christian education seems to swing between two unhealthy extremes: mindless learning of Bible facts and an emotion-filled philosophy that neglects the authoritative Word of God. Healthy Christian education is both true to the Word of God and relevant to the needs of the person and the world. Emotionalists claim, "If it feels so good, it must be true." On the other hand, rationalists assume that if people know the truth intellectually they will automatically be good people. Insights from Piaget bring balance to Christian education.

One of Piaget's most important contributions was to provide a philosophical and empirical connection between external and internal knowledge. How does objective knowledge from outside the individual relate to the subjective meaning-making activity of the individual? How does Bible knowledge relate to being a godly person? How does one avoid cramming raw facts down the throats of children, or at the other extreme, merely using the Bible as a tool for feeling good about oneself?

THE PRACTICAL PROBLEM

Insights from Piagetian theory might suggest a rethinking of the theory and practice of Christian education. But is such a radical rethinking really needed?

The church around the world is growing rapidly. The ratio of Christians to non-Christians is higher than it has ever been since the first coming of Christ. Both the percentage of Christians and the number of Christians in the world is higher than ever in history. Christianity is growing rapidly everywhere.

Bible-believing Christian education professors and publishers are increasingly aware of developmental psychology and at the same time are able to integrate psychology with historic orthodox theology. This is an encouraging trend.

But families are falling apart and seminaries seem to be less and less relevant to the needs of the church. Ethnocentric and racial hatred is sweeping the world. Bible teaching in the Sunday School often seems strangely unrelated to the frustrations of life. Economic and ecological prophets of doom are sounding more persuasive, while prophets of the Lord are often ignored. Hundreds of thousands of new Christians are not growing in their faith. While the number of Christians in the world is higher than ever in history, the number of non-Christians is also higher than ever before because of rapid population growth.

Though there are encouraging trends in the field of Christian education, the overall picture provides many hints of a discouraging state of affairs. Bible-believing Christian educators must not relax, but must work and pray for a quiet revolution in the field. We cannot go on as we are! Christian education is in need of a gracious, Bible-based revolution. Piaget suggests a theory and practice of education that might be a beginning.

THE INFLUENCE OF PIAGET

Piaget suggested a general skeleton for thinking about knowledge, and that general structure is being modified and fleshed out by modern researchers. Piaget himself would have been disappointed if fresh thinking about his theory ceased when he died. While he was alive, Piaget encouraged his students to go into new directions, to use the basic insights from his theory to understand new problems (Shulman, Restiano-Baumann, & Butler, 1985, p. xi). Piaget's theory was dynamic and changing while he was alive, and fresh thinking about his theory needs to continue.

Robert Kegan, a neo-Piagetian, believes that "in Piaget we discover a genius who exceeded himself and found more than he was looking for" (1982, p. 26). Kegan has enlarged Piaget's theory to include personality development, with implications for clinical psychology.

While Piaget's theory is incomplete and developing, his insights about thinking and growing may be some of the most important of the century. Several scholars have lauded the impact of Piaget and concluded, "Assessing the impact of Piaget's work on developmental psychology is a little bit like assessing the impact of the automobile on American society" (Dolezal, 1984, p. 3), or, "assessing the impact of Piaget on developmental psychology is like assessing the impact of Shakespeare on English literature or Aristotle on philosophy—impossible. The impact is too monumental to embrace and at the same time too omnipresent to detect" (Beilin, 1992, p. 191).

OVERVIEW OF PIAGET'S LIFE (1896–1980)

Piaget was born in 1896 in the small Swiss university town of Neuchâtel. "His father was a historian who specialized in medieval literature, and his mother was a dynamic, intelligent, and religious woman" (Gainsburg & Opper, 1988, p. 1). Piaget was a brilliant child. He published his first academic paper at age ten. By the time he was twenty-one, he had earned a doctorate in natural sciences from the University of Neuchâtel, had published twenty-five professional papers, and was considered one of the world's experts on mollusks. By the time he was thirty, Piaget held a job in the Rousseau Institute in Geneva and had a worldwide reputation (Gardner, 1981, p. 56). Piaget was a disciplined person who organized his thinking on long walks and wrote down his ideas the next day. During the summer months he would retreat to a hideaway in the Alps, take long walks, write, and come down in the fall with another book. For Piaget, writing was the way he organized his thoughts. When traveling, he would sometimes go to the airport several hours early so he could have uninterrupted time to write (Gardner, 1981, p. 57). By the time he died, Piaget had written or coauthored about fifty books and hundreds of articles.

After finishing his doctorate, Piaget shifted his interests to psychology and began to work in a laboratory with Binet to standardize intelligence tests. Piaget was intrigued with incorrect answers children gave to questions on tests (Wadsworth, 1989, p. 3). For example, many older children would be able to distinguish between the right and left hand of a picture of a boy standing on his head, whereas children a year younger would almost always be confused by the question.

Piaget spent many hours observing his own children, watching them learn to perceive the world in radically different ways every few months. Earlier Piaget had discovered that the shape of mollusks would change when put in a changed environment and concluded that mollusks could assimilate changes because of the need to adapt to the environment. He now observed that the process of adaptation in children had common elements to adaptation in mollusks.

He worked at the Centre International d'Epistémologie Génétique in Geneva for the rest of his life. His theories have continued to generate much interest and research.

Piaget argued that in order to understand an idea, a person in one sense has to invent that idea. Invention of ways in which the world works is a challenging task with many pitfalls. Piaget's theories went counter to Freudian psychoanalytic theories that encouraged parents to avoid frustrating the developing child in any way. He felt such theories led to an excess of unsupervised liberty (Piaget, 1973, p. 6). Piaget felt that children do not learn unless faced with an optimum level of dissonance.

He also disagreed with the ideas of Skinner and of programmed instruction. "Programmed instruction is indeed conducive to learning, but by no means to inventing . . . unless the child is made to do the programming himself" (Piaget, 1973, p.

7). Piaget would also disagree with Mager-type behavioral objectives. He would likely prefer problem-posing educational objectives.

OVERVIEW OF PIAGET'S THEORY

The Process of Growth

Piaget is best known for exploring the mechanism and the stages of cognitive development from birth to adulthood.

Piaget has generated important studies on the factors that promote development. Two important factors are social interaction and the process of exploring tensions, or "disequilibration." People tend to grow and develop as they struggle with problems in a social setting.

Interestingly, people tend to make the most progress in learning when things don't make sense! For example, a small child may have one single mental category for animals—the family dog. Everything with four legs, a tail, and a wet nose is a dog. When the child sees the neighbor's cat, which has four legs, a kind of tail, and a sort-of wet nose, the child labels the animal a dog. The process continues until the child sees a cow, or any animal that doesn't fit the "dog" category. The cow has some of the characteristics of a dog, yet is very different. The cow doesn't fit the child's mental category. This causes "disequilibration." The problem prompts the child to construct a broader mental category for animals and produces cognitive development.

Adults also grow as they explore tensions and create new categories. This process is enhanced through interaction with other adults. This means that small groups can provide an ideal setting for healthy growth. For example, when a Presbyterian and a Pentecostal think together over a passage in the Book of Acts, it is very possible that interesting "disequilibration" will take place. As they explore the tensions of their differences in interpretation, both will see things they never saw before in that passage. Interaction with people who have different perspectives can be a powerful stimulus to growth.

Ultimately, growth toward Christlikeness is a gift of God. Each Christian has spiritual gifts, so the group itself can become a means of grace. Though groups can facilitate growth, godly development is a result of God's grace.

Piaget has described the strategies used by children to make sense of their world. The mind at birth is not a passive blank slate, but has built-in structures or *schemata* for organizing information. The child takes in information from the surrounding environment and puts that information in a mental file folder. Piaget calls this process *assimilation.* Children transform or rewrite the information to fit existing mental categories. But not all the information a child receives seems to fit the existing file folders. When young children hear the story of Pontius Pilate, they put him in the mental file folder labeled "pilot." Maybe this is why one child drew a picture of the flight to Egypt of Mary and Joseph and baby Jesus in an airplane, with Pontius as the pilot. Such a picture makes sense, given the child's limited number of mental file folders. But eventually the child begins to figure out that there may be two kinds of pilots, and such an understanding results in confusion or disequilibration in a puzzling situation (LeBar & Plueddemann, 1995, p. 201). The child realizes the need for *accommodation,* or the need to add more file folders to accommodate the new category. So the child has one category for airplane pilots and creates another category for a person named Pilate. Learning as defined by Piaget is not solely an inner or outer process, but is the interaction of the inner thinking of the child with the outer world.

Stages of Growth

Piaget spent many hours observing his own children in natural settings and found that growth takes place in spurts or stages. These stages are "great leaps" followed by times of calm and integration. He described four major stages. Many researchers have confirmed these general patterns of developmental stages in people from many cultures.

Sensorimotor stage (ages 0–2)

The sensorimotor infant makes sense of the world primarily through physical observations—by seeing, hearing, and touching. If a baby is playing with a rattle and the rattle should fall from sight, the baby will not look for it. For babies, objects seem to cease to exist when they are out of sight.

In some ways, the sensorimotor age is the most complex of the developmental stages. Piaget discovered at least six substages in infants. At birth, children react entirely with their reflexes, and by the time children reach two years of age they have begun mastery of language and have discovered how to perform scientific experiments with concrete objects. Each day produces dozens of miracles both for the child and the parent.

Preoperational stage (approximately ages 2–7)
The child at this stage has the new capacity to make sense of the world through language and fantasy. Preschoolers learn through intuition rather than through systematic logic, and they have a creative imagination. Children aren't little "thinking machines"—thinking and feeling are always tied together.

In some ways preoperational or intuitive thinking is the most interesting and creative stage. Since children are not burdened with abstract logic, cars can fly, dragons can hide under the bed, and the moon follows them as they go for a night walk. Elkind (1979) calls children at this stage "cognitive aliens." Children speak a different language and make up words such as "mouth brow" for mustache. A three-year-old neighbor told her mom I was "lawning" when I was mowing the lawn. "We cannot take anything for granted insofar as the child's knowledge or understanding is concerned" (p. 147). But children are logical thinkers. Their rules of logic are just based on different ways of knowing the world.

While preoperational children are "cognitive aliens," Elkind (1979, p. 151) calls them "emotional countrymen." Children may have difficulty seeing the perspective of a parent or another child, and thus have difficulty with cooperative play. But while preoperational children are least like adults in their thinking, they are most like adults in their feelings.

Concrete operational stage (approximately ages 7–11)
The elementary-school-age child has the new capacity to use mental logic but is limited to situations that are real and observable. Ten-year-olds in my Sunday School class assume that "tent-making" missionaries are missionaries who live in tents.

Children at this stage learn facts easily, are very literal, and see social issues in terms of black and white, right and wrong. They love the *Guinness Book of World Records* and have numerous collections of rocks, stamps, and sports cards.

Formal operations stage (often 12 and up)
In adolescence and adulthood an important way of making sense of the world is through abstract thinking. Adolescents and adults have the ability to solve hypothetical problems with logical thinking. Many principles of Scripture cannot be fully understood from the perspective of concrete operational thinking. But complex concepts such as the Atonement take on deeper meaning when adults are able to see the abstract conflict between justice and mercy.

In one important sense, people can have a mature faith at any level of cognitive development, but for a more adequate understanding of Scripture, formal operational thinking is probably needed.

Piaget found that growth is promoted through interaction with other children and with parents. And progress in stage development is motivated or enhanced as the child encounters perplexing situations.

The theories of Piaget provide valuable insights for teaching children about God and the Bible. Piaget would suggest that we encourage young people to struggle with problems rather than give them easy answers. He would also suggest we give children plenty of opportunity to explore for themselves and to interact with other children.

Growth in Perspectivism

According to Piaget, the process of growth is like the widening ripples caused by a stone falling into a pond (Plueddemann & Plueddemann, 1990). Each stage of human development leads to wider horizons and broader perspectives. The more mature person can appreciate a point of view from a greater number of perspectives, making it possible for empathetic and caring relationships with people of different perspectives. As people grow in the ability to see problems from the perspective of the other person, they can better "rejoice with those who rejoice and weep with those who weep." Perspectivism makes discussion possible as people listen and interact with each other's views. Missionaries who can present their messages from the perspectives of people in other cultures are more likely to be effective.

Parents know that small children are egocentric, seeing the world from their own limited perspective. A wise parent knows it does no good to tell a hungry baby to wait sixty seconds for milk. God didn't create screaming babies with the mental capacity to contemplate the future.

As children grow older, their awareness of the points of view of other people increases, but the depth of their interaction with others is rather shallow. This is why young children tend to interact in what is called "parallel play." They are aware of other children playing near them, but they "play alone together" (Selman, 1976). Minimal interaction for children begins to take place at about the age of seven. They can now discuss concrete situations with each other and begin to take the perspectives of other children. But they are still not able to discuss abstract concepts such as "sharing." For the seven-year-old, sharing means letting another person use one particular object. So a child may remember to share an umbrella, but not a jump rope. Sharing in the abstract is a difficult concept for children.

From about the age of twelve, perspectivism grows rapidly. Teens experience a revolution of worldview when they are able to see themselves as others see them. Such perspectivism is a strong motivation for boys to begin combing their hair and for girls to pay special attention to what they wear. Teens are growing in their ability to participate in group discussions because they are better able to analyze and reflect on comments from others in the group. Teens often question the religious upbringing of their homes because they are able to reflect on what life might be if they were raised in Muslim homes. Perspectivism can lead to doubt or to a stronger, personally owned faith.

Many adults are capable of genuine perspectivism, but some adults have difficulty "wrestling" with new ideas from different perspectives. Adult Sunday School classes often end in argumentative discussions with one person not really hearing the point of the other adult. Class comments are often a string of unrelated observations from different members of the group. People may respond dogmatically to complex questions with overly simple answers. Piaget never assumed that all adults would reach formal operational thought, so genuine dialogue among adults is not something to be taken for granted.

Moral Reasoning

Why do people do what they do? The level of cognitive development is reflected in why people do or do not obey rules.

Piaget observed children playing marbles and wondered about their attitudes toward rules. Children seldom learn rules for playing marbles in a formal setting with rewards and punishment set by adults (Duska & Whelan, 1975, p. 9). Piaget wanted to know how children thought about rules, how rules could be changed, and if children actually followed the rules.

Before the age of two, children play marbles without rules, but practice many of the skills of playing the game of marbles. After the age of two, children learn from older children that there are rules to the game, and they imitate those rules. Piaget called these children *egocentric* because they assume their rules are followed by all people in the world. They believe that their particular rules are sacred and should not be changed. "They believe that the rules of marbles have been handed down from adults, and some even believe that God may have originally formulated them. Any alteration in the rules is considered a transgression" (Duska & Whelan, 1975, p. 10). Children feel an obligation to play by the rules, but often play with little cooperation with other children.

At about seven years of age, the child begins to play marbles according to rules set by the group, and becomes legalistic in enforcing obedience to the rules. Piaget called this *heteronomous obedience* to rules. Rules can be made by the children if they all agree to a particular set of rules.

Twelve-year-olds often develop ability for abstract reasoning, and the making of rules becomes a most important task in playing a game. Rule-making becomes a social activity, rather than blind obedience to external rules. Children may have a serious desire to cooperate, so they actually abide by the rules to which they mutually agree. Piaget called this *autonomous reasoning.*

Younger children understand doing good as doing what one should do, obeying the rules of adults. Younger children seldom consider the intentions of people as to why they do what they do. For example, if a child, because of clumsiness or by accident, breaks fifteen teacups, that child is considered a worse offender than a child who out of anger intentionally breaks only one teacup. Older children pay more attention to intentions.

Piaget's understanding of the moral thinking of children supports the idea that children do not merely absorb character traits from adults, but are actively involved in making sense out of moral behavior from their developmental perspective.

Piaget's work on the moral reasoning of children stimulated much of the thinking of Lawrence Kohlberg and James Fowler in the fields of moral reasoning and faith development.

RELIGIOUS THINKING IN CHILDREN

David Elkind built on understandings of Piaget when he conducted research about how children think about religious issues. He was not interested in what children were taught in formal education, but what they really thought about religious ideas in a spontaneous setting. He investigated children's conceptions of prayer, God, and religion. His method was to ask questions. "The only requirement in formulating questions is that they be so absurd, to the adult way of thought, that one can be reasonably certain children have not been trained one way or the other regarding them" (1979, p. 259).

He asked questions such as: *Can God be president of the United States? Can God talk French? How did God get His name? Does God have a first name?* Along a similar line he would ask a Baptist child: *Can a dog be a Baptist? How can you tell if a person is Baptist? Can you be an American and a Baptist at the same time?*

Elkind found stages similar to those of Piaget. He found young children to be undifferentiated in their thinking (Baptists have blond hair), older children to be concretely differentiated (They don't allow dogs in our Baptist church so a dog could not be a Baptist), and young teens to be abstractly differentiated

(Yes, one can be both American and Baptist).

An understanding of Piaget can be helpful in understanding the broad task of religious education. People grow as they interact with people, with the physical world around them, and with knowledge. People are not merely empty sponges to be filled with knowledge but are active in the process of growth. Education is not something one gives to another such as teachers giving an education to a student. True education is the reflective interaction between the student and the environment.

IMPLICATIONS FOR MINISTRY ACROSS CULTURES

The church around the world is in serious need of Christian education that is related to the worldview and needs of culture and at the same time is under the absolute authority of the Word of God. Good teaching in another culture is most challenging.

Piaget would argue that most cultural differences are variations on a set of common themes. There may be thousands of different ways of looking at life, but Piaget would contend that such differences build on similar deep structures in the person.

Traditional IQ tests are thought to be culturally biased, but Piaget redefined intelligence. Piaget claimed that the foundational structures of intelligence are genetic, and thus are potentially available for every human being in every corner of the earth. Piaget did not promote an elitist or Western definition of intelligence. The rate of development may be slowed or optimized by cultural influences, but highest levels of intelligence are possible for every culture (Ashton, 1975; Dasen, 1976; Price-Williams, 1981). The doctrine of Creation affirms that every person is made in God's image with all the potential implied by that creation.

Since the fundamental components of teaching and learning are the same in every culture, basic principles of teaching are appropriate in every culture.

IMPLICATIONS OF PIAGET FOR CHRISTIAN EDUCATION

Christians need to evaluate and modify Piaget's theories in light of the authoritative Word of God and must be empowered by the Holy Spirit for effectiveness in Christian education. While Piaget made no claim of being a follower of Christ, his insights can remind the Christian educator of basic biblical principles.

- Piaget helps us to see that *the purpose of education is development.* The ultimate goal of human development is for people to glorify God by becoming like Christ in every aspect of life. The task of the Christian educator is to foster the development of people so they will become like Christ—people who more fully love, know, and glorify God. Too often, Christian educators become sidetracked with idolatrous purposes such as building bigger programs or merely transmitting knowledge. Church growth and program development must always be means toward the greater goal of Christlikeness, or they become idols.

- Piaget helps us see that *learning is a social activity.* Christians should not need to be reminded that good education must involve the body of believers, the church. People develop as they interact with other people. People do not learn the most important things in life by sitting in a pew taking notes from one-way communication. Good lectures and powerful preaching may be stimuli for significant education, but Piaget reminds us that people must interact with each other in order to grow. Education that merely fosters passive reception of information will seldom develop people.

- Piaget helps us to see that *learning is a disequilibrating and re-equilibrating process.* We grow as we wrestle with the issues and problems of life in light of the Word of God. Life is filled with frustrations and challenges. We are influenced by sin at every stage of spiritual growth. We will always face tensions between the way we live and the way we should live. The good news of the Gospel must always be the answer for the bad news of our human situation. The purpose of knowledge, even knowledge of the Bible, is that it be a tool for helping us to resolve the deepest dilemmas of being human.

Through the power of the Word of God and by the Spirit of God these three principles could spark renewal in the church around the world. The purpose of Christian education is to promote the godly development of people. We must involve the whole body of Christ in this process, using God's Word as a means for resolving life's tensions. If these principles are indeed revolutionary, let us be gracious and humble in implementing them, but let the revolution begin!

FOR FURTHER READING

Ashton, P.T. (1975). Cross-cultural Piagetian research: An experimental perspective. *Harvard Educational Review, 45* (4), 475–506.

Beilin, H. (1992). Piaget's enduring contribution to developmental psychology. *Developmental Psychology, 28* (2), 191–204.

Duska, R., & Whelan, M. (1975). *Moral development: A guide to Piaget and Kohlberg.* New York: Paulist Press.

Elkind, D. (1984). *All grown up and no place to go.* Reading, MS: Addison-Wesley.

Gardner, H. (1981). *The quest for mind: Piaget, Levi-Strauss, and the structuralist movement* (2nd ed.). Chicago: University of Chicago Press.

Jacob, S.H. (1984). *Foundations for Piagetian education.* Lanham, MD: University Press of America.

3

The Power of Kohlberg

Catherine Stonehouse

In 1945 Lawrence Kohlberg graduated from high school and headed for war-torn Europe. The horror and injustice of the holocaust struck him with force. He quickly completed his military duty and became a volunteer on a ship trying to transport Jewish refugees illegally to a new life in Palestine. He experienced the capture of that ship and the death of several infants in the takeover. As Kohlberg continued to work for holocaust survivors, he wrestled with major moral questions (Kohlberg, 1991, p. 12). His was no casual interest; a lifelong quest to understand the moral was born out of firsthand struggle with gross injustice.

Moral questions motivated him as he began his university career. In the developmental understandings of John Dewey and the empirical work of Jean Piaget, Kohlberg discovered the foundation for his own exploration of moral development (Kohlberg, 1991, pp. 13–15).

Kohlberg's research began with a study of ninety-eight American boys, ages ten to sixteen. For thirty years he interviewed those original subjects every three years to track the development of their moral reasoning. Many cross-cultural studies were also done. From this extensive research, Kohlberg's theory of moral development was formed and refined (Kohlberg, 1991, p. 15).

SOME BASIC ASSUMPTIONS

Kohlberg believed the study of moral development must be guided by moral philosophy. One's moral philosophy should then come under the scrutiny of the empirical findings of research (Kohlberg, 1991, p. 14). Since all researchers are impacted by their philosophies, absolutely objective research does not exist. The best approach, then, is to identify and acknowledge basic assumptions up front and honestly critique those assumptions in the light of the data. To interpret Kohlberg adequately, we need to understand some of the basic assumptions that guided his work.

In conflict situations, many factors influence moral decisions and actions. Kohlberg would acknowledge the role of motives, affects, and strength of will, but saw moral reasoning as one of the most powerful factors in morality (1969, p. 397). As a cognitive-developmentalist, he believed a strong and important cognitive component is woven through social and behavioral development. For example, changing thought patterns seem to impact development in motives and affects (p. 390). He found that the maturity of moral judgment was a powerful predictor of moral action (p. 397).

Kohlberg chose to focus his studies on the development of moral reasoning. Since all research must set limits to be manageable, Kohlberg's choice was a legitimate one. His findings on the development of moral reasoning provide us with useful insights into an important piece of morality.

Cognitive-developmentalists distinguish between the content and structure of thinking. *What* I believe to be right or wrong is the content of my moral judgment. *Why* I believe something is right or wrong reflects the structure of my judgment. Content may change, expand, or remain the same, but structures undergo development. The structure of thinking or moral reasoning changes in quality and follows an invariant sequence in its changing patterns (Kohlberg, 1969, p. 372). That marks the change as development.

Three persons may say it is wrong to steal (content) but all give different reasons for their judgment (structure). One may say, "Stealing is wrong because you'll get punished for doing that." Another claims, "Stealing is wrong because the law says so." A third might say, "I would not want someone to steal my things, and it is wrong for me to do to others what I would not want them to do to me." Moral content is important, but knowing only the content is not enough if we want to understand the dynamics of morality.

Kohlberg's research probed the structure of moral reasoning. We do not present him as the authority on moral content, but look to his findings for insights regarding the structures, the development, of moral reasoning.

Two components, social perspective-taking and justice operations, make up the structures Kohlberg examined (Kohlberg, Levine, & Hewer, 1984, p. 251). Perspective-taking is the ability to put oneself in the shoes of another. Justice operations are the ways in which one understands equality, equity, and reciprocity or the give-and-take in a situation of moral conflict. Differences in these two components lead to very different ways of judging moral decisions.

With these background understandings in place, we turn to look more specifically at the work of Kohlberg.

RESEARCH AND FINDINGS

Methodology

Everyone with any knowledge of Kohlberg's research has probably heard of Heinz, the poor man whose wife is dying. A drug that could cure her is available at a very high price. Since he is unable to pay for the medicine, should Heinz steal the drug to save his wife's life? The Heinz story is one of several dilemmas in the Moral Judgment Interviews that Kohlberg used to gather his research data. After hearing the dilemma, the interviewee was asked how the person in the dilemma should respond and why (Gielen & Lei, 1991, p. 64). The interviews gave researchers a way of listening to the moral reasoning of many people. Kohlberg's theory of moral development levels and stages was formed through his study of the data from these extensive interviews.

	Level I	Level II	Level III
Source of Authority	Self-interest.	External standards —models and rules.	Internal principles.
Definitions	Right is what adults command or what brings reward. Wrong is what I am punished for— what brings pain.	Right is what good people do or what the law says one should do. Wrong is what good people do not do or what the law says one should not do.	Right is living our moral principles and being just. Wrong is violating a moral principle and being unjust.
Intentions	Oblivious to intentions.	Make allowances for intentions. Lenience tempered by sense of duty.	Consider intentions, but also concerned about justice.
Justice	What adults command. Later, equal treatment.	Defined by society.	Equal consideration for all.
Value of Persons	Valued in material terms. "Persons are valuable for what they do for *me*."	Valued because of relationships of affection and for their contribution to society.	Valued because they are persons. Human life is sacred.
Stimulus to Right Actions	Fear of punishment and desire for reward.	Desire to please important persons and perform one's duty to society.	To be true to oneself one must act upon the moral principles to which one is committed.
Ability to Take Another's Perspective	Understands the perspective of persons in situations which he or she has experienced.	Understands the perspective of friends, family, and eventually society.	Understands the perspective of a wide range of persons including minority groups.

Table 1

The Pattern of Moral Development

Kohlberg found a pattern in the way people reasoned about moral issues. As they developed morally, the quality of their reasoning changed, not in a random fashion, but along a common path. The speed of development varied, but not the sequence in which persons began using different kinds of moral reasoning. Young children showed little or no ability to take the perspective of others. But the ability to take the perspective of an ever-widening circle of persons characterized maturing moral judgment. A predictable pattern emerged in the development of understandings such as right and wrong, the source of moral authority, the value of persons, justice, and motivations to do right.

The pattern of development reflected three levels of moral reasoning, which Kohlberg called the Preconventional, Conventional, and Postconventional or Principled levels. Within each level he found two distinct stages (Kohlberg, 1969, pp. 375–376, 378–382; 1981, pp. 17–20, 409–412). Table 1 provides a summary of the levels. We will look briefly at the characteristics of each level of moral development.

Level I — Preconventional

Moral reasoning involves determining what is right and what is wrong. Children using Level I moral thinking decide an act is wrong if they are punished for it. If an adult commands it or if things work out to their advantage, it is right. They build their understanding of right and wrong out of their own experiences. This understanding is therefore specific and, to the amazement of adults, not generalized and transferred to other situations.

The desire to avoid the pain of punishment and gain the pleasure of reward stimulates Level I persons to do the right and avoid the wrong. They have not as yet discovered other reasons for acting morally.

Young children are egocentric, only aware of their own perspectives on a situation. They do not realize others are seeing things differently. Because of this they do not question the accuracy of their perceptions. As children develop in Level I, they discover the perspectives of other children in the concrete give-and-take of their lives. They learn what they have to give to get what they want. Persons are valued in concrete terms. Their worth is based on what they can do, especially for "me."

Level I moral reasoning judges the degree of wrongness by the physical consequences of the action and the quantity of wrong done. The intentions of the actor are not considered. The girl who broke ten cups hurrying to obey her mother is judged naughtier than the girl who broke two cups stealing cookies. Why? Because ten is more than two. One bright four-year-old, after further questioning, changed his answer. "The one who broke two," he said, "because she did two things." The content of his answer changed, but not the structure of his reasoning. His mind still focused on the quantity of wrong done: disobedience plus broken cups, as opposed to only broken cups.

The developing concept of justice is the centerpiece in Lawrence Kohlberg's understanding of morality. Children begin by judging anything an adult commands as just. Adults hold the power in a child's world, and young children do not question the justice in the use of that power. As children develop, fairness becomes very important to them. Equal treatment is fair. Their sense of justice is offended when they are not treated equally.

Young children depend on self-interest as their source of moral authority because that is all they have to work with. They have not discovered the system of external moral standards that guides their families or society. During Level I they are learning through experience what works for them. If their world is structured according to the moral standards of their society, they will probably experience living by those unknown standards. Through that experience they discover that there are external guidelines helpful for judging right and wrong. With this new perspective they move into Level II.

Level II—Conventional

At the beginning of Level II, young people look to important persons as their source of moral authority. They try to be like those models. Kohlberg called this the Good Boy—Nice Girl stage. Right is what good people do, wrong is what they do not do—and the young person wants to be good. When judging the consequences of actions they are deeply concerned about damage to relationships.

As they continue to develop, they discover the rules and laws by which good people live. They come to value highly society's laws as they see the needed order that laws bring to community life. Right becomes keeping the law, maintaining order, and doing one's duty for society.

Level II moral reasoning requires the ability to take the perspectives of friends and family, those with shared experiences. Considering the dynamics of expectations and relationships is important. Development at this level leads to an understanding of persons in one's social system and the contributions they should make to society.

What motivates Level II persons to do right? The desire to please those who are important to them. They also want to be known as good people. The law-oriented Level II person does what is right to maintain the order created by law and to be a good citizen.

As young people move into Level II, they become aware of the intentions behind actions. At first they overuse intentions. They excuse almost anything if the person meant well. But as they grow in their understandings of society, they discover the importance of being responsible for actions as well as intentions.

Persons are valued for the warmth and affection they offer or because they are loved. As the understanding of the social order develops, groups and society increase in importance, and persons are valued for their contribution to society. Interpersonal relationships and group involvement are highly valued at Level II.

Justice is embodied in society. Group or societal rules define what is just, and keeping those rules ensures justice. Level II persons are loyal to the social order and work to bring others to that same loyalty.

Level III — Postconventional

Principles are at the heart of Level III moral reasoning. As persons live by laws and wrestle with applying those laws in complex situations with conflicting interests, they realize specific laws are sometimes not enough to guide moral decision-making. They discover that just laws are specific expressions of moral principles. An understanding of those basic principles is needed to resolve moral conflict.

The principles can also be used to judge the justice of laws and rules. Level III persons believe unjust laws need to be changed and value the procedures that make change possible. Right is defined as living out moral principles; wrong is violating those principles.

One day an expert in the law asked Jesus to choose the greatest commandment. Jesus responded by stating the two principles from which the whole law flows: love the Lord your God with your whole being and love your neighbor as yourself (Matt. 22:35-40). Jesus identified the basic tools for Level III moral reasoning—principles.

As persons develop in Level III, moral principles are owned and internalized. Those internalized principles become the source of moral authority. In this context, it is interesting to note how God describes the new covenant He will make with Israel. "I will put My law in their minds and write it on their hearts" (Jer. 31:33). The people of God are called to be governed by internalized laws.

Level III persons are motivated to right action through their commitment to moral principles. To be true to themselves and their commitments, they must do what is right. Kohlberg found greater consistency between the moral reasoning and moral actions of Level III persons than with the earlier levels (Kohlberg, 1969, p. 395). Internalized principles seem to bring consistency and integrity.

From a Level III perspective, human life is sacred and all persons must be respected as having worth. Justice calls for each person to receive equal consideration. Level III persons are able to take the perspectives of those who are quite different from themselves. If development continues, they take on a special concern for the poor and powerless. They speak for those who have no voice. They judge intentions in the light of justice for all. Kohlberg found very few examples of this mature moral reasoning, so few that he had to acknowledge his Stage 6 within Level III to be a theoretical speculation needing further empirical study (Kohlberg et al., 1984, p. 215).

Age and Moral Development

Normally, Level I describes the moral reasoning of children; Level II, preadolescents and adolescents. Each level is important. Living by the reasoning of one level lays the foundation for the next. Levels I and II are normal and appropriate for children and youth. Kohlberg and his colleagues found very few examples of people using Level III moral reasoning before the age of twenty-four (Kohlberg & Higgins, 1984, p. 458). Most American adults continue to use law-oriented Level II reasoning, never moving into Level III (Kohlberg, 1969, p. 384). Unfortunately, some adults use only Level I moral reasoning.

EXPANDING AND REFINING THEORY

Justice, Care, and Responsibility

Kohlberg worked with a group of colleagues in his extensive research projects. Through their interests and the concerns they identified, the focus of research expanded. Carol Gilligan, one of Kohlberg's colleagues, became interested in the responses women and girls gave to moral dilemmas. She believed the predominately male interviewers were not picking up on the concerns being raised by women. Using Kohlberg's research methods, Gilligan began studying the moral development of women and girls.

Gilligan found that women based moral judgments on an understanding of their responsibility to care for persons. Women and girls did not seem to focus on fairness and justice or rights and rules for moral judgment to the extent that men and boys did. From her research, Gilligan charted the development of an ethic of care (Gilligan, 1982).

Kohlberg responded to Gilligan's work by acknowledging the need to enlarge the study of moral development to include issues of care and responsibility (Kohlberg et al., 1984, p. 212). He did not, however, accept the idea of a separate development for the ethic of care (p. 358). To resolve personal, real-life moral dilemmas, consideration of both justice and care must be addressed (pp. 343–344). With our understanding of justice we choose what we believe to be the right or moral solution. With our understanding of care we decide what our responsibility is in the solution.

Moral Reasoning and Moral Action

Across the years, Kohlberg and his colleagues wrestled with the relationship between moral reasoning and moral action. They developed a formula identifying four functions that lead from moral reasoning to moral action (Kohlberg & Candee, 1984, pp. 536–37).

Interpretation of the situation

Persons interpret situations based on how adequately they can understand the perspectives and needs of each person involved in the moral conflict. Situations are interpreted using the level of moral reasoning one has developed.

Decision-making

Based on the interpretation of the situation, one decides what should be done, what is right, just, or moral.

Follow-through — moral judgment

It is possible to decide what should be done and walk away from the situation. Moral action is not connected to moral reasoning until one addresses the question of responsibility or obligation. I must ask, "Am I responsible to act in this situation?"

Follow-through — nonmoral skills

People who follow through with moral actions are those who have the ability to design a plan of action. They must be able to pay attention to the task in spite of distractions and persevere until it is completed. Kohlberg referred to these skills as ego control. They are needed to translate moral judgment into moral action.

Moral Reasoning and Religious Thinking

What is the relationship between moral reasoning and religious thinking? Kohlberg believed the functions of morality and religion could be differentiated but were intimately related, especially in Christianity and Judaism (Kohlberg & Powers, 1981, p. 321). His theory of moral development outlines an understanding of justice and how persons think morally, but leaves unanswered the question, "Why be moral?" That question, Kohlberg suggested, needs a religious answer (p. 322). Religion provides the meaning or purpose for moral action and supports or encourages moral judgment and action (p. 336).

In attempting to deal with religious matters and moral development, Kohlberg added a Stage 7 to his developmental progression. Stage 7 describes an ethical and religious orientation centered on *agape*. Universal responsible love, forgiveness, and compassion are freely given. *Agape* does not compete with justice principles; rather, it inspires one to go beyond the demands of justice. Acts of *agape* are acts of grace to the recipient. They cannot be justly demanded but are freely given (Kohlberg, 1981, p. 308; Kohlberg & Powers, 1981, pp. 351–352).

Causes of Development

What causes moral development? How can we cooperate with those causes to facilitate development? These are questions of interest to educators.

Kohlberg found that cognitive development is a necessary but insufficient cause of moral development. Concrete logical thought is necessary for Level II moral reasoning and abstract thinking (Piaget's formal operations) for Level III (Kohlberg, 1969, p. 391). However, cognitive development can occur without progress in moral development. Other factors must also be at work, but encouraging the development of thinking skills is important to moral development.

Kohlberg designed moral dilemmas such as the Heinz story to test moral reasoning. The dilemmas have also been used to engage students in the discussion of moral issues. Development can be facilitated through such discussions (Kuhmerker, 1991, pp. 91–92). Exposure to slightly more advanced moral reasoning helps to stimulate development. Kohlberg found that persons prefer reasoning one stage beyond their own; they do not generate those higher level solutions when asked what ought to be done, but they choose the more advanced response when given several options (Kohlberg, 1969, p. 387). Messages tend to be misinterpreted if they are two stages or more beyond the reasoning a person uses with ease (Kohlberg, 1969, p. 402). Kohlberg postulated that young people would be helped not only by hearing moral reasoning, but also by seeing moral actions at a stage just beyond their own (1969, pp. 403–404).

Role-taking opportunities are the fundamental social stimulus in moral development (Kohlberg, 1969, pp. 399–402). By taking various roles, persons experience the relationships, responsibilities, and conflicts related to those roles. Writing in 1980, Kohlberg (p. 459) identified the privatism of youth as the major hindrance to their development. Being a participating member of the family, peer group, and other institutions gives opportunity for role-taking. The more involved persons are in decision-making responsibilities, the more they must take the roles of others. Then they better comprehend the perspectives of others, which stimulates development. Families and groups that encourage interaction and communication enhance development.

Moral development research indicates that life experiences that demand personal moral responsibility are necessary preparations for using principled moral reasoning (Kohlberg & Higgins, 1984, p. 455). Some understandings essential for mature judgments come only through experience. Persons cannot be talked or rushed into development if critical experience is missing.

In the crucible of life experience, role-taking, and exposure to more advanced moral reasoning, persons discover the inadequacies of their old ways of judging. The resulting inner conflict demands resolution and becomes the motor of development.

VALUES FOR CHRISTIAN EDUCATION

The moral issues Kohlberg explored are important to Christian education. Kohlberg himself observed that Christianity and Judaism:

> view God's principle concern as being not for cultic worship but for love and justice. They emphasize that to be in harmony with God people must act morally, but they also stress that people must rely on God in order to live a moral life. (Kohlberg & Powers, 1981, p. 321)

To learn from Kohlberg's findings does not exclude continued dependence on God for moral strength and guidance. Insights from moral development research, I believe, can help us be more effective Christian educators.

Christian teachers and parents have often thought that if they indoctrinated children and youth with moral content, moral living would result. Kohlberg helped us see that moral content is only one part of what is needed. Effective moral education calls for helping students develop the ability to make moral judgments in the situations they face, accept their moral responsibility, and know how to develop a plan for moral action. Our task is much bigger than delivering moral content, as important as that content is.

The invariant sequence of development which Kohlberg describes in his moral levels and stages helps us in planning for teaching. From the pattern of moral development we can know the kind of moral reasoning used most often by various age-groups. We know what moral messages learners will likely be able to understand and those they will probably distort to fit their own level of reasoning. We can also anticipate which messages may attract them to move on in development.

Knowing the pattern of moral development helps us accept without undue concern moral reasoning that is normal for children. We can be patient as they exercise their present skills and prepare to move on in development. But knowledge of the pattern also triggers concern when a person's moral development stops. If a child of seven does right to avoid punishment and gain reward, we don't worry; but when a twenty-seven-year-old does right only when there is threat of punishment, we are properly concerned.

Kohlberg's research provides us with insights into the experiences that will facilitate development. Children, youth, and adults need to be active participants, not just passive observers and receivers in the life of the church and the family. As they take on various roles and carry age-appropriate responsibilities, they grow in their abilities to see things from the point of view of others. An expanded perspective makes possible more adequate moral judgments.

In almost every Sunday School class, teachers ask, "What should Tommy—or Sue or Jeff—do?" Too often we stop with the "what" and never probe the "why." Students need the opportunity to practice moral reasoning through discussing moral dilemmas and being pushed to explain why certain actions are right or wrong. In such discussions students will often hear moral reasoning a step beyond their own and be attracted to the new way of thinking.

As persons develop and begin to discover the inadequacies of their understandings, they may question moral standards and their own faith. Those questions are often frightening to parents and teachers. What the learner needs is a friend and guide who sees those questions as a sign that the motor of development is running—a friend who will be there to give support and point toward new and better ways of understanding.

FOR FURTHER READING

Kohlberg, L. (1981). *The philosophy of moral development: Moral stages and the idea of justice.* San Francisco: Harper & Row.

Kohlberg, L. (1984). *The psychology of moral development: The nature and validity of moral stages.* San Francisco: Harper & Row.

Kuhmerker, L., with Gielen, U., & Hayes, R.L. (1991). *The Kohlberg legacy for the helping professions.* Birmingham, AL: Religious Education Press.

Munsey, B. (Ed.) (1980). *Moral development, moral education, and Kohlberg: Basic issues in philosophy, psychology, religion, and education.* Birmingham, AL: Religious Education Press.

4

The Power of Fowler[1]

Perry G. Downs

One of the more controversial applications of developmental theory is the suggestion that faith develops in predictable stages. The idea of faith stages is not new, but what is new is the attempt to apply the rigors of structural analysis to such a non-empirical topic as faith.

James W. Fowler (1940–   ) is widely regarded as the seminal researcher in the psychology of religion, and his is the dominant theory of faith development. Educated at Harvard, he taught at Boston College and Harvard University before taking his current position as the Director of the Center for Research in Faith and Moral Development at Emory University.[2]

While at Harvard, Fowler was introduced to the developmental research of Lawrence Kohlberg, who later became his colleague and friend. Fowler was working to understand the psychological aspects of how people make meaning in their lives, and Kohlberg introduced him to the possibility of stages for this aspect of development. Fowler settled on the term *faith* to describe the aspect of human experience he was describing.

Fowler argues that faith is a universal human phenomenon because all people believe in something. The content of faith may not be at all religious, but he contends that all people set their hearts and convictions on something or someone. Everyone, he believes, has faith.

The focus of his research is to separate the *content* of faith (what people believe) from the *structure* of faith (why they believe it), and then to examine the deep structures of *how people believe* rather than *what people believe*. He is attempting to identify and describe the predictable, developmental patterns of how people hold their faith.

James Fowler describes himself as a "classical liberal Protestant."[3] Influenced strongly by the theologies of Paul Tillich and H. Richard Niebuhr and the *a priori* epistemological categories of Immanuel Kant, Fowler has developed a construct of faith that brings together a variety of issues. He offers the following brief definition and explanation of faith:

> Faith is a composing, a dynamic and holistic construction of relations that include self to others, self to world, and self to self, construed as all related to an ultimate environment. This view has been scorned by some critics for not providing a more unitary and precise definition of faith. . . . It tries to evoke an awareness of faith as a multidimensional, central form of human action and construction. Faith involves both conscious and unconscious processes and holds together both rational and passional dynamics. Faith holds together both religious and nonreligious directions and forms. (Fowler, Nipkow, & Schweitzer, 1991, p. 21)

While Fowler sees faith as a universal human phenomenon, when this definition is applied to Christian faith specifically, God is the ultimate environment, and relationship to Him and to others is transformed. Life and life issues may now be understood through the lens of the Gospel, with the assurance that the sovereign God loves us and controls both our ultimate destiny and our current situation. We now see ourselves as *simultaneously justified and yet sinners* (Luther) and other people as having great dignity and worth, but in peril as sinners before a holy God. It is rational in its cognitive acceptance of the biblical perspective and passional in its love for God and neighbor.

Fowler has suggested six stages of faith through which human faith may progress. Because structural developmental stages are not controlled exclusively by chronological growth, not all people progress to the later stages. The stages and normal age brackets are as follows:

Stage Zero — Primal Faith (Infancy)
Prior to the development of faith, the infant's predisposition to trust is formed through relationship with parents and others as a way of offsetting the anxiety that results from separations that normally occur during infant development.[4] Fowler calls this a "pre-stage" because it is not accessible to the normal modes of empirical inquiry used for faith development research.

Stage One — Intuitive/Projective Faith (Early Childhood)
A highly imaginative stage, the young child is strongly influenced by images, stories, and symbols, which are not yet controlled by logical thinking. Perceptions and feelings are powerful teachers regarding those parts of life that are both protective and threatening. Images of faith are shaped by the significant adults in the world of young children.

Children reared in Christian homes learn that church is a good place to be by the attitudes of their parents. Prayer, a joyful spirit, and personal contentment by the parents will help form in the child an attitude that emotionally proclaims, "This is my Father's world." While not yet able to provide logical descriptions, intuitive/projective faith knows certain realities about its environment.

Stage Two — Mythic/Literal Faith (Childhood and Beyond)
Emerging concrete operations (Piaget) allow these people to think logically and order their world by means of categories of causality, space, and time. Faith at this stage is *mythic* in the sense that it can now capture life-meaning in stories, but *literal* in that it is generally limited to concrete thinking. There is still a relative undeveloped interiority of the person, with limited self-awareness. As a result, a person in this stage has difficulty taking the perspective of other persons.

Stage Two faith tends to understand God in terms of moral

reciprocity, keeping score of who must be forgiven and who must be punished. As a result, people in this stage must either ignore or deny various segments of life experience.

The child in Stage Two understands Christian faith in rigidly literal terms, believing that heaven consists of an amazing housing development ("In my Father's house are many rooms . . .") with streets paved with gold. Children in this stage are unable to see spiritual realities apart from the literal constructs, and are therefore limited in the way they can think about and respond to biblical truth. An important task of mythic/literal faith is to sort out reality from make-believe.

Mythic/literal faith is highly appropriate for young children, but should be set aside in later years. Jesus' approval of child-like faith (Matt. 18:2-3) affirms *humility*, not childish ways of thinking. Unfortunately, some congregations tend to "lock in" at this stage. Probably reflecting a desire to take Scripture literally, these groups are so rigidly literal in their thinking that the deeper teachings of Scripture elude them. Such faith is not appropriate for adults. Literalism should be a stop along the way, not a destination.

An interesting phenomenon in mythic/literal faith is what Fowler describes as "eleven-year-old atheism." As the new modes of thinking emerge, children are not quite able to reconcile their understanding of the world with the concept of God. Their literalness cannot yet accommodate the idea of an invisible God who is sovereign over created order. Such cognitive conflict may result in a temporary crisis of faith as they try to bring their worlds of ideas and experiences together.

Stage Three — Synthetic/Conventional Faith
(Adolescence and Beyond)

A strong relational component to faith emerges in Stage Three, as adolescents see themselves in relationship with others. This stage is *synthetic* in that the beliefs and values of the previous stages are synthesized into some sort of coherent perspective. It is *conventional* in that it tends to adopt the belief systems and forms of a larger community. An emerging sense of selfhood develops, and self-identity is constituted by roles and relationships.

Stage Three people tend to be highly committed to the church because for them the church becomes an idealized extended family. Social and political activities, as well as religious and educational ones, are more often than not rooted in the context of the church. Because of extreme identification with the church, conflict and controversy within the body tend to be highly threatening. Moreover, Stage Three people will experience dissonance when authority figures are in conflict.

People in this stage perceive God as an extension of interpersonal relationships who can be counted upon as a close personal friend. Stage Three faith has no problem believing that God has a perfect parking spot for me right in front of the store because He deeply loves me and is interested in my best interest. God loves, not only the individual, but the whole group with whom this person has identified. Synthetic/conventional faith is quite sure regarding who are the true people of God, and who are not.

A limitation of this stage is an overdependence on significant people within the community of faith. Pastors, youth leaders, or other significant persons are a source of both judgments regarding truth (What do we believe about . . . ?) and self-worth. A *third-person perspective,* which allows us to see ourselves and our group as others might see us, is lacking. In addition, Stage Three is highly susceptible to the *tyranny of the they,* which allows external control to become all-important.

Synthetic/conventional faith can be a great comfort because it provides a sense of community and belonging that is missing in much of contemporary society. Also, categories tend to be sure, with clear delineations between truth and error and "the good guys" (us) and "the bad guys" (them). An ecclesiastical theology that stresses community and relationships and strong leaders tends to create a context that holds people in Stage Three faith.

Stage Four — Individuative/Reflective Faith (Young Adulthood)
Stage Four is marked by a double development of self and of religious thinking. The experience of selfhood is in contrast to the community self of Stage Three. Self-authorization emerges with the possibility of making choices based solely on the self,

apart from the dictates and expectations of the group. Third-person perspective-taking becomes possible. Self and the larger community of faith are now seen in relation to society as a whole.

Self is now separated from the group, and the individual stands over against the group, asking why the group believes and acts as it does. The eager "fitting in" of Stage Three is replaced with a conscious criticism (not necessarily negative) of Stage Four. It is *individuative* in the sense that the person now establishes his or her own identity (individuates), and *reflective* in that it is marked by a conscious thinking about (reflecting on) the assumptions and practices of the group.

Growth into individuative/reflective faith is usually marked by a sense of guilt and loss as the comfort of Stage Three is left behind. The faith community that has nurtured and supported the person is now the object of separation and critique. Especially those communities that foster synthetic/conventional faith will not tolerate these changes easily, creating more guilt and a sense of loss.

My own movement out of the more rigid fundamentalism of my youth was especially painful. As I began to question some of the more extreme beliefs of my group (such as "wearing a beard violates biblical standards"), I believed I was growing in my understanding of what it meant to be Christian; but my faith community told me I was "going liberal" (the worst charge to be leveled against a fundamentalist). It was a lonely time as I tried to determine if I was growing in faith as I thought I was, or losing my faith, as my friends believed I was.

The primary limitation of individuative/reflective faith is its overreliance on its own perspective. A certain arrogance allows one to set oneself over against a group and critique it. What sometimes emerges is such a privatized faith that no external judgment is tolerated. Church is seen as totally pragmatic at this stage, existing only to serve the needs of the individual. Stage Four faith will demythologize religious rituals, asking for the meaning behind the rituals. Such seeking can be important to the integrity of the group, but can also be indicative of failure at any level to submit self to the authority of the group, God, or the Gospel.

Stage Five—Conjunctive Faith (Midlife and Beyond)

Conjunctive faith becomes aware of the limitations of self and is less sure of the judgments and assessments of Stage Four. A deeper self-awareness and a greater awareness of the grandeur of God lead to a better understanding of the relativity of our perspective. The Stage Five believer appreciates both divine immanence and transcendence and holds the theology of incarnation and holiness in a new, more paradoxical relationship. It becomes axiomatic that truth is multidimensional and reasonable to assume that other people have insights we do not have. The Stage Five person seeks and values significant encounters with other people and groups in a new quest for understanding.

Conjunctive faith is increasingly aware of the possibility of idolatry within even its own doctrinal statements, so it is marked by greater tolerance to outside perspective. A critical question remains regarding the extent of tolerance necessary to be clearly within the boundaries of Stage Five. Fowler's own theological content allows him greater leniency in this regard than would more conservative theological positions. He insists, however, that it is possible to hold to evangelical theology and still have conjunctive faith. People "earn" this stage by the hard work of living reflectively through the earlier stages.

Conjunctive faith has a new sense of humility that lessens the self-assurance of Stage Four. The new openness allows for, and seeks dialogue with, groups outside of one's own community, which can be essential to cooperative efforts among a variety of groups. When coupled with proper biblical constraints, Stage Five can be profoundly helpful in allowing persons to see the multiple facets of truth, and the limitations of any human perspective.

Stage Six—Universalizing Faith (Midlife and Beyond)

Stage Six requires a radical decentralization of the self and a radical new quality of participation with God. All matters of paradox and polarities are set aside for a new identification with the work of God and His kingdom. A new quality of freedom emerges where matters of self are now subsumed into identification with the "ground of being."

A new expectation of life focuses on matters of love and

justice, with divisions and oppression set aside. Universalizing Faith has "a disciplined activist incarnation—making real and tangible—of the imperatives of absolute love and justice of which Stage 5 has partial apprehensions. The self at Stage 6 engages in spending and being spent for the transformation of present reality in the direction of transcendent actuality." (Fowler, 1981, p. 200)

DEVELOPMENTAL STAGES AND CHRISTIAN FAITH

When Fowler discusses faith, he is referring to a common human attempt to make sense out of life. For him, faith is in a sense a hermeneutical grid through which persons interpret life and attempt to find meaning. He has attempted to separate out from the process of *faithing* (his word for exercising faith) content from structure, examining the *how of faith rather than the what.*

Of course, Fowler is not without his critics. Concerns about his work tend to cluster in two broad categories. The first concern is that such a personal and mystical experience as faith cannot be reduced to predictable developmental stages. Because faith is a gift of God, and because human beings travel such diverse pathways to faith, it is inappropriate to attempt to reduce faith to predictable stages. To do so violates both the mysterious work of God and the uniqueness of persons. The possibility of faith stages is rejected in principle. Many Christians agree with this criticism.

The second cluster of critiques center around the application of structural analysis used by Fowler. Has he really been able to separate content from structure and describe a truly universal structural pattern to faith? Is his research sufficiently disciplined to avoid contamination from his own theological perspective? I shall return to this concern later.

When evangelicals discuss faith, they usually mean something specific—acceptance of a specific content in ways that involve their minds, emotions, and wills. They speak of *the Faith,* referring to a specific content held in a specific way. Is Fowler's conception of faith compatible with this perspective?

I believe that it is both reasonable and helpful to assume the validity of faith development theory. The possibility of stages of faith can be rather difficult for American individualism to accept, but it does not necessarily do injustice to the mystical work of the Spirit in the lives of people. Faith stages are broad categories and descriptions, not rigid confining boxes. Part of the orderliness of God's creation could easily be that human beings develop in the structure of faith in orderly ways.

But has Fowler successfully separated content from structure, allowing for any content of faith to be held? Just as Kohlberg's theory requires the emergence of justice as a primary content of the later stages, so Fowler requires the emergence of a content of faith strongly similar to the advanced theology of Paul Tillich. Fowler recognizes this fact and explained it as follows:

> Despite the growing empirical verification, however, its theoretical framework and grounding indisputably rest on theological foundations and reasoning. These foundations have convictional status and finally rest on the faith commitments of the theorist and of the faith tradition of which he or she is a part. They can be rationally explicated, however, and are subject to statement in largely formal and functional terms. To a degree not yet fully tested, they seem capable of being stated in terms derived from other traditions and cultures not Christian or Western. It is a principle thesis of this chapter that the acknowledgment and rational explication of these broadly theological foundations do not jeopardize the theory's claim to scientific integrity. In this regard there are parallels with the conviction-laden philosophical rationales for normative and descriptive theories of cognitive development and for developmental theories of moral and religious reasoning. (Fowler, Nipkow, & Schweitzer, 1991, p. 33)

It is difficult to be totally right, as it is difficult to be totally wrong. Fowler has done excellent work in bringing together a variety of issues and weaving them into a description of the construct of faith. Moreover, he has come a long way in clarifying research and scoring procedures for determining a person's faith stage. He offers descriptions of the stages that allow for a variety of contents, and he has listened attentively to his critics, evaluating and responding to their concerns in reasonable ways. Also, he is aware of the determinant role his own theology plays in his theoretical constructs.

It is precisely at this point that I must part company with Fowler. His use of Tillich and Niebuhr, with their assumptions about the nature of God, the role of human experience, and the substance of the Gospel, lead him, in the higher stages, to constructs that are not compatible with God's self-revelation in Scripture. Ultimately, we are not called to identification with the *Ground of Being,* but to a profound thankfulness for the grace of a holy God who both sought and enabled our redemption. We are called to *know Him* (John 17:3) and *serve Him* (Rom. 12:1) out of grateful hearts.

Fowler rightly recognizes, as we must also, that a theory of faith development cannot be totally scientific and value-free. Rather, it must of necessity begin with a description of the endpoint of faith, that normative state toward which all faith must lead. He acknowledges that

> any developmental theory involving an accounting of qualitative transformations in human knowing, valuing, committing and acting, must derive its *Tendenz* and normative direction from some faith vision of the excellence to which humans are called and for which we are potentiated. (Fowler, Nipkow, & Schweitzer, 1991, p. 36)

Ultimately, evangelicals must offer an amended version of his stage descriptions and validate them empirically to make this theory compatible with a distinctively biblical perspective. A more biblically derived vision of the ultimate stages of faith would yield a theory more useful for our purposes, but one that is exclusivistic in its orientation. That does not mean that we have nothing to gain from Fowler's theory as it currently exists. It does mean, however, that more work needs to be done from an evangelical perspective.

CONTRIBUTIONS TO CHRISTIAN EDUCATION

Even though faith development theory as it currently exists has some theological problems, we can draw much good from this work. If we remain mindful of the weaknesses and keep our own theological moorings firmly in place, the work of James Fowler and his associates yields some important insights for Christian education and the process of spiritual growth. The following seem especially important to me:

(1) Faith as a Universal Phenomenon

Faith development theory presents a "high" view of humankind, arguing that everyone has faith. Faith is not something only religious people have; everyone is engaged in a quest for meaning that is mediated through faith. All people engage in faith when they attempt to find meaning in their existence.

Since all people have faith, Christians need not feel inferior because we are people of faith. The distinction between the Christian and the secularist is the *content* of faith, not the *fact* of faith. A careful probing of another person's perspective will yield an ultimate core of beliefs and relationships that make up that person's faith.

There is grist for the apologetic mill here as the reasonableness of the choice of faith content is examined. Is the Gospel a more adequate faith content than the stock market? Does it make better sense to put one's trust in and loyalty to Jesus of Nazareth than any other center of value and power? Can we offer a better content for faith than those without Christ?

I am not thinking about winning religious or philosophical debates. I am thinking about speaking to a very real life need that Fowler has described. God has designed us as thinking/ feeling/believing creatures; we all must believe in something. The Gospel speaks to that need for transcendence, offering a content for the human propensity for faith to embrace and a more adequate object of faith than any other option open to humankind. Fowler has done a great service in helping us to see that all people have faith.

(2) Description of Faith as Different from Religion and Belief

Influenced by Wilford Cantwell Smith (Smith, 1963), Fowler offers a critical distinction between *faith* and *creed*, which is especially needed by the evangelical church. Our concern for doctrinal purity has so consumed us that we have tended to reduce the concept of faith to creedal statements, referred to as a *Statement of Faith*. Such statements list specific content to be believed by persons associated with its community of origin. It is assumed that if one can sign the statement, one has faith, because one concurs with this doctrinal position.

But Fowler reminds us that faith is dynamic, evolving, and relational—an integral part of our lives. It shapes the way we see and make meaning of our lives, controlling our values and perceptions and exercise of power. He reminds us that faith is not static, but dynamic, influencing the way we see and relate to the world around us. He offers a corrective to those who would reduce faith to a cognitive list of beliefs, that, if one asserts them to be true, guarantee one's salvation.

Fowler is much closer to the historical concept of *belief* than the modern perspective. Contemporary usage has reduced belief to a purely cognitive construct without its subsequent affective and volitional components. But historically, belief has meant *by-life,* meaning that what one believed was what one lived by. It was unthinkable to claim that one's belief did not shape one's life. Fowler is reminding us again of the true nature of faith and belief.

(3) A More Complete View of Faith

Fowler's research can help Christian educators view people more completely. He shows us that faith is tied closely to self-image and worldview. Psychologists have long understood the importance of self-image in the development of the person, but Christian educators have tended to leave that concern to the domain of the therapist. Fowler helps us realize that one's emerging self-perceptions will influence how one shapes and experiences one's faith.

People who only understand and view themselves primarily in terms of roles and relationships (I'm a Sunday School teacher; I'm a mother; I'm a member of First Church) will find it very difficult to progress beyond a Stage Three faith. The higher stages require an ego-strength not all people can exercise. Because faith is partly a human phenomenon (that is, a gift from God but exercised by human beings), we need a whole-person perspective to understand how people may be experiencing their faith.

Responsible Christian education tries to understand the whole person, not being limited only to those concerns that are spiritual. Because faith involves the whole person, it must be understood in the total context of development. Faith is not an isolated aspect of the human personality but is the outcome of various aspects of the personality being integrated into a unified perspective. Such understanding can guard against superficial understandings of this complex theological/psychological phenomenon we call faith.

(4) Sensitive Listening to Faith

Christian educators must learn to listen sensitively as people discuss their faith. Historically, evangelicals have attended to content, but have ignored structure. We've been so concerned with guarding *what* people believe that we have failed to listen to *how* they believe. We've ignored the possibility of stages of faith, striving only to make faith *stronger* without being concerned with making faith *more mature.* We've tended to police its content and tried to strengthen its power, but have neglected its maturity.

Fowler helps us to sense the maturity of faith. Becoming conversant with his stages can help us listen with greater sensitivity to the way people describe their faith. It can help us hear with deeper insight the way people understand and experience their faith.

There is always the danger of abusing developmental stages, quickly categorizing people as to their stages, and then attempting to manipulate them into higher and more adequate stages. Besides being disrespectful of persons, such an attitude is also ignorant regarding the nature of developmental psychology. If Fowler's stages offer new ways to put people in "pigeon holes" and a new hierarchy of spirituality, then there will be more harm than good to the church.

But the point of faith development is to help us understand better the ways people experience and exercise faith. If we can hear with greater sensitivity the structure of faith reported by people, we can understand better both those ideas and experiences which can bring comfort as well as those which might be disruptive or might stimulate growth.

(5) Describing Mature Faith

Closely related to the previous point, Fowler's stages can help Christian educators understand the maturity of the faith of their people. Instead of focusing only on strength, educators can also assess maturity.

Lower stages of faith are not inappropriate for young persons. A young adolescent in Stage Two faith can have a strong faith (a deep commitment to God) that is perfectly appropriate for his or her age. But if this same person continues in a Stage Two structure well into adolescence or adulthood, the faith can be said to be strong, but immature. That is, it is not developmentally appropriate for the person's age and place in life.

Children who believe God will protect them from all harm have a strong belief in the sovereignty of God and specific childlike perceptions of what His love for them entails. Such belief is appropriate for children. But when they become adults, if they still believe that nothing "bad" can happen to them because of their faith, they are both misguided and immature. A more mature faith can differentiate between God's redemptive involvement in life situations (Rom. 8:28) and an ironclad guarantee that believers are exempt from life's trials.

Christian educators who are sensitive to the stages of faith are able to hear structure as well as content, and maturity as well as strength. They understand people more deeply, and have a more realistic perspective of the health of their congregations. Moreover, they have better possibilities for designing educational approaches appropriate to their peoples' maturity. Fowler has offered a way of determining the relative maturity of faith, describing the stages through which a maturing faith will progress. His descriptions are not without error and theological bias, but they are helpful for describing how people grow in faith.

FINAL STATEMENT

There are a variety of ways to discuss spiritual maturity. Most tend to be either highly mystical or highly individualistic.

James Fowler has offered a reasonable way to view faith developmentally. His theory is not perfect, but it does provide some helpful categories and important insights for Christian education. Even though further work is needed, there is real power in the work of James Fowler. We are well advised to listen to his findings and discover ways to contribute to the research base, so that we can help develop a theory that more adequately accommodates biblical pictures of faith and maturity.

FOR FURTHER READING

Fowler, J. (1981). *Stages of faith: The psychology of human development and the quest for meaning.* San Francisco: Harper & Row.

Fowler, J., Nipkow, K., & Schweitzer, F. (Eds.) (1991). *Stages of faith and religious development: Implications for church, education, and society.* New York: Crossroad Publishing Company.

Dykstra, C., & Parks, S. (Eds.) (1986). *Faith development and Fowler.* Birmingham, AL: Religious Education Press.

Smith, W.C. (1963). *The meaning and end of religion.* New York: Macmillan.

NOTES

1. This chapter is adapted from *Teaching for Spiritual Growth: An Introduction to Christian Education* by Perry G. Downs (Grand Rapids: Zondervan Publishing House, 1994). Used by permission.

2. As of this writing, Fowler's books include *To See the Kingdom: The Theological Vision of H. Richard Niebuhr.* Nashville: Abingdon, 1974; *Stages of Faith: The Psychology of Human Development and the Quest for Meaning.* San Francisco: Harper & Row, 1981; *Becoming Adult, Becoming Christian: Adult Development and Christian Faith.* San Francisco: Harper & Row, 1984;

Faith Development and Pastoral Care. Philadelphia: Fortress Press, 1987; *Weaving the New Creation: Stages of Faith and the Public Church.* San Francisco: Harper & Row, 1991.

3. This description and following specifics are taken from his presentation to the National Association of Professors of Christian Education (now known as the North American Association of Professors of Christian Education) October 22–25, 1987, Danvers, MA.

4. This understanding of infancy is strongly influenced by Erik Erikson's concepts of psychosocial development and its concerns for Basic Trust vs. Basic Mistrust and Margaret Mahler's conception of the psychological birth of the human infant.

5

The Power of Erikson

Les L. Steele

This chapter seeks to introduce the reader to the life and theory of Erik Erikson. More importantly, it seeks to explore the implications of Erikson's theory for Christian education. With this in mind, we will explore certain aspects of Erikson's theory and leave others unattended. The reader is encouraged to consider Erikson further by reading other sources such as those listed at the end of this chapter.

The chapter will first give biographical information on Erikson, which gives the reader not only a glimpse at his life but also clues to the direction he takes with his theory of psychosocial development. From biography, the chapter turns to theory. Here we will describe some of the more central aspects of Erikson's theory. Finally, the chapter considers insights from Erikson for religion and, specifically, Christian education.

BRIEF BIOGRAPHY OF ERIK H. ERIKSON

We begin by painting a general landscape, not a detailed account, of Erik Erikson's life and work. On June 15, 1902, Erik was born to Danish parents near Frankfurt, Germany. Prior to his birth his parents had separated, leaving Erik to be nurtured by his mother. They moved to Karlsruhe, Germany, where Erik became ill. His mother took him to a local pediatrician, Dr. Homburger, who attended to his health and to his mother's loneliness. They married, and Erik was raised in a home that allowed for exploration and growth. Erik took his stepfather's name as his middle name, hence, Erik Homburger Erikson.

Erik did not do well in the German educational system, primarily because he was bored with school and interested in other things. He managed to graduate from Gymnasium with a solid education in the arts and sciences as well as Latin and Greek. After graduation, he chose to be a wandering artist or, as he describes himself, an early beatnik, wandering Europe for several years as an artist and thinker. These years were formative for his own sense of self as well as his theory. At age twenty-five, he returned to Karlsruhe to study art.

In 1927, Erikson went to Vienna to teach children in a school related to Sigmund Freud's Psychoanalytical Society. The school was quite progressive in nature and allowed students and faculty alike to engage their own interests while providing a solid education. During this time, Erik was convinced to begin training in psychoanalysis. An integral part of such training is to undergo psychoanalysis yourself, so Erik began analysis with Anna Freud. He also studied with a Montessori Group in Vienna because of his interest in children and education. In 1929, he met Joan Serson, an American/Canadian, and married her months later.

Erik and Joan Erikson remained in Vienna for another four years to finish training. These were not good times in Europe; fascism abounded all around Vienna and soon it would take control. Erikson completed his analytic training in 1933 and graduated from the Vienna Psychoanalytic Society. Though they hoped to settle in Copenhagen, he and his wife realized the danger of the times and fled to America with assurance from a colleague in Boston that there would be a position for Erik.

By December 1933, the Eriksons were in Boston and Erik began work as a child analyst. Despite the fact that he did not have any formal degrees, he held appointments at Massachusetts General Hospital and Harvard Medical School.

Erikson would later hold a variety of positions in different parts of the country. In 1936 he was a professor at Yale, and in 1939 he moved to work at the University of California at Berkeley. Throughout the years, his clinical observations were giving rise to his theoretical insights. He did several research projects, including studies of the Sioux and Yurok Indian tribes. Erikson's clinical work, research projects, and papers culminated in the publication of his first book, *Childhood and Society* (1950), in which he articulated his eight stages of the human life cycle.

The following years would bring many other projects and publications, as well as a growing reputation as a leading thinker in human development. He was intrigued with the notion of personal identity and how historical and cultural factors affected identity. He was also keenly interested in how religion operated in human development. This is best expressed in two of his books on religious leaders. He later published *Young Man Luther* (1958), a psychohistorical study of Martin Luther, where he expresses his deep appreciation for the valuable role religion plays in human life. He also published *Gandhi's Truth* (1969), a psychohistory of Mohandas Gandhi that also investigates the role of religion in the human life cycle.

Erikson's life story has much in common with his life work. His own adolescent wanderings provide insight for his interpretation of adolescence in Western cultures. His breadth of knowledge provides an approach as much like the humanities as the sciences. His keen observations of life provide a compelling methodology unencumbered by the rigidity of carefully controlled, purely empirical studies. His study of religion in the human life cycle gives him great appreciation for the significance religion plays in human becoming.

ERIKSON'S THEORY OF
PSYCHOSOCIAL HUMAN DEVELOPMENT

We turn our attention to the theory of psychosocial development that Erikson articulates. We will consider the sources of his theory, the essentials of the theory, and a description of the stages of the theory.

Sources of Erikson's Theory

Erik Erikson is first and foremost a clinician rather than a research psychologist. He uses his observations of clients along with research to create his theory. For some, his approach is not scientific enough in that he does not find it necessary to be confined by the parameters of quantitative empirical research. He does not believe in the false hope of objective knowing supposedly available through the scientific method. Instead, he affirms what he names "disciplined subjectivity." This approach acknowledges the subjectivity of observers while they attempt to draw conclusions about human behavior. Erikson claims this frees him from the unnatural confines of rationalism and allows for a full theory of knowing that appreciates both the rational and intuitive.

Erikson draws on a variety of sources to develop a holistic theory of human development. This approach has given rise to criticism of his work. Particularly, his work in psychohistory has provoked both historians and psychologists.

Finally, Erikson's theory begins with Freud and yet is quite different. Generally speaking, Erikson is much more hopeful about human nature; he shifts our thinking from human pathology to normal, healthy human development. He sees human development in the larger social context. He also moves individuals from what could be considered a victim's role to being responsible selves.

We should be attentive, as Carol Gilligan has pointed out, that Erikson's theory may contain a male bias due to his similarities to Freud.

Essentials of Erikson's Theory

A beginning point for Erikson is the epigenetic principle. *Epigenesis* means that the human personality has a ground plan that gives direction and a general pattern to human becoming. This does not, however, imply any sort of genetic determinism. The epigenetic principle states that there are points of ascendancy for each of the stages of human growth. Ascendancy implies there is a generalizable time in the life cycle in which the sources of human development coincide to bring special attention to the particular psychosocial crisis. This does not imply that the issues of a particular stage suddenly appear and then suddenly disappear; they are present in the infant as they are present in the elderly. Finally, epigenesis implies the growth toward a functioning whole. Each of the psychosocial crises the human encounters is not to be understood as an isolated event from the totality of the personality. Each crisis becomes incorporated into the human personality. The earlier crises become foundational for the later crises.

Essential to Erikson's theory is his emphasis on interaction. Some theories of human development are atomistic and reductionistic; these theories assert that the human personality is a result of either nature or nurture. If nurture only, then the personality can be understood as simply the accumulation of experiences and identifications with significant others. An interactionist approach rejects such an understanding.

Interactionism, according to Erikson, asserts that the human personality is the result of a variety of factors and influences and the personality is never simply the result of past experiences or single influences. Erikson describes human development as the dialectical interaction of *soma, psyche,* and *ethos.* *Soma* means the body; our body types, sizes, and capabilities influence who we become. *Psyche* implies the sense of self; unique personality traits and aspirations interact in the creation of the human personality. *Ethos* implies the cultural setting in which the personality develops; the setting provides either support or resistance to the developing person. Erikson also acknowledges the interaction of the historical moment on human development. In the case of Martin Luther, Erikson argues that the time was ripe for the life and words of Luther.

Erikson's theory is a psychosocial interactionist theory that acknowledges the complementary role of the various elements of human development and the contradictory role of the elements. His theory clearly takes an interactionist life span approach that seeks to describe the growing healthy personality.

Erikson's Psychosocial Stages

Before describing Erikson's stages, some comments on the stage theory are necessary. First, what is important is *how* persons go through the stages, not *if* they will. Fixation at a stage is not possible in Erikson's theory. Persons will encounter the stages as long as they live. Second, the stages are building blocks. The earlier stages provide either strength or weakness for persons to negotiate later stages.

Erikson, consistent with his interactionist and dialectical understanding of human development, describes the stages in bipolar terms. The psychosocial crises are identified as X versus Y. This illustrates the inherent tensions in human development. The ideal resolution of each crisis is not a total victory for the positive pole; rather, it is in coming to a favorable ratio of each pole of the crisis. This implies that the positive element is primarily reached, yet some negative is maintained. In infancy this means resolution mainly in the direction of a basic sense of trust, yet some element of mistrust must be exhibited. Individuals who are overly trusting and naive often become easy victims.

Each of the stages described by Erikson includes a variety of components. There is the basic psychosocial crisis to be resolved. There is also an "ego strength" or "antipathy" that depends on the resolution of the stage crisis. If the crisis is favorably negotiated, then a strength or virtue in the personality arises. If it is an unfavorable negotiation, then an antipathy or weakness in the personality results. Erikson also describes the "radius of significant others" that affect the developing person. For the infant, this is the maternal/paternal figures; for the play-age child, a few friends; for school-age children it is parents, siblings, friends, and teachers. The radius extends as the individual develops and grows. Erikson also postulates "ritualizations" or "ritualisms" as ways people relate to one another at particular points in the life cycle. Ritualizations are positive and healthy ways of relating, while ritualisms are the unhealthy and negative ways people attempt to relate. There are several other dimensions that Erikson explores at each stage, but these are the central aspects of the stages.

The Stages
Basic trust versus basic mistrust
An infant must discover whether or not his basic environment is trustworthy. If the basic needs of the infant are met and he senses loving, caring parents, then the infant gains a sense of

basic trust. He also is coming to a sense of his own trustworthiness. Can he trust himself or is he untrustworthy? If a positive resolution is negotiated, then the infant will develop a sense of hope as well as trust.

Autonomy versus shame and doubt
In early childhood, children reach out and attempt to assert a sense of autonomy. This is observed in very basic acts such as the first "no!" and learning to control one's bladder and bowels. If children negotiate a sense of autonomy, then they will exhibit a healthy sense of will to live and flourish; if a negative resolution, then children will feel undeserved shame and doubt themselves.

Initiative versus guilt
In the play age or preschool years, children extend their borders to include friends and preschool teachers. As they extend, they "move out," plan activities, and attempt to win friends. At times they may overextend and intrude into others' lives in unwelcome ways. Overly aggressive children often initiate too much. If, however, a favorable ratio of initiative is reached, then children will develop a sense of purpose to complement their sense of hope and willfulness; if a negative ratio, then children will develop a sense of guilt over their inability to limit their initiatives. This may be deserved guilt, but it may also be undeserved.

Industry versus inferiority
At the school age, children have a desire to develop skills and abilities that help them feel useful, competent, and good about themselves. They enjoy mastering tasks and facts; if this occurs, then a corresponding sense of competency yields a grounded sense of self-esteem. Sports, music, or academic success often serve as the source of industry. If children are unable to master skills and feel useful, then they develop a sense of inferiority and low self-esteem. They feel as if they have nothing to offer and therefore are worthless.

Identity versus role confusion
In adolescence, individuals are attempting to discover their sense of self or identity. They ask, "Who am I? What do I

believe and value? Who are my people?" If a sense of identity is achieved, then individuals develop a sense of fidelity in their lives. They can be faithful because they know something of who they are. If not, they remain confused and unable to commit to themselves or others. They do not know what they value or where they are to go; confusion results.

Intimacy versus isolation

As young adults emerge from adolescence with a sense of identity, they now face the issue of giving that self away in loving, caring, intimate relationships. If they are able to be intimate, they develop the strength of love in their lives. If, however, they emerge from adolescence confused about themselves, they may be unable to be truly intimate. This isolation leads to superficial relationships or a total lack of social involvement.

Generativity versus stagnation

In middle adulthood, individuals are confronted with the challenge of giving themselves away to others. Can they be generative? Can they generate offspring, ideas, or in some other way contribute to the upcoming generation? If not, they face stagnation and self-absorption. They act in very selfish ways.

Ego integrity versus despair

In older adulthood, our attention is turned to making sense out of our entire life span. Can we, as we recall our lives, come to a sense of wholeness or integrity about our lives, with both the good and bad, the successes and failures? People who can look back and laugh at their failures and be proud of their successes have a sense of peace and hope. They are perceived as wise people who can teach us much about life. Others, however, are not able to be at rest with their lives and live in despair, unable to change the past and unable to face the future. These individuals tend to live bitter, frantic lives void of wisdom and full of dread.

IMPLICATIONS

Erikson and the Religious Dimension of Life

Unlike Freud and others in psychoanalytical theory, Erikson has an appreciation for the potentially positive role of religion and understands the significant role religion can play in communicating the importance of trust and hope in our world. For Erikson, the church is the institution in culture that helps us regularly remember to trust, to have faith, and to hope. Parents can find grounding in these qualities as well as parent their children toward trust and hope.

Erikson believes in the integrity of persons, reminding us that our lives are integrated wholes: that our psychosocial development affects our growth in faith and, conversely, our religious life affects our psychosocial development. This is an essential relationship to understand as we attempt to strategize ministry to persons.

Paul states in 1 Corinthians 13:13, "And now these three remain: faith, hope and love. But the greatest of these is love." As Erikson describes the development of healthy persons, these qualities are found at major turning points in the human life cycle. Beginning at infancy, Erikson identifies hope as the ego strength that allows infants to trust. Trust nourishes hope.

The nurturing our parents give to us serves as a prototype for our budding understanding of God. If we find parents trustworthy, then we begin to understand God as trustworthy. Life becomes hopeful and hope-filled.

Hope in turn is an important precursor to faith. The ego strength that arises from a favorable resolution of the identity crisis is fidelity, or faithfulness. Hope in infancy provides fertile ground for our faithfulness. Faith in adolescence is the result of our being devoted to someone worthy of our allegiance. No wonder adolescence is the typical age for religious conversion. This is the time we consider to what we will be faithful. The Christian Gospel tells us God in Jesus Christ is the One faithful to us, and to God our faithfulness belongs.

Love is the ego strength that arises with a favorable resolution of the intimacy versus isolation crisis. Erikson's notion of love is not the romanticized idea perpetuated by society. Love is a commitment to give yourself to another, knowing full well that it involves costs to you. This is the love that God gives us and asks from us; it is grounded in commitment and arises out of hope and faith. When hope and faith come together in a person, the response is to give it away in love.

There is power in Erikson's theory to help us understand the inherent potential of persons to grow toward God.

Erikson and Ministry

Erikson's work has stimulated many to consider issues of faith and ministry in the light of psychosocial development. Erikson suggests a movement from concrete morality in childhood to an ideological morality in adolescence and then to a mature ethical stance in adulthood.

Several interpreters have worked to press the psychosocial stages in directions that help us understand religious growth across the life span. John Gleason (1975) appropriates Erikson's theory in order to understand religious development. He begins by suggesting particular theological doctrines that he finds to correspond with Erikson's stages; for example, in trust versus mistrust, Gleason finds the doctrine of God to be a crucial theological task with which to deal. He applies insights from his work both to counseling situations and Christian educational issues.

Donald Capps (1983; 1987) has pressed Erikson's theory into service on a variety of fronts. Primarily, Capps has worked with the application of Erikson's theory to pastoral counseling and care. He finds Erikson useful as the counselor attempts to assist persons in growing through life. The counselor can serve as a moral counselor, a ritual coordinator, and a giver of wisdom. Each of these roles is derived from the specifics of Erikson's theory.

Approaches to Christian education

More specifically, Erikson may help us to consider approaches to Christian education. Several Christian educators have appealed to Erikson in order to develop their ideas on Christian education. A classic example of this is *The Struggle of the Soul* (Sherrill, 1954), written a few years after Erikson released his first book. Sherrill is informed by Erikson as he attempts to describe the ways in which faith and human growth interact across the life span. Among several metaphors that he articulates, Sherrill finds "pilgrimage" to be most helpful.

Robert Havighurst, known for his insights on developmental

tasks and "teachable moments," made use of Erikson's theory in his book *The Educational Mission of the Church* (1965). More recently, *Christian Child Development* (Cully, 1979) refers often to Erikson to help us understand ways to educate children in faith.

Erikson's work can give us insight as we articulate a philosophy of Christian education. One aspect of developing our approach is to consider the question of human nature; what does it mean to be a maturing Christian human being? Erikson gives us much to help develop a response to this question. He provides for us a way to think of the direction of human growth that is part of our growth in faith. His descriptions of ego strengths and the positive structures of each cycle resonate with Christian qualities of character. These all help us in initially articulating an approach to Christian education.

Age-appropriateness
Erikson can also help us identify age-appropriate educational designs. We must always ask if our curriculum, our teaching approach, and our objectives connect with the lived experience of the student. Particularly, we are reminded to give attention to the affective domain in learning. Consider again hope, faith, and love. If hope and trust are crucial issues for infancy and early childhood, then Christian education must take care to nurture trust and hope in parents and children. This is done by creating parent support groups and by making sure nursery personnel and environments are conducive to nurturing trust and hope.

Faith and fidelity are the psychosocial and religious concerns in adolescence. Christian education informed by Erikson will recognize the mutually supportive interplay between religion and identity formation. *Conversion and Personal Identity* (Gillespie, 1991) articulates the significance of this relationship with special reference to conversion. While conversion and identity formation are not the same, they do interact. Conversions can bring about a center for the adolescent identity and, conversely, the identity search can be the catalyst for finding meaning in life. Christian education must provide means of identity exploration that may appear unrelated to spiritual growth but are indeed important.

Love is the primary issue for young adults. Christian education informed by Erikson's thought will design models that assist young adults in understanding the true nature of love and relationships. Erikson's own definition of love is amazingly reminiscent of the biblical concept of *agape* love. He stresses the self-giving nature of love and the importance of commitment even in the face of differences and disillusionment. Christian educational strategies with young adults will help them understand primary relationships as well as assist them to avoid the dangers of elitism by which young adults can be very exclusive of others.

These are but three examples of how Erikson's theory can help us in identifying needs and developing educational strategies to meet these needs.

Erikson can also be helpful in designing individual educational plans. Some people are nurtured in the church and as such have the opportunity to experience a lifelong educational process in their faith. Others come to faith later in life and may have missed some aspects important to maturing faith. If some come to us as young adults, they may have needs to affiliate and develop relationships. They may need to work on prior tasks such as trust, learning the ways of being in the church, and what it means to have a Christian identity.

These are but brief and suggestive ideas to illustrate the usefulness of Erikson to our tasks as Christian educators. I find Erikson's theory to be immensely helpful in both the larger question of Christian maturing and the particular question of designing educational approaches.

FOR FURTHER READING

Capps, D. (1983). *Life cycle theory and pastoral care.* Philadelphia: Fortress Press.

Coles, R. (1970). *Erik Erikson: The growth of his work.* New York: De Capo Press.

Erikson, E. (1985). *The life cycle completed: A review.* New York: Norton.

Erikson, E. (1993). *Young man Luther: A study in psychoanalysis and history.* New York: Norton.

Gillespie, V. (1988). *Religious conversion and personal identity.* Birmingham, AL: Religious Education Press.

Steele, L. (1991). *On the way: A practical theology of Christian formation.* Grand Rapids: Baker.

Wright, J.E., Jr. (1982). *Erikson: Identity and religion.* New York: Harper & Row.

6

The Power of Perry and Belenky

Richard E. Butman and David R. Moore

THE POWER OF PERRY

William G. Perry, Jr., along with his many colleagues at the Bureau of Study Counsel of Harvard University, has argued that there is a strong relationship between college education and adult thinking processes. Based on interpreted interviews with Harvard and Radcliffe undergraduates in the late 1950s and early 1960s, he assumed that there was a common, underlying pattern to mental maturation in students in the pluralistic liberal arts college milieu. His approach has been widely described as the Perry scheme of cognitive and ethical development (Perry, 1970; 1977; 1981). Specifically, Perry and his associates found evidence for a sequence of development through nine positions (essentially equivalent to levels or stages in other models). Subsequent work has modified Perry's inferences, which were based primarily on advantaged male students at an elite residential university. Especially influential has been the recent theorizing of Belenky, Clinchy, Goldberger, and Tarule in *Women's Ways of Knowing* (1986).

Few would doubt that higher education can powerfully influence cognitive development. As Pascarella and Terenzini

(1991) have noted in their massive review of more than 2,600 empirical studies on how college changes students:

> If one theme underlying changes in values and attitudes during college is that they tend to be supportive of or at least consistent with observed changes in cognitive growth, a second theme is that the changes also coalesce around a general trend towards liberalization. Considering consistent changes in the areas of sociopolitical, religious, and gender role attitudes and values, it would appear that there are unmistakable and sometimes substantial freshman-to-senior shifts towards openness and a tolerance for diversity, a stronger "other-person orientation," and concern for individual rights and human welfare. These shifts are combined with an increase in liberal political and social values and a decline in both doctrinaire religious beliefs and traditional attitudes about gender roles. (p. 559)

The clear movement in this liberalization of attitudes and values is away from a personal perspective characterized by constraint, narrowness, exclusiveness, simplicity, and intolerance, and toward a perspective with an emphasis on greater individual freedom, breadth, inclusiveness, complexity, and tolerance (pp. 559–560).

Far less is known about the specific ways in which a particular institution's educational and interpersonal climate or culture may modify these broad generalizations (for an exception, see Van Wicklin, Burwell, & Butman, 1994). Still, Pascarella and Terenzini suspect that the differences between institutions may not translate into large differences in how students are affected (i.e., the similarities may significantly outweigh the differences).

This chapter will briefly describe Perry's approach to the study of cognitive and ethical development in early adulthood and explore relevant insights and implications for Christian educators. Indeed, the Perry scheme has been a dominant development model in higher education for nearly three decades. In discussing the limitations of this approach for developmentally informed Christian educators, the work of Belenky et al. (1986) will be presented as a potential way in which to enrich and enlarge our understanding of those factors that facilitate or retard cognitive growth in the "critical years" of young adulthood (see also Butman, 1993).

PERRY'S MODEL OF INTELLECTUAL AND ETHICAL DEVELOPMENT

Perry's scheme consists of nine positions and four broad orientations to the nature of knowledge (also called categories). As described by Gilligan, Murphy, and Tappan (1990), the sequence of development goes "from the early absolutism of adolescent logic, through its full flowering in the forms of multiplicity and relativism, to the development of a new equilibrium of identity and epistemological commitment within contextual relativism" (p. 211). In essence, Perry sees the relativistic and postrelativistic positions (5–9) as adding a "post-formal-operational" stage to Piaget's sequence of cognitive development (see chapter 2 in this volume). The sequence can be viewed as somewhat linear, since students do not seem to skip levels but may go through all of them (i.e., simple dualism, multiplicity, relativism, commitment in relativism), although more recent modifications see it as an "ever-widening and increasing helix or spiral" rather than as a series of stages. Intellectual growth is not inevitable in the collegiate context, according to Perry. "Temporizing" (a pause in growth), "retreat" (regression to a previous position), and "escape" (fatalistic acceptance or gamesmanship) may slow the rate of change. Adult commitments may never form in the collegiate years or beyond, a phenomenon that has been described as "persistent foreclosure" by Erikson (see chapter 5).

For Perry, a major epistemological shift occurs when the adult learner recognizes the apparent contextual relativism of all knowledge. There is a limit to formal logic, which Perry refers to as "reason":

> Reason reveals relations within any given context; it can also compare one context with another on the basis of meta-contexts established for this purpose. But there is a limit. In the end, reason itself remains reflexively rela-

tivistic, a property which turns reason back upon reason's own findings. In even its farthest reaches, then, reason will leave the thinker with several legitimate contexts and no way of choosing among them — no way, at least, that he can justify through reason alone. . . . . If he is still to honor reason he must now also transcend it; he must affirm his own position from within himself in full awareness that reason can never completely justify him or assure him . . . he must commit himself through his own faith. (1970, pp. 135–136)

Perry, like Piaget, recognizes that there is a structural component of thought. His postformal scheme of intellectual and ethical development assumes that choices must be made, and that tacit assent needs to become affirmation (i.e., commitment in relativism), thereby ushering in the "period of responsibility" (p. 205). *Commitment,* then, is central to Perry's view of continued intellectual and ethical maturation. Although Christians will certainly differ on the nature of authority (e.g., the essential content of the Scriptures which we obey), we can certainly appreciate his insights about the process of making and keeping commitments. Unfortunately, terms like "dualism," "multiplicity," "relativism" or "commitment in relativism" are easily misunderstood.

Dualism (Positions 1 and 2)
Perry assumes that students enter college in positions 1 or 2, which he terms *dualism.* Dualists believe there is absolute truth and falsehood and assume they should be rewarded for being good and right. They tend to look toward professors as possessors of absolute truth. The students believe that it is the responsibility of those in authority to give the right answers or the information needed to discover the right answers. If that individual fails to give clear-cut answers, the authority is seen as incompetent, untrustworthy, or even a "heretic."

In its initial expression, the dualistic Christian college student might say something like this: "If I study hard, read every word, and learn the right answers, everything will be fine" (after Perry, 1981). Somewhat later, the "internal dialogue" might sound closer to this: "The true authorities must be right, and all the others must be wrong. Good authorities sometimes give us problems but that is so they can help us find the right answer." For the extreme dualist there is little to no tolerance for uncertainty or ambiguity. The "learner" is a rather passive participant in the educational process. Thinking tends to be rather concrete and is often rigidly compartmentalized.

Obviously, being "bombarded" with numerous authorities can create significant tension for the student in a diverse and pluralistic setting, especially when those individuals admit that they don't know all the "answers."

Multiplicity (Positions 3 and 4)

A second group of positions (3 and 4) is usually termed *multiplicity*. It is almost inevitable in the collegiate environment that the student will be exposed to many alternative ideas. In multiplicity, the student begins to recognize that there may be a number of solutions for specific problems, but lacks a coherent system for selecting among them. As the word implies, the students begin to accommodate their thinking to account for the possibility of multiple perspectives for any given problem or question. As Moore (1982) has observed, learning shifts from primarily a focus on the "facts" (i.e., what to learn) to discovering a way to find out the right answers (i.e., how to learn).

In its more developed forms, the learner assumes that everyone has a right to individual opinions, especially when the authorities do not know the "right" answers. According to Perry, "success" in multiplicity tends to be viewed as giving authority figures what they want. Further, personal worth tends to be heavily dependent on how these same individuals evaluate their efforts. Students are certainly vulnerable both academically and personally in these positions. For Perry, multiplicity is closer to the understanding of "relativism" in our subculture (see Buchanan, 1991).

Relativism (Positions 5 and 6)

In contrast, Perry views *relativism* (positions 5 and 6) uniquely. Relativism is defined as the recognition of the contextual nature of right and wrong solutions to given problems and questions.

The relativist assumes that knowledge will change and that not all ideas are equally valid. Logic emerges as a powerful tool in assessing alternatives. The learner recognizes that choices must be made despite the incompleteness and uncertainty of knowledge and that acceptance and rewards can by no means be guaranteed.

Thinking contextually, or becoming a "constructor of knowledge," is a potential blessing and burden for the adult learner; a potential blessing in that it opens up new possibilities for growth and learning, and a potential burden in that there is far less certainty and closure in a period in which so many important life choices and commitments must be made (see Taylor, 1986, for an especially sensitive treatment of the "risk" of commitment for the reflective Christian). It is not surprising, then, that "temporizing," "retreat," or "escape" become rather tempting options. Without a sense of efficacy and social support, we suspect that the intellectual and personal burden may simply become overwhelming. With the right kind of "challenge in the context of support" (see Perry, 1981), the student becomes an active learner who values relationships and responsibilities (see discussion on "scaffolding" in chapter 7).

Commitment in Relativism (Positions 7 through 9)
Commitment in Relativism (positions 7 through 9) is the logical extension of this period of active experimentation and risk-taking, not unlike Erikson's proposed shift from psychological moratorium to identity achievement (see chapter 5). Matters of epistemological and intellectual reflection potentially take on a more explicit lifestyle and worldview orientation. Adult learners progressing through these positions of commitment realize that while there are multiple perspectives in this pluralistic world, and while much knowledge is contextual, there are nevertheless some answers and some commitments that are more "right" than others. Forging "wholehearted but tentative" commitments will most likely make them feel vulnerable. What potentially emerges is a kind of "convicted civility" that reflects the perspective of Oliver Wendell Holmes: "I do not give a fig for the simplicity on this side of complexity. But I would give my life for simplicity on the other side of complexity" (Parks, 1986, pp. 50–51).

Mature wisdom is not escape from complexity and mystery, but active engagement with the problems and questions of the day without relying exclusively on authority-bound and dualistic ways of knowing. Similar themes are clearly evident in the work of Erikson (see chapter 5) and Fowler (see chapter 4).[1]

Perry's scheme, like that of Piaget, is a *structural* model. In other words, it focuses on the *forms* (i.e., structures) of thought rather than on the specific content of such thoughts. Although it might be tempting to view it as a stage model only, it is more accurately a "dialectical, relational and recursive" approach (see Perry, 1981). The scheme assumes that the adult learner proceeds through positions in sequence, and that learners at "lower" positions cannot really appreciate the reasoning or thinking at "higher" positions. Still, it does not need to be viewed in an arrogant, elitist, or even ethnocentric manner. Students at different positions approach problems and questions differently, but this is certainly no guarantee that their "character" is better.

The work of Perry has immediate connection to the practice of Christian education. At the end of this chapter, concrete implications of the Perry scheme of intellectual development are discussed. In the next section a modification of Perry's work is discussed. This adaptation addresses some gender-related issues, noted by several researchers, and has received a wide reading in educational circles. The interest in this work by Christian educators goes beyond the empirical investigations per se and focuses on the epistemology and alternative way of knowing and embracing truth proposed by these researchers.

THE POWER OF BELENKY

The work most often cited in the ethical and moral reasoning differences between the roles and functions area is no doubt Belenky et al.'s *Women's Ways of Knowing* (1986). Like Perry and his colleagues at Harvard, Belenky and her colleagues based their model on in-depth, interpreted interviews with 135 women, 90 of whom were college students. Based on their content analyses of the transcribed interviews designed to assess cognitive and psychosocial development, they developed an alternative model consisting of five major "perspectives" or "positions" they believed more accurately reflected their data and experience.

Silence

Women in this position are characterized by extreme self-denial and dependence on external authority for guidance and education. Specifically, they do not see themselves as "knowers" and all too often are "without voice." In the Perry scheme, they could not accurately be described as even dualists, since their approach to learning is like a kind of academic learned helplessness (that is, they don't even seem to try). Tragically, they were almost completely lacking in self-identity and unable even to conceive of further self-development. There was a disproportionate amount of abuse or abject poverty in their backgrounds, according to the researchers, and they constituted a small minority of those interviewed. We suspect, however, that the concept has wide applicability in cultures where women are clearly oppressed or "invisible" (see the sensitive discussion of these themes in Coles and Coles' *Women of Crisis II: Lives of Work and Dreams,* 1980).

Received Knowing

These individuals see themselves as knowers and are gaining a voice. Still, their thinking is rather dualistic, in that they echo the voice of authority figures rather than asserting themselves. Their primary means of learning is by listening to others; learning is still a very passive process. Their moral judgments tend to conform to societal conventions, and their self-concepts depend very heavily on what others think of them.

Received knowers see knowledge as very distant from themselves, as something to be discovered from authority figures who possess this etheral entity. They approach the educational environment somewhat like a sponge who sees her role as soaking up as much knowledge as possible from the experts. No doubt there is a time and a place for such a mind-set, but as a steady diet it can actually become anti-developmental, thwarting the maturation process. Conformists do not usually become intellectual risk-takers.

Subjective Knowing

This parallels the movement from dualism to multiplicity. Specifically, the transition is from passivity to action, in that the self is emerging and growing. Subjective knowers perceive truth to be very private and personal, and they begin to value and respect their own intuition and opinion. Like students in multiplicity, they begin to trust their inner voice as a source of authority, but they are still very reluctant to express it. Discerning truth tends to be a rather solitary activity, intrapsychic rather than interpersonal.

Procedural Knowing

In contrast to subjectivists, procedural knowers have a somewhat lower view of their intuitions and opinions. Like the emerging relativist of Perry, they are discovering that not all perspectives are equally valid, and that truth can (and should) be shared (versus simply kept private). Toward that end, the procedural knower actively seeks knowledge through deliberate, systematic analysis. Sometimes this occurs in a manner marked by detachment from the process of learning (separate knowing). At other times, the knower is not separated from the known (connected knowing), and the process of learning is more interactional and reciprocal, based on mutual respect and trust. Belenky et al. (1986, p. 102) assume that this process is not gender-specific but may be gender-related. Again, note the contrast between Belenky et al. and Perry in terms of the relative emphasis on the relational dimension of knowing.

Constructed Knowing

This stage is similar to the final stage in Perry's scheme. Like the committed relativist, the constructed knower has reached the vital understanding that knowledge is not some distant, ethereal entity to be discovered in isolation. Indeed, the constructed knower sees her role as a learner to be not a passive sponge, simply receiving knowledge from authorities, but rather an active "builder" who is in the process of constructing.

Becoming a constructed knower involves a process of integrating subjective (intuition) and objective (procedural) knowledge. Ideally, rationality is teamed with passion and emotion and energy. Personal involvement and investment in the process of learning is high—and is seen as shared responsibility. We would add that constructed knowers are probably self-confident yet humble, possessors of strong convictions yet civil in their interactions with others. Their "firm but flexible" commitments value and appreciate the diversity of other perspectives.

Constructed knowers also have a very different view of self and the overall process of learning. They are in the search for (and have begun to find) a unique and authentically personal voice. Knowledge, they discover, is not some distant ethereal entity—indeed, with significant effort, it can be constructed and built. Learning therefore becomes active rather than passive, a function of deep personal involvement and investment as well as shared responsibilities.

TOWARD AN INTEGRATIVE PERSPECTIVE

It should be clear to the reader that the approach of Belenky et al. is less hierarchical than that of Perry. Despite this important difference, both models reveal strikingly similar beliefs about the nature of human development. The key phrase that seems to emerge from Belenky et al. is that of "developing one's voice," a view of one's self as not only a knower but as someone who is capable of constructing new knowledge and insight. A similar process can be seen in Perry's scheme in the progression from dualism, in which students simply receive knowledge from authorities, to the position of commitment in relativism, in which the individual finally sees herself as capable of construct-ing meaning and knowledge.

Perhaps what is most helpful and unique about the Belenky et al. approach is its emphasis on the relationship between a positive self-concept and the articulation of one's voice (i.e., cognitive development appears to parallel identity develop-ment). For silent women, intellectual development was greatly thwarted by their nearly nonexistent self-identities, whereas constructed knowers emphasized the vital importance of their own emerging self-identities in their cognitive development.

Taken together, both approaches offer us valuable insights into the development of self, voice, and mind within a collegiate context. Perhaps the greatest potential area of cognitive development is not so much a change in attitudes as *a change in the way one's attitudes are held*—with greater confidence and tolerance (Berger, 1993, p. 422). Perhaps college students become more accepting of diversity because they are less threatened by the inevitable differences of opinion. Consequently, they are more likely to be open to dialectical reasoning, to share their voice, and to forge commitments in the context of their communities. Surely our Christian communities can appreciate the need for greater clarity about these most important processes.

Constructed knowers are self-confident yet humble persons. They are rigorous in their pursuit of truth and yet at the same time can appreciate and respect the complexities of differing viewpoints. Still, constructed knowers are not halfhearted in their convictions, but they are also civil toward those with whom they disagree. As Perry has observed in his description of committed relativists, they do not simply mouth and espouse beliefs; they act on them in word and deed. The constructed knower is an empathetic individual, one who is not only able but willing to listen actively and respectfully to others, including those with whom she disagrees.

Constructed knowers are not only concerned about the expression of their voices, but are committed to assisting others in developing and expressing their own convictions, especially in the formative stage. They see it as their responsibility to connect with others, to teach them, and to share with them. Indeed, with greater intellectual maturation, we view this as a matter of intellectual integrity and the responsible stewardship of our minds. In Belenky et al. (1986), the teacher is viewed as a midwife who assists in giving birth to the ideas of others, an analogy that is incredibly powerful to us. Contrast that with the notion of teachers as bankers, who see their tasks as "depositing" discrete pieces of information into the minds of their students.

In short, the constructed knower values the interpersonal as well as the intellectual. One's intellectual pursuits are seen as an ongoing process of perpetual growth and development, of lifelong living and striving to achieve her full potential and become all she can be.

IMPLICATIONS FOR CHRISTIAN EDUCATORS

We see many parallels between what it means to be a constructed knower or committed relativist and what it means to be a mature Christian. Suffice it to say that we think it is vital that Christian educators make prominent the goal of promoting holistic development. Obviously, the content of Christian education is crucial. Our foremost concern, however, has to do with the often undervalued or even neglected contextual variables that Perry and Belenky et al. so clearly address.

Recall some of the qualities of constructed knowers mentioned in the previous section. They are marked by humility and empathy for others. Consider the words of Philippians 2:4: "Each of you should look not only to your interests, but also to the interests of others," which compel us to care for others as well as for ourselves for God's sake. The constructed knower possesses "firm yet flexible commitments" but also is civil and loving toward others who hold differing viewpoints (see the excellent discussion of convicted civility in Mouw, 1992). The constructed knower does not simply espouse views and beliefs but puts them into action (see James 2:17, "faith, by itself, if it is not accompanied by action, is dead"). Further, the constructed knower is marked by passion and compassion (see Regas, 1987), qualities any Christian should learn to cultivate and express. The constructed knower desires to empower others and serve others and to use his or her gifts (including the development and expression of one's voice), goals that all Christians should be able to endorse as an expression of their Christian commitment. The imagery of life as a journey or sojourn in Belenky et al. is also strikingly reminiscent of passages in Scripture that view the spiritual life as a walk or a run. Finally, the constructed knower values diversity and community, something that "world Christians" ought to view highly. The repeated references in Scripture to the interdependent members of the body of Christ certainly come to mind. These parallels do not make the theorizing of Perry or Belenky et al. inherently Christian, but the overlapping concerns are certainly striking or at least suggestive of the possibility of common grace and common truth (see Holmes, 1983).

How can Christian educators promote this kind of psychological and spiritual development in their students, be it in formal (classroom) or informal and unstructured situations? First of all, it might be useful to stop viewing their students as "tabula rasas" or "empty bank accounts" with no prior knowledge or experiences to offer the instructor or other students. Rather than adopting this banker model of teaching, educators could adopt a more transformational model like that of the midwife or mountaineer. Contemporary discussions of the need for more effective role-modeling or mentorship (see chapters 13 and 16) or improving higher learning in our classrooms (Angelo, 1993) are certainly needed. Effective teachers see each adult learner as having the potential for constructing knowledge rather than simply receiving it. There is a world of difference between slowly and patiently attempting to draw insights and values out of the student versus depositing or even shoving knowledge into the student. Obviously, support and instruction are crucial, but it is ultimately the student's "baby" (midwife analogy) or "journey" (mountaineering analogy). Ideas, like "embryonic" faith commitments, must be slowly and carefully nourished toward greater differentiation and maturity. Offering "challenge within the context of support" (see Perry, 1981) seems essential for growth. Too much support seems to foster continued dependence on external sources of authority, whereas too much challenge without support runs the risk of prompting disengagement, escape, and retreat (see Van Wicklin, Burwell, & Butman, 1994).

Both Perry and Belenky et al. stress the need to encourage the application of values and commitments (i.e., "How then will you live your life?"). The importance of praxis in the educational context and beyond cannot be stressed enough in Christian circles (see Westfall, 1991, for a helpful discussion). All too often our subculture stresses orthodoxy ("right thinking") to the neglect of orthopraxy ("right living"). Perry seems especially sensitive to the need for authentic commitments to have clear behavioral manifestations ("You don't just have the truth—the truth must have you!"). With reference to faith commitments, it is vital that Christian educators become exemplars of the values and beliefs they espouse, since students today seem especially sensitive to perceived inconsistencies between what the teacher says and what he or she does.

Although it may seem obvious to some readers, it also seems essential to give students opportunities to practice expressing and articulating their voice. Ideally, the local community of believers is a safe and supportive environment where emerging views, beliefs, and commitments can be tested and find acceptance. This in and of itself has the potential to promote a sense of efficacy and self-confidence. The Scriptures are the ultimate authority upon which the truth of values and beliefs must be evaluated, but the responsible Christian educator must be patient and respectful as students work their faith out "with fear and trembling." We suspect that this will mean teachers will speak less — and the students will express themselves more, however tentative and cautious their initial efforts might be.

In order for men and women to become mature, connected knowers, we need an atmosphere of community where questions can be raised and heard, where voices are freely expressed and not silenced, and where students are given the opportunity to think aloud, including the freedom to express their doubts and struggles related to their faith commitments (see Yancey, 1992). Authentic, personal convictions are not formed in isolation, especially in the critical years of young adulthood. Christianity cannot be "inherited" — from parents or even dedicated teachers, although it certainly may become incorporated (see Butman, 1993). For one's faith to be truly meaningful it must be his or her faith, and eventually expressed in the context of a group of fellowshipping and worshiping believers.

We suspect that for many college students, although certainly not for all, this can only come through a period of questioning, doubt, soul-searching, and seeking (see Parks, 1986). This kind of dissonance or disequilibrium seems essential for the development of a mature faith (see the discussion of individuative-reflective faith in chapter 4). We suspect that our subcultures and societies are profoundly ambivalent, or even overtly hostile, toward this mind-set. The evangelical church has not always been a safe place to articulate and express one's voice, especially when it is met with silence, shame, or a condescending authoritarian retort like, "You just don't have enough faith." Perhaps what Belenky et al. and Perry would have us see is that such questioning may be vital, even life-sustaining, for the authentic expression of emerging commitments and contextualized knowing.

A FEW CAUTIONARY REMARKS

It is crucial for teachers to be patient with students. Christian education can be a slow and often tedious process that may not bear fruit for years or even decades. Learners' progress, or even lack of it, is not ultimately a teacher's responsibility. Our students are certainly different, and some are clearly "easier" to teach than others, but this is no basis for our treating them in a condescending, patronizing, or preferential manner.

It is natural to want to have a classroom or community full of mature, constructed knowers with fully cultivated and sanctified imaginations. Not many of us will ever have such an experience. Each student is unique and therefore on his or her own developmental timeline. Well-meaning but pushy attempts to speed up development may be counterproductive and frustrating for both the student and the instructor. The right combination of structure, support, and challenge is an ongoing assessment task for the Christian educator, and this delicate balance is difficult to achieve. Students need to be gently led to grow and mature. They do not need to be carried or shoved. In a very real and powerful sense, it is the students who must give birth to their own ideas and convictions, and they are the ones who must ultimately decide which paths they will travel on in the journey of life.

It is also important for teachers to be patient with themselves. An educator must be careful not to judge his or her personal worth as an educator (or a person) according to how developed his or her students are. It is clearly destructive to conclude that one is a failure as a teacher because a student had a "miscarriage" (midwife analogy) or "lost his way" in life's journey toward greater maturity (guide analogy). Educators must strive to provide the best possible learning environment in which the students may develop. Teachers must, however, be careful to allow students the freedom to make mistakes and learn (often through trial and error).

As Christians, we are called to "put on" a number of traits that are powerful prescriptions for any helping relationship. In the words of Colossians 3:12: "Therefore, as God's chosen people, holy and dearly loved, clothe yourselves with compassion, kindness, humility, gentleness and patience." Indeed, in our work as Christian educators, we are to image God in our work (see chapter 16 in Jones & Butman, 1991). When it comes to the issue of cognitive development, we must remember that secular brilliance is not the same thing as true wisdom. God is the beginning of wisdom, the source of all wisdom, and wisdom incarnate. The specific content of what we believe does matter and has eternal consequences.

Although we may differ on the way in which important truths should be discovered or found, we can certainly agree with Foster (1978, p. 1) that "Superficiality is the curse of our age. . . . The desperate need today is not for a greater number of intelligent or gifted people, but for deep people." Apart from the specific content of those beliefs, we are convinced that the process of making and keeping commitments is not unrelated to the task of becoming truly deep people. If either model assists us in this task, it certainly has the potential to at least become powerful.

FOR FURTHER READING

Belenky, M., Clinchy, B., Goldberger, N., & Tarule, J. (1986). *Women's ways of knowing: The development of self, voice, and mind.* New York: Basic Books.

Gilligan, C. (1982). *In a different voice: Psychological theory and women's development.* Cambridge, MA: Harvard University Press.

Parks, S. (1986). *The critical years: The young adult search for a faith to live by.* San Francisco: Harper & Row.

Pascarella, E., & Terenzini, P. (1991). *How college affects students.* San Francisco: Jossey-Bass.

Perry, W. (1970). *Forms of intellectual and ethical development in the college years.* New York: Holt, Rinehart and Winston.

Perry, W. (1981). Cognitive and ethical growth: The making of meaning. In A.W. Chickering (Ed.), *The modern American college* (pp. 76–116). San Francisco: Jossey-Bass.

NOTE

1. Those wanting additional information should write for the "cumulative bibliography and copy service catalog for the Perry scheme of intellectual and ethical development" (c/o Dr. Bill Moore, Coordinator, Perry Network, 1520 14th Ave. SW, Olympia, WA 98502).

7

The Power of Vygotsky

Cynthia Jones Neal

"Mommy, I can do it!"

"No, I'm gonna teach you. You have to do it my way."

"No, Mommy, let me do it!"

This interaction occurred during a session in which a mother was attempting to teach her three-year-old child a task. Just prior to this interaction, the mother had watched her son perform the task by himself with a fairly high rate of accuracy. One might expect that a sensitive teacher, having just observed the child's abilities, would approach the teaching with the idea of building on his present skills. However, this mother simply intruded, took over the task, and commanded the child to follow her instructions. After two minutes of this "teaching," the three-year-old pushed the task away and said to the mother, "You do it." This child, who initially had worked quite competently alone, had now simply given up.

This, unfortunately, is only one incident among many that I have found in my observations of parents teaching their children (Neal & Diaz, 1989). Quite frequently, we, as teachers, however well intentioned we may be, are guilty of the same overwhelming intrusiveness. In this chapter, I will demonstrate how a particular quality of teaching, specifically, scaffolding, built from Lev Vygotsky's theory, has relevance to our desires, indeed mandate, to educate our children in the Christian faith.

Vygotsky's socio-contextual theory has particular application, given that the Christian faith has relational and dynamic qualities, and it will serve to further our understanding of the ways we might effectively support our children in their faith development. To develop the concept of scaffolding, two basic Vygotskian frameworks will be discussed: the notion of development-in-context and the notion of the zone of proximal development.

OVERVIEW

In recent years the work of Lev Vygotsky has provided contemporary developmental and cognitive psychologists with novel theoretical and empirical research models. It is a theory that incorporates the relevant connections between growing children and their culture, a theory that emphasizes the formative role that mastery of the tools and tasks of the culture play. A socio-contextual theory such as Vygotsky's asserts that knowledge is shaped, organized, and has meaning through communal acts. Therefore, development can be understood only when embedded within a social-historical context.

Many developmental theories view the individual apart from the environment and yet "influenced" by it. Piaget refers to his theory as an interactionist theory. While most theories agree that there is an interaction between the individual and the environment, there is disagreement as to the function or nature of that interaction. Vygotsky advanced the notion that development occurs in context (culture) and in turn transforms the context. According to this theory we dare not view the child or attempt to explain the child apart from the social context. Examining the child while ignoring the context distorts our understanding of the nature of the child and the community.

Two essentially different modes of analysis are possible in the study of psychological structures. . . . The first method analyzes complex psychological wholes into elements. It may be compared to the chemical analysis of water into hydrogen and oxygen, neither of which possesses the properties of the whole and each of which possesses properties not present in the whole. The student applying this method in looking for the explanation of some property of water—why it extinguishes fire, for example—will find to his surprise that hydrogen burns and oxygen sustains fire. These discoveries will not help him much in solving the problem. (Vygotsky, 1962, p. 3)

Psychology winds up in the same kind of dead end when it analyzes human nature by reducing the units of study into smaller, decontextualized parts. Vygotsky asserted that a second mode of analysis was required, that our unit of study must be the child-in-context. We who hold to the Christian view of the *imago Dei,* which assumes being relational is part of being made in God's image, can find alliance with this second mode of analysis, child-in-context. We are a people-in-relationship. The contexts with which we live include important relationships. We cannot understand the developing human person apart from the relationships that help shape that development.

VYGOTSKY'S VIEW OF DEVELOPMENT

According to Vygotsky, individual differences in children's development can be explained by the individual differences in the social context in which children learn to master the tasks and experiences that the culture defines as meaningful. In other words, individual differences in cognitive processing can be understood and explained by the social milieu with which the child interacts. Some of these differences are manifested in a child's attentional, memory, and self-regulatory processes (what Vygotsky labeled higher psychological functions). These psychological functions have social origins. What begins as a biological function is transformed through the shared, social interactions into a higher intrapsychological function. One way to illustrate this concept is noting the developmental progression of a child's attentional capacities (Diaz, Neal, & Amaya-Williams, 1990). Contrast or movement "captures" the infant's attention. With age, there is a shift from this "captured" or other-regulated phenomenon toward voluntary or self-regulation; the child develops the ability to sustain attention in the face of distracters (particularly in the classroom setting).

The use of signs (e.g., language, symbol system, etc.) mediates these higher mental processes (Wertsch, 1985). A qualitatively new level of psychological functioning emerges. Vygotsky and Piaget disagreed on the importance of these mediational means or tools; in particular, language. Whereas Piaget de-emphasized the role of language in cognitive development, Vygotsky viewed language as foundational to all higher cognitive processes.

Development-in-context

In order to understand Vygotsky's view of development, we must examine the social interactions that govern our experiences. What are the contexts in which we live? Bronfenbrenner proposed that development is best conceptualized by a series of "nested structures, each inside the next, like a set of Russian dolls" (1979, p. 3). The immediate setting, the microsystem, contains the developing person. This is the home, the classroom, the church, and so on. The second structure, the mesosystem, refers to the interconnections between immediate settings, or microsystems, for example, how the communication between home and school affects the child's ability to learn, the connection between the church and home. The third structure, the exosystem, includes those events that may not contain the developing person but affect him or her (parental employment, decisions human service agencies make with regard to foster care, etc.). The fourth structure, the macrosystem, contains the "blueprint for the organization of the society" (p. 4). This includes the resources, lifestyles, opportunities, and patterns of social interactions embedded in the other systems, for example, how the government decides to prioritize federal funding for human services, beliefs about the quality of life, perspectives on separation between church and state.

Although we could legitimately discuss the Christian culture within all levels, beginning with the macrosystem serving as the broader theological and belief context, it is at the level of the microsystem that the building blocks for faith development are formed. This is the system most relevant for our purposes of understanding Christian education. Both the home and the church are part of the process of faith development, sometimes working in concert, sometimes at odds. As can be seen from the Scriptures, the family and its community (the church) are the major places in which faith development occurs (Deut. 6:1-9; 31:12-13).

Jesus modeled the relational and dynamic quality of faith when He welcomed the children.

> Then little children were brought to Jesus for Him to place His hands on them and pray for them. But the disciples rebuked those who brought them. Jesus said, "Let the little children come to Me, and do not hinder them, for the kingdom of heaven belongs to such as these" (Matt. 19:13-14).

The children are to be a part of the faith community and share in its life. When we leave Christian education to a traditional classroom setting, we remove faith from context. Faith primarily means to believe, trust in, rely on, be persuaded by (Liddell & Scott, 1974). As a verb, it is an active mode of being and committing. Faith is always relational and dynamic. Classrooms must become faith communities inviting students to work together, share experiences, connecting truth (biblical knowledge) with lived experience (Palmer, 1983). The separation of the Christian faith from relationships and dynamic life leaves an artificial understanding of the Christian walk. There is a real danger in judging children's understanding of the Christian faith by their answers on workbook sheets. Additionally, it would be tragic if the community of faith were out of touch with children's lives outside the classroom, never seeing how or if their faith understanding has an impact on their world or guides their behaviors.

I query students each semester as to how many children they know by name or even spoke to during the last Sunday service at their church. An embarrassed silence generally follows, except, of course, for those students who teach Sunday School! It is a sad commentary when Christian education is relegated to the Sunday School teacher, thereby relieving the rest of the congregation of the responsibility for the faith development of the children of the church. It is someone else's job. That is in direct contrast to the scriptural understanding of faith. Fostering an evolving faith community requires us to unite the learning of biblical doctrines and creeds with the collaborative sharing of our faith experiences ("communal process" of gaining knowledge).

Robert Coles discusses the environments that best facilitate moral development. He raises important issues that I believe are meaningful correlates when discussing that which promotes faith development. In fact, we could simply substitute the word *faith* where Coles writes *moral*.

1. Moral life is best understood by actual behaviors that arise from real experience, not verbal responses to hypothetical moral dilemmas.

2. Moral responses reflect a person's character, personality, and particular social situation in ways that are complex and not reducible to abstract propositions.

3. Children typically understand their actual moral behavior as having a narrative meaning in the context of their life.

4. Morally structured stories or narratives, often of a religious kind, provide strong support and inspiration for children, and their own moral responses are often deeply rooted in their previous experience with narratives (Vitz, 1990).

In sum, when deciding the best method to educate others in the Christian faith, one must preserve and build from the cultural context within which faith is learned. Through the relationships that are developed, our homes and churches impress upon us how faith is lived. If indeed we are people in relationship with others and learn from our relationships with others, then our narratives, our stories of faith, must be integral parts of our education. Parker Palmer reminds us of the crucial role of the church community, "The community is a discipline of mutual encouragement and mutual testing, keeping me both hopeful and honest about the love that seeks me, the love I seek to be" (1983, p. 18).

As a Christian educator, I must also understand the context out of which this learner standing before me comes. What is his or her story? What is going on at home? What woundedness is present in my learner? The mesosystem, according to Bronfenbrenner, is that necessary level of communication and connection between the microsystems. The church and family need to work in concert, both microsystems recognizing the importance of nurturing the faith of our youngest disciples.

ZONE OF PROXIMAL DEVELOPMENT

A useful framework to help us understand differences in cognitive development was introduced by Vygotsky (1978) as the zone of proximal development. Wertsch and Rogoff (1984) have conceptualized the zone of proximal development as

> that phase in development in which the child has only partially mastered a task but can participate in its execution with the assistance and supervision of an adult or more capable peer. Thus, the zone of proximal development is a dynamic region of sensitivity to learning the skills of culture, in which children develop through participation in problem solving with more experienced members of the culture. (p. 1)

Ideally, the more skilled adult builds on the competencies children already have and present them with activities supporting a level of competence slightly beyond where the children are now.

The zone of proximal development is an important concept because it embodies the essential features of Vygotsky's theory: that of learning in context, the importance of mediational means to transform shared cognitive processes into internal psychological capacities and the emphasis on cultural practice as a source of thinking. Vygotsky did not believe that internalization was merely a function of transfer of knowledge or skills first shared with a more competent teacher. He believed that the very tools of the collaborative learning process are internalized, subsequently transforming and producing new, elaborative cognitive functions (Ratner, 1991). In other words, the learner internalizes and subsequently is transformed by the process. The goal is not for the learner to become just like the teacher. "The focus, therefore, is not on transferring skills, as such, from those who know more to those who know less but on the collaborative use of mediational means to create, obtain, and communicate meaning . . ." (Moll, 1990, p. 13).

I believe we could discuss this process with the principles of faith as well. Our goal is that the children become aware of and transformed by the principles of faith. According to Vygotsky, "an individual is formed through the internalization of activities carried out in the bosom of society and through the interaction that occurs within the zone of proximal development" (Rosa & Montero, 1990, p. 83). What a beautiful metaphor with which to describe the transformation that can occur within the bosom of our church society! This is not a transfer of the adult's faith but a very transformation of the learners—faith that will guide their thoughts and behaviors.

This raises the question concerning an endpoint in faith development. We as Christian educators must recognize that the very internalization process transforms the faith of the learner. Personal faith, ever changing in complexity and ever growing in intimacy with our Creator God, is what we eagerly desire for our learners. The emphasis, then, is on the joint activity of the learner mediated by teachers with the expressed goal of helping the children "obtain and express meaning in ways that would enable them to make this knowledge and meaning their own" (Rosa & Montero, 1990, p. 14).

This joint activity requires the church to think in terms of community building both inside and outside the classroom. Curriculum should be carefully scrutinized. Is there an emphasis on rote memorization versus conceptual understanding? Do the children spend time learning the books of the Bible at the expense of learning and experiencing concepts such as forgiveness and servant leadership? How well are we listening to our learners? Are we encouraging discussion, disagreement? Are the learners creatively interacting with each other? Is there regular use of journaling, group work, questions? We must also examine the way we structure Christian education outside the classroom. What are the supports necessary to facilitate mentoring relationships?

I observed one successful mentoring program. All the adolescents were encouraged to choose adult mentors to spend time with outside the church setting. These youth have benefited tremendously from these relationships as, indeed, have the adults. A variety of activities are shaped by the mentor and the adolescent with occasional corporate programs with all the dyads.

Active participation and respect for individual differences are principles shared by both Piagetian or Vygotskian theories. Nevertheless, an important distinction remains. Vygotsky highlighted the role of assisted learning as opposed to a Piagetian emphasis on a more independent learning style. Collaborative participation in learning within the zone of proximal development is an important feature that results from a Vygotskian theoretical position. Scaffolding, as an application of Vygotsky's theory, is an essential tool for the Christian educator.

SCAFFOLDING AND ITS INTEGRATION WITH CHRISTIAN EDUCATION

In this final section I will endeavor to bridge the two Vygotskian constructs of development-in-context and zone of proximal development with the relevance of this distinctive quality of teaching.

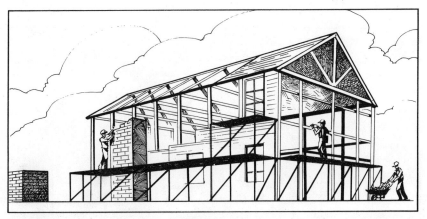

Figure 1

Anyone who has worked with young children has experienced their struggle for autonomy and independence. This struggle is often demonstrated by those infamous words, "Me do it!" Knowing what tasks the young child is capable of accomplishing, as well as knowing when continued help is necessary on the part of the adult, is a major component of competent teaching. More importantly, in order for a child to begin taking over the regulation of his or her behavior, teachers must be able sensitively and gradually to withdraw from the regulatory role. This relinquishment of control requires teachers to be able to discern the level of independent functioning children can competently handle. This competent and sensitive teaching describes the quality of interaction called scaffolding.

It may be helpful to conceptualize scaffolding in terms of the analogy it suggests (Bruner, 1983). When we consider a scaffold that builders use when building a structure, we can imagine a steel framework around the building being erected. As the illustration demonstrates (see Figure 1), the scaffold supports the work at that current stage of construction. The next illustration (see Figure 2) reveals the necessary adjustment

Figure 2

made, the different position the scaffold now occupies as the building progresses. The scaffold is a temporary framework of support for the builder, used until the structure is capable of standing on its own. The scaffold is then withdrawn. Admittedly, this is a crude analogy; builders erecting a building clearly cannot capture the intricate workings that transpire between teachers and children. The construct we do want to capture is the role teachers play in assisting children in taking over that regulatory function so essential for later development.

Scaffolding is described as the gradual withdrawal of adult control and support as a function of children's increasing mastery on a given task (Diaz, Neal, Amaya-Williams, 1990). An important skill of the effective scaffolder is the ability to accurately judge the level at which a child is working. Adjustments of support are made optimally based on a child's behavioral cue. Rogoff (1990) likens this role to that of apprenticeship.

> Vygotsky's model for the mechanism through which social interaction facilitates cognitive development resembles apprenticeship, in which a novice works closely with an expert in joint problem solving in the zone of proximal development. The novice is thereby able to participate in skills beyond those that he or she is independently capable of handling. Development builds on the internalization by the novice of the shared cognitive processes, appropriating what was carried out in collaboration to extend existing knowledge and skills. (p. 141)

Appropriate adjustment involves assessing the focus of attention, the level of skill development, and the amount of responsibility the child is able to take over during the course of the interaction. The essential feature of scaffolding is that the focus is on the learner. The teacher has a set agenda—principles to learn, tasks to complete, concepts to understand. However, the method of teaching is to allow the learner's behavior to guide the instruction. Proverbs 22:6 tells us, "Train a child in the way he should go, and when he is old he will not turn from it." Clearly we are mandated to "train." And yet, we are told to pay attention to the child's way—"according to his way." In Deuteronomy 6:20 we find a similar focus: "In the future, *when* your son asks you . . ." — again we are told to pay attention to the child's readiness. This is not abdication of the teaching

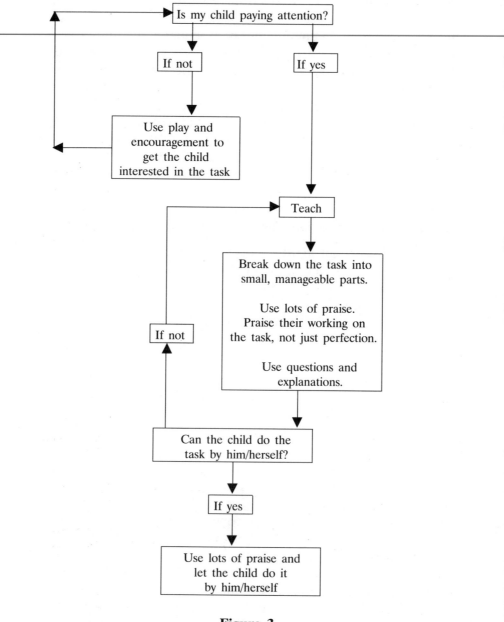

Figure 3

responsibility. It is the call for teachers to observe the child's "way" or style of learning, the child's level of understanding. We should pay particular attention to the mistakes the child makes. Not just for the purpose of correction, but to give the teacher a window into the child's understanding. When the child indicates mastery, the competent scaffolder withdraws, allowing the child to perform independently (see flowchart in Figure 3).

Jesus is an exemplar of this gradual withdrawal when He demonstrates the change in His relationship with His disciples. He no longer plays the role of master; the disciples are now regarded as friends: "I no longer call you servants, because a servant does not know his master's business. Instead, I have called you friends, for everything that I learned from My Father I have made known to you" (John 15:15). When teachers are supporting their children's learning, adjusting the structure as children gain in skills and understanding, and transferring responsibility as children indicate readiness, development is enhanced.

The attributes of the scaffolder include warmth, praise, high quality of verbal teaching (questions, explanation, direct relinquishment), breaking down the task, and allowing the learner to struggle (Neal, 1990). These are all parental qualities found in the developmental literature that facilitate social and cognitive development. These scaffolding tools help the learner internalize the necessary mediational means for transforming the cognitive capability. These are necessary characteristics of the discipler as well. I believe that a competent scaffolder is a discipler. Learning about something so dynamic as faith requires more than a drill and practice routine or a rote memorization strategy. Faith development occurs in relationship woven from the fabric of dialogue and apprenticeship or mentoring. Disciplers take the disciples from their own levels of understanding, challenging and stretching the learners through mediational means such as questions and explanations toward becoming those who are able to make faith commitments of their own. Jesus modeled this scaffolding for us when He met the disciples on their way to Emmaus (Luke 24:13-32).

One can readily notice how Jesus used questions to draw

out His companions' current level of understanding. He allowed their mistakes to become apparent. However, He used their misunderstandings as a springboard to give a clearer picture, a more full interpretation of the prophecies in the Scriptures concerning Himself. Although He used questions and explanations, He also allowed them to struggle in their discovery process. He walked with them along the way—their way. He did not disclose His identity initially. I suspect that might have clouded the issue, which was that they needed to understand the Scriptures. It was not until their eyes were opened, when He broke bread, that full realization came for them. At that point, Jesus left. The structure was in place. The scaffold was no longer needed. They had come to the place of understanding and knowledge for themselves. No longer did they need a king; they had met their Savior. Continued support, confirmatory as well as challenge, would come from the presence of the Holy Spirit in their lives.

Encapsulating Vygotsky into a single chapter is a formidable task. Obviously, only a fraction of his theory is present. I have tried, however, to raise what I believe are some of the most relevant aspects for Christian education. Faith development occurs and is understood by our narratives in mentoring or discipling relationships. Learning and growing in faith require a communal or collaborative effort. The greatest changes occur when we challenge our learners within the zone of proximal development through dialogue and example. The Bible remains the sacred text which we explore and from which our narratives have meaning. We need to walk with our learners as they struggle to make the Christian faith their own, using mediational means that transform them rather than producing automaton conformity. This process is very similar to the "connected teaching" concepts or teaching as midwifery (described in chapter 6). When we scaffold, focusing on our learners' levels of understanding, building on their strengths, using their misunderstandings to adjust our level of support, our learners will begin the process of creating knowledge and meaning for themselves. If our knowledge of Scripture and faith development is to transform our lives, it must be internalized and owned. "(O)ur epistemology is quietly transformed into our ethic. The images of self and world that are found at the heart of our knowledge will also be found in the values by which we live our lives" (Palmer, 1983, p. 21).

As Christian educators, we yearn for those we have mentored to truly be the Lord's disciples and to possess a faith reflected in the choices they make and the values by which they live. Although we always stay in relationship with our learners, we ultimately desire to work ourselves out of a job. When we scaffold our learners, we are "making disciples" (Matt. 28:19) who will, in turn, disciple/scaffold others.

FOR FURTHER READING

Bronfenbrenner, U. (1979). *The ecology of human development.* Cambridge, MA: Harvard University Press.

Luria, A.R. (1979). *The making of mind: A personal account of Soviet psychology.* Cambridge, MA: Harvard University Press.

Moll, L. (Ed.). (1990). *Vygotsky and education.* Cambridge, MA: Cambridge University Press.

Ratner, C. (1991). *Vygotsky's sociohistorical psychology and its contemporary applications.* New York: Plenum Press.

Vygotsky, L. (1978). *Mind in society: The development of higher psychological process.* Cambridge, MA: Harvard University Press.

Section 2

Developmentalism from the Perspective of Age Groups

8

Children and Developmentalism

Julie A. Gorman

W hen I was a child, I talked like a child, I thought like a child, I reasoned like a child. When I became a man, I put childish ways behind me."

The Apostle Paul, 1 Corinthians 13:11

"In Sunday School they told us what you do. Who does it when you are on vacation?"

Jane

"Dear God,
Who draws the lines around the countries?"

Nan

"Dear God,
Instead of letting people die and having to make new ones why don't you just keep the ones you got now?"

Jane

"Dear God,
I like the Lord's Prayer best of all. Did you have to write it a lot

or did you get it right the first time? I have to write everything I
ever write over again."

Lois (Hample & Marshall, 1991)

Developmentalism is probably more consciously perceived
and accepted in the teaching of children than at any succeeding
age. After all, the child's enlarging vocabulary, increasing size,
and changing skill capacities are impossible to ignore. How does
the developing nature of the child reconfigure our attempts to
teach that child?

THE SIGNIFICANCE OF LEARNING STRUCTURES

Theoretical frameworks, particularly the work of Piaget, offer
major considerations for the communication of spiritual truth so
the child can understand it and then implement it in life. As
Christians, we are committed to the transmission of truth, the
content of Scripture. However, developmentalism suggests, and
research has borne out, that the simple declaration of truth or
moral principles does not result in changed values, attitudes, or
actions. Developmentalism declares that the valuable content of
Scripture must be combined with an awareness of the stage the
child is in so as to match the teaching of content to the capacity
of the child.

This suggests that, while all parts of the Bible are true, not
all parts are suitable for teaching to children. It also suggests
that truth, to be understood, must be reframed in the experience of the child. "The Lord is my Shepherd" means little or
nothing to a child of the twentieth century whose nearest association with shepherd is the German shepherd dog who lives
down the street. The truth is relevant but must be repackaged
for children to grasp it with understanding. The passions and
acts of David and Bathsheba, while comparable to present-day
TV series, are nonetheless out of the experience of a fourth-
grader. Yet the child can understand and identify with the overwhelming desire of "I want what I want when I want it—even
when I know I shouldn't." Paraphrases or simple translations
are welcomed wherever teachers and parents aim for understanding of God's Word. This dual focus of being sensitive to

the child and rephrasing truth to make it understandable in the child's world grows out of the awareness of the priority of acting in sync with the capacities available in the child within the stages of growth.

Sequence in learning also affects our teaching for spiritual growth. As each stage gathers understanding and assimilates insight in preparation for the next stage, so in spiritual development we must expect transformational stages to occur. Each stage is a valuable increment in the process. None is regarded as less insightful or unnecessary. When a child responds to an invitation with, "I came because I love Jesus and want to tell Him," this is not a disappointment. Rather, it is a valuable responsive progression in the process of surrendering one's life to Him. Such is a vital stage on the way to knowing God as Savior and Lord. It is saying "yes" to Jesus with the understanding that is there. Neither is this kind of declaration to be rushed into premature birth by putting into the child's mouth words that are not yet comprehended by the heart. Developmentalism says timing is important.

Sequential learning sensitizes us to what has already been constructed and then builds on that, leaving no gaps. It also suggests that the child is continually increasing in capacity for broader and deeper comprehension and response. For many believers, childhood is a time for coming to know Christ — that is the goal. However, developmentalism, with its constantly enlarging capacities and assimilation of more truth, challenges us to help children go on to "grow up in Christ." This means knowing the meaning of increasing surrender to His lordship, discovering widening dimensions of His guidance, becoming aware of the broadening subtleties of sin. The developmentalist never sees the child in a static state, but rather as always increasing in ability and insight. Christians who work with children need to challenge children to the edge of their capacities in the world of spiritual development.

CONCEPTUALIZATION IN VERY YOUNG CHILDREN

How a child thinks has many implications for the teacher of spiritual truth. Piaget hypothesized that very young children (before age two) "think" by experiencing a series of disconnected episodes much like the projection of individual slides on the screen (Beadle, 1970). While they are able to imitate (babies will smile back when smiled at even as newborns), their reasoning capacities seem to be more of a trial-and-error experience. Repetition of simple words will finally issue in a response, but often with inaccurate labeling when a new object is encountered (such as calling a horse, "doggie").

The Tyranny of Transductive Thinking

The process of conceptualizing is so familiar to most of us that it seems strange to think of not being able to do so. A concept is an image or representation by which objects may be classified. For instance, when you see the words "six o'clock," those particular letters, when joined together, stand for a certain configuration of numbers on a clock, which in turn frames a period of time that cannot be seen or held or known in anything but an intangible way. Time exists only in our minds.

The young child finds difficulty in classifying and tends to think in precepts (specifics) rather than concepts. The child relates ideas on a one-to-one basis, moving from one particular to another. A large truck goes fast because it is heavy. A small truck goes fast because it is light. A black truck goes fast because it is black. This is called *transductive thinking* because the thinking moves across from one particular to another particular. The car that gets to the finish line first is the fastest regardless of the amount of distance covered (Williams & Stith, 1974). Children are notorious for wanting the largest piece of cake (or whatever) even though they cannot eat any more than a small piece. Because the child thinks with centering, the focus is on one aspect, failing to factor in any others.

Nonsensical Syncretistical Thinking

Transductive thinking results in persons in this period linking together items, events, or experiences that do not belong together. In first grade, a teacher established the rule that any child having to go to the bathroom must raise his or her hand, to which a puzzled child asked, "Teacher, how does that help?" If the phone rings and the child stumbles on the way to answer it, she will often blame the phone for making her fall down. Children seek for causes, and their limited understanding may create illogical linkage, such as the child who observes the car wreck and asks, "Did the car run into the tree because it was angry at the tree?"

This inaccurate thinking carries over into spiritual truth, as seen in the boy who thought God sent the thunderstorm because he refused to eat his beans at dinner that night. (Many adults still hold to this childish thinking when it comes to spiritual thought, fearing that the flat tire on Monday morning was the result of not going to church on Sunday.) But the wise teacher views wrong answers as natural steps to right understanding and probes the child's understanding of God. "Would God have sent the thunderstorm if you refused to eat your chocolate cake?" "What does a thunderstorm mean?" "Does God send storms to punish and frighten us?"

Myopic Mind-set: An Egocentric Point of View
Listen in on a preschool conversation.

"Give me the car."

"I'm going to my grandma's house today."

"This car is the fastest one."

"My grandma has a cat."

Each of the above two preschoolers assumes the other is interested in what he is interested in and operates out of the stance that "everybody thinks as I do."

Egocentrism is not self-centeredness. It is lacking the capacity to see self as different from others. Young children are unable to see things from the perspective of another. They do not know there is another perspective. Their way of thinking and seeing is the way it is. Different points of view or mentally placing oneself in a position to visualize an object from a different vantage point is impossible. "Now how do you think Derek feels?" is an unanswerable question, just as, "If you were Lisa, you would want somebody to share with you" becomes enigmatic. "Share your toys" is more likely to be accomplished because the child wants to please adults and learns by experience that not sharing is displeasing.

Kohlberg's structures take into account this egocentric element in the amoral stage in which the child has little judgment of right from wrong except on the basis of personal consequences, "what happens to me." The Preconventional Level Stage I child (overlapping the preoperations and concrete concepts period) operates with a blind centering on Authority as knowing what is good and what is bad. "It is bad if I get caught and punished and good if I am rewarded." There is no way others are taken into account.

Perspective on Power: Humanistic/Artificial

The egocentric viewpoint of being at the center of the universe and having the only perspective there is factors in thinking that the events that occur in the natural world are caused by people—often the child himself. This artificial humanistic thinking assigns tremendous responsibility to people. Remember the old warning, "Step on a crack and you'll break your mother's back." In a more serious vein, children of divorce often live for years with the conviction that they caused the separation of parents. If they had been more obedient, more responsive, more . . . the parents would still be together.

CONCEPTUALIZATION DURING CONCRETE PERIOD

During the concrete concepts period the child's thinking increases in complexity but is still attached to substantive, concrete elements. Working with concrete ideas, the child can begin to classify, "Which doesn't belong in this series?" He can begin to grasp time by working with concrete representations of minutes and hours and numbered days on a calendar. "Hands-on" experiences, concrete objects, and activities are vital when teaching concepts of spiritual truth. Pictures, drawings, clay, models, investigations, and drama help reshape and build new ways of understanding.

The Ambiguity of Abstracts

Though seven- to ten-year-olds can use the vocabulary of abstracts, the children have difficulty with them as mental concepts and need concrete situations to explain and expand their awarenesses. Abstracts (intangible vocabulary words that conceptualize many specifics) abound in Scripture and in our principles for life—"mercy," "justice," "sin," "responsibility," "salvation," and "grace." As children seek to "make sense" out of words not understood, they often modify them to fit in with their system of understanding, a habit that causes adults to smile. Thus "surely goodness and mercy shall follow me . . ." becomes "good Mrs. Murphy shall follow me. . . ." Or the pledge of allegiance to the flag is rephrased, "I pledge a legion to the flag of the Republic of Richard Sands; one nation and a vegetable with liberty and justice to all" (Stith, 1967).

Hard-to-Grasp Generalizations

The child at early ages of this stage has difficulty in understanding generalizations—drawing abstract concepts from concrete happenings. "Do good to those who wrongfully use you" and "Live by faith" are examples of generalizations. Memory verses are often generalizations given in hopes that this generalized principle will be applied in a relevant situation. In teaching children, it is important to begin with a concrete situation or happening from their lives that poses a dilemma. This is spoken to by concrete content from the Scriptures (this is why stories are good for children's learning—they portray concrete happenings). While summarized in a generalization memory verse, we must always bring that concept back to concrete, relevant happenings in the child's life. Imagine a lesson on responding to people who mistreat us.

1. Begin with a concrete situation: "A child finds on the playground the homework paper of a child who has called him a name. What does he want to do? Why? Suppose this is a test from God? Now what does he want to do? Why? Why is it so tough not to want to get even? Do you think God gets even?"

2. Move to the concrete story of Joseph and his brothers. "What changed Joseph's attitude? What rule did he live by? What were the results?"

3. Summarize the concept in the verse, "Do good to those who wrongfully use you. . . ."

4. Move back to concrete happenings in a child's life. "Let's suppose this happens to you with your older brother or sister. . . . What is a way to practice this verse in that situation? Here's

another situation. . . . What is a way to live out the command of this verse?"

The Challenge of Conservation Learning

In Piagetian terms, this deals with the ability of the child to grasp that a principle or an attribute will remain constant even though the situations change. Children learn this in clay as they use the same amount of clay to make a large round object or a long thin object. Or by pouring water from a tall, narrow glass into a broad, flat dish and then pouring it back again, recognizing that the amount stays the same. Educators have found that this concept is best learned through handling of physical objects. Richards declares:

> The reason conservation is important is that much of ministry with children has assumed that children will be able to acquire an abstract, symbolic concept such as "forgive" or "share" or "trust" and to actually conserve that concept across situations and apply it appropriately in their own daily experiences! Such an approach to teaching children, relying on teaching concepts or principles that children are expected to be able to apply on their own, is, to say the least, unrealistic. (1983, p. 114)

Thus we must "pour the principle" back and forth between many situations and, as a response, to many dilemmas before the child begins to comprehend that it is applicable in different forms. The more concrete the experience, the more likely the child is to reshape thinking to incorporate that principle. Simply teaching the lesson with a moral at the end is pointless.

Symbolism: Truth in Disguise

In like manner, symbolism is often used in teaching children because as adults we can conceive of something "standing for" something else. The hazardous area is again the abstract. Something literal or concrete represents something abstract. Although there are "like" elements, the child often has difficulty conserving the qualities of one in the realm of the other. So-called "object lessons" often hold the interest of young learners because of the visual objects used or the "magic" involved. But afterward they are more concerned with "How did you do that?" than the "moral" or principle it was to teach. There is no carry-over into life, and no transformation of life occurs.

This limitation affects the teacher of the Bible, for there are many symbols given in Scripture, but always to adults and usually in the context of something meaningful to them, for example, Living Water to the woman at the well, the Bread of Life to those who had experienced the feeding of the 5,000. Many adults have a hard time explaining the parable of the wise man who built his house upon the rock. Jesus addressed this story to a people who lived in a land of shifting sand and who heard Him share this story in the Sermon on the Mount. At the end of His illustration He gives the clue to its interpretation: wisdom is in hearing and putting into practice. Children enjoy singing the motion song that portrays these wise and foolish builders but are not able to explain its meaning unless someone has helped them process what it is actually teaching. Children's songs are notorious for symbolism. "This Little Light of Mine" (what does this mean to a literal minded child? a flashlight?), "Fishers of Men" (they love the casting action), "Take Jesus into your heart," "Sin is black" (this in an age when black is beautiful).

Many symbols have been used to explain the Trinity, sin, salvation, heaven. Children have no difficulty with imagination because that moves from a concrete object representing something else concrete. (Toss a ball at a child, saying, "This is a bomb," and the receiver cries out, "Kaboom!") But symbolism moves from the concrete to the abstract. (Toss a ball, saying, "This is responsibility"; the receiver doesn't know how to respond.) This conservation limitation means we spend time questioning and reframing to help children shape meaning from the symbols they use.

The Change with Classification
The young child begins this important skill of grouping according to similarities early, when he discovers that small furry animals with thin tails are known as cats while small furry animals with bushy tails who sit up are known as squirrels. However, not until middle years are children able to classify according to two concrete qualities (e.g., both red and round) and not until the

end of childhood (formal operations) can they work with hypothetical thought and classify objects that overlap into two categories but that are absent.

This suggests that explanations of the Trinity where God is
seen as Father, also Son, and also Spirit are impossible to comprehend until the processes of formal operations are present.
This principle also has implications for when we teach the
books of the Bible so they become more than mere words—but
make sense in their grouping.

An Expanding Sociocentric View

As seven- and eight-year-olds develop reasoning powers, experience others, and see their varied responses, children's thinking
begins moving in the direction of recognizing, "I cause an effect
on others. Other persons are different from me, seeing things
differently. They process and feel and experience also." This is
a sociocentric view as opposed to an egocentric view. Such capacity introduces the element of intent and motive. Whereas
formerly, during egocentric days, the one element that determined guilt or innocence was the extent of the damage, now
intent enters the picture. The child begins to realize that size of
the consequence is not the sole basis for determining moral
evaluation. Intent to do harm that results in little damage will
now be declared worse than unintentional harm of greater mag-
nitude.

"That's OK. You didn't mean to," reveals the child's growing understanding. The child begins to take responsibility for
"willing" the harm, not just causing it.

Such expanding reasoning introduces two higher stages of
moral reasoning, each of which sees children being able to place
self in the position of others and realize they may intend and
think differently. In Kohlberg's Stage 2, eight- to ten-year-olds
reason self-centeredly that right is what they value and getting
even is good because self is justified. At the same time, not
getting even is good because you might not want that person to
get even with you someday. They are developing a sense of
fairness, a realization that the other person held a motive that
was different from the result. Called "moral reciprocity," children realize that others operate out of different perspectives

but reason what is right according to what benefits or seems right to them.

Kohlberg's Stage 3 broadens to include others' motives and perspectives and seeks to live up to expectations of others. "Being nice" determines certain right and wrong responses. Right is doing what significant others want. The ability to reason morally is a tremendous asset to spiritual development. When the young child says, "He shouldn't do it because he might get caught," you realize that "not getting caught and punished" means to the child in this framework that the response is all right. As children become aware of the intentions and responses of others outside themselves and want to factor that into their concept of "rightness," they move closer to taking responsibility for actions and to working with God as valued Authority who works for and in me to do right. This capacity to care is extremely important along with "intention" and motivation. While young children can be empathetic and identify with children expressing feelings, what appears to be more difficult is developing the capacity to care by modifying actions to respond to the needs of the other person.

Inhibiting behavior appears to be developmental also. Young children learn to inhibit "jumping the gun" with a physical response. During grade school years they learn to inhibit emotions until they can be expressed to the right people in the right places. Inhibiting one's own behavior so that another may be helped requires development of a consciousness, a will, and a knowledge of what will help and what will hinder another.

DISEQUILIBRATION AND SYNTHESIS

Human beings long for harmony, unity, balance, and congruence. We dislike problems, irregularities, incongruities, and deviance. We mistakenly feel that life would be great if only we could maintain the former and avoid the latter. But developmentalism enables us to see that the interplay of each of these causing the other is what prompts growth and lets us know we are alive.

As children experience new data from the environment, new social encounters, and changing mental capacities, they are faced with constantly reorganizing and restructuring views of reality—the locus for operating in the world. Paul, in 1 Corinthians 13, speaks of putting childish ways of reasoning, thinking, and talking behind him. Ever-expanding horizons beckon us to continual reorientation.

The Scriptures are one of the primary reshapers of our ways of reasoning and responding. These authoritative principles outside of us often cause disequilibration in our ways of thinking and operating. As Christians, our goal is that the objective revelation of the Word of God be taught so as to become the personal inner reality out of which the learner operates. To do this within the child's world of living, we must "translate the great truths of faith into thought units that can be experienced by boys and girls! . . . Because Scripture is a reality revelation, the great realities it portrays can be experienced on every level" (Richards, 1983, p. 122). These truths that guide the child's choices call for a reshaping of ordinary ways of thinking.

When truth is presented on a child's level, the child is faced with new and radical ways of operating—ways that often call for a reshaping of assumptions and contrasting patterns of action. For example: the value of not getting even when previously having learned to look out for oneself, of trusting another after being raised to be self-sufficient, to be community-minded in a world that says to be independent. Learning begins when the child recognizes that a problem exists. The good teacher takes time to raise the problem, to elicit the child's questions, and to work through the process of reconstituting the child's frame of reality with this new piece of information. This takes time and lots of back-and-forth dialogue. It means talking about, "What about this is difficult to believe? difficult to want? difficult to put into practice?"

"Why did Ananias and Sapphira lie when they must have known they should be honest?" To help the child work this new reality into becoming the child's own is far more difficult than telling the child that this is the way one ought to operate or being satisfied with mere repetition of memorized words. We want to know "why" children choose to operate as they do.

Developmentalists suggest that the teacher's role is far greater than "cut and paste" on a child's mind. We must take seriously the importance of raising issues that are of concern to children, of seeing Bible truth as reality that serves as a basis for choices in their spheres of living. Bible truth is not just a "story" — it is a way of life that God has designed for us to walk in. Ideas, values, ways of acting that do not fit, are springboards to further insight and growth.

THE ASSET OF ACTIVE LEARNING

A great gift of developmentalism is its stress on the active involvement of the child if anything of significance is to be learned. Knowledge is constructed during those interactive moments between mental processing and environmental intrusion. This includes more than telling. If the teacher is reading or speaking, the learner must be given something to actively listen for or recognize. It suggests hands on, try out, experiment, fit to your situation, build on your experience methodology. It means we cannot substitute formulas or just words for understanding. This requires involving the learner in expressing concepts, in explaining reasons — not in just giving the right answer. As one little girl explained, "Of course I don't believe in a Santa Claus," while her teacher nodded. But then she added her reason for the statement: "One man couldn't carry all those presents." Active learning calls Christian teachers to view themselves in tandem with the learner, with the learner being as actively involved in processing the content as the teacher — if not more so. So-called "activities" are not wastes of time — they are shared experiences of learning where the learner takes part in her own learning.

THE MINEFIELD OF MORAL REASONING

Kohlberg's work has helped us become aware of the importance of knowing how children process what is right and wrong — not just hearing them verbalize it. Hartshorne and May's research demonstrated that programs in moral education have very little influence on how children will act. Lying, cheating, and stealing were found to be situational, with children refusing to lie in certain situations and lying easily in others (Damon, 1988). This suggests that teachers should not be content with verbal affirmations, "lying is wrong," but that they follow this up with why, and present numerous varieties of situations where the choice of truth-telling is difficult.

The varied evaluations of what constitutes right and wrong suggest the necessity of giving children accurate truth when we teach the Bible. If we teach accurate concepts — even though they are inadequate — the basic truth remains. For example:

"God loves me even though I sin."

"God is fair whether I understand that or not."

"Sin is more than disobeying parents."

"Some things are wrong whether I get punished or not."

"Doing right is obeying God even when I may not please someone else."

"All have sinned, even parents and teachers."

"You can't earn forgiveness with God."

Christians must go beyond Kohlberg. Moral judgment and moral development must include more than moral reasoning. The content of those judgments and the will to act in line with that content go beyond moral reasoning. Concern for how the child processes right from wrong is to be combined with concern for the content of that rightness and wrongness. Being able to *reason* "correctly" does not mean that the child will choose to *behave* differently. The essence of morality originates with God, never with human beings' best efforts and reasoning.

Believers are concerned that children know a relationship with God that will cause them to want to respond in a godly way. Morality is more than rules — it is a relationship. Certainly the implantation of the Spirit in a life gives inner impetus to right doing and right thinking. As Christians we must not expect children who do not have this new life in the Spirit to act as though they do. "Teaching them to be Christians" is impossible without their first having experienced the radical transformation of the Spirit of God.

How can we foster internalization to follow through in doing right? By examining moral issues and locating difficult hurdles to following through (e.g., fear of losing esteem in the eyes of important others). By giving children hands-on experiences that provide meaning to abstract concepts such as "justice," we provide not only information but also emotion, attitude, and action. Framing "right" in many different settings, facing squarely "bottom-line issues" as to why we choose to do wrong in certain situations, giving opportunity to do right, and constructing a healthy, loving relationship with God as Friend and Lord—all these nurture right living and being righteous. We cannot *give* children moral values or conceptions. We can only help them construct their values and concepts.

SPOTLIGHT ON SALVATION

A most important milestone in spiritual development is that of moving by faith into new life with God. How is this most prized experience impacted by developmentalism? Certainly the language we choose is determined by the developmental level of the child. "Asking Jesus to come into your heart" creates problems for literal thinkers. Abstracts such as sin, grace, even salvation, must be explained with numerous illustrations. Symbolism is to be avoided.

The understanding of the process involves many profound truths (the holiness of God, the sinfulness of man, the judgment on sinners, the necessity of atonement, the substitution of the righteous One, the acceptance of Jesus' death for me, my acceptance by God as being "in Christ"). It is foolish to think that with one or two presentations, the child who has never heard the Gospel will understand and respond to it. Children may make many commitments, saying "yes" to Jesus in related areas ("I love Jesus." "I feel bad I took the money"), all as preparatory to moving into the kingdom. Ronald Goldman, drawing on the cognitive limitations of Piaget's research, suggests that children not even be exposed to scriptural truth before formal operations are available (Goldman, 1964). But children are more than minds. Salvation is incomprehensible. Scripture reminds us that it is received by faith. While not totally understanding the concepts, the child can respond by faith with trust in a God who is loved and who does understand.

The Word of God is more than truth to be comprehended— it is truth to be lived. In the living of it the comprehension increases. Jesus claimed that those who followed Him would know truth and thus be set free. That following is a step of faith that leads to insight. The child raised in a Christian home and exposed to the Gospel over a period of years cultivates an open, believing perspective and a receptive heart as these values are embraced by significant others and lived out as reality.

Here are some things we know about children that will affect how we deal with them in explaining salvation.

1. The child will be focused on the present—not the future. Immediate tangible benefits are important. (Avoid concepts like heaven, streets of gold. Instead, what does salvation mean for the child now?)

2. Recognize and adapt to the child's incomplete intellectual development.

• Has difficulty with abstracts, generalizations, symbolism.

• Thinks concretely—needs many specific situations, needs many different explanations from different angles.

• Has difficulty verbalizing what is known and difficulty interiorizing truth. Do not put words into child's mouth. Ask questions and wait.

• Needs time to process and integrate. Do not push. The Spirit convicts, not people.

3. To be capable of repentance, the child must know right from wrong. Know child's perspective in moral development.

• Children believe that what those in authority say is right. Show child God's authority.

• Children feel they are usually wrong, whereas adults are usually right. Recognize their own inadequacy and weakness. Distinguish between childish behavior (tiredness, lack of coordination so glass breaks) and willfully choosing wrong. Is the child old enough to take responsibility for his or her choices?

• Children want to please, so they may answer as they think you want to hear. Do not put words into their mouths. Ask enough questions.

• Children may feel guilt over being caught (consequences) but not over sin. Why is child repenting?

• Children use words they do not understand completely and may make statements that mean something different to the adult than to them. Ask many questions. Do not take words for granted.

● Children are sensitive and receptive to God. Take time in a relaxed atmosphere to talk about spiritual insights. Talk only as long as the child wants to talk and invite him or her to come back for more.

Viewed developmentally, the years of childhood are exciting surges. Each child struggles in the direction of maturity. And Jesus' response was, "Let them come to Me." Do not hinder them with adult ways and values.

FOR FURTHER READING

Coles, R. (1990). *The spiritual life of children.* Boston: Houghton Mifflin.

Damon, W. (1988). *The moral child.* New York: The Free Press.

Flake-Hobson, C., Robinson, B., & Skeen, P. (1983). *Child development and relationships.* Reading, MA: Addison-Wesley.

Kagan, J. (1984). *The nature of the child.* New York: Basic Books.

Labinowicz, E. (1980). *The Piaget primer.* Menlo Park, CA: Addison-Wesley.

Richards, L. (1983). *A theology of children's ministry.* Grand Rapids, MI: Zondervan.

Siegler, R. (1990). *Children's thinking* (2nd ed.). Englewood Cliffs, NJ: Prentice Hall.

Stith, M. (1969). *Understanding children.* Nashville, TN: Convention Press.

9

Adolescent Development

Frances Anderson

ADOLESCENTS:
MADE IN THE IMAGE OF GOD

The creation account in the first chapter of Genesis records that God created human beings, male and female, and blessed them. Then God looked at all that He had made and He was pleased ". . . it was very good" (Gen. 1:27, 31). Adolescents are a part of God's good creation. They, too, bear His image and bring Him pleasure. Why then, do they seem to bring parents, the church, and society so many problems?

One way to answer that is to say that adolescents participate in the fallenness of creation. They, too, choose to go their own way, not God's. They know the rebellion, the separation, and the loneliness of living apart from Him and others. It is also helpful to examine this question by looking at the way adolescents develop and change en route to adulthood.

ADOLESCENTS: TRAPEZE ARTISTS

A picture coming from the work of Erik Erikson will serve as an underlying theme for considering the adolescent's long passage from childhood into adulthood. Erikson pictures the adolescent as a trapeze artist swinging between childhood and adulthood.

> Like a trapeze artist, the young person in the middle of vigorous motion must let go of his safe hold on childhood, and reach out for a firm grasp on adulthood, depending for a breathless interval on the relatedness between the past and the future, and the reliability of those he must let go of, and those who will receive him. (1968, p. 90)

As young adolescents begin the swing toward adulthood, the trapeze bar is still on the side of childhood. However, once that bar has been grasped, the process will continue, and that movement is back and forth. One moment young adolescents want the privileges and security of childhood. The next, they seek independence, wanting no reminders of the past. Movement is uneven and unpredictable, but it is also certain. What is going on in the lives of adolescents during this time? What is the safety net for them as they swing out into the adventure of adolescence? What happens when they do not perceive that the adult world is reliable and will indeed receive them as valued persons?

Being a trapeze artist calls for risk—for choices that will build identity, confidence, and skill in the adventures of life. By understanding the developmental process, adults can be helped to affirm the image of God in adolescence, to look with awe at the creative work of development in youth, and to say with the Creator God, "It is very good!"

DEVELOPMENT: CONTINUITY, DIVERSITY, AND INTERACTION

It would be hard to isolate one single moment in which the child starts on the road through adolescence to adulthood. There will be both private and public events that give indication of the beginning of that journey. Whatever its beginning, it is continuous with, and builds upon, the development of the childhood years.

One of the subtle but striking characteristics of adolescent development is the diversity of the various ages each adolescent juggles within himself or herself. A girl with the chronological age of thirteen may have an intellectual age of sixteen, a physical age of eleven, a social age of ten, and a spiritual age of fifteen. She is academically ahead and is receiving affirmation for this area of achievement. However, inside she is painfully aware that among her peers she is the only one who has not started menstruation and breast development. This may well keep her from some of the social interaction of her peers, but also may contribute to her dependence on her church group and her faith experience with Jesus.

A boy with the chronological age of fifteen may have the physical age of eighteen, the intellectual age of thirteen, the social age of seventeen, and the spiritual age of twelve. In contrast to the girl, this young man is struggling academically, but finding fulfillment possibly in athletics and in social interaction with girls. His faith experience has not kept pace with other areas of growth.

Environment influences every level of development. Some adolescents develop in an environment with a team of significant people as models and support. Others swing on the trapeze between childhood and adulthood with little or no support. When no one seems to care, the difference in development will be great.

Thus a description of adolescent development is more general than specific. Anyone who works with adolescents must respect individual growth and development, knowing that it can bring both pleasure and pain to the person. While descriptions of different developmental areas are most easily given separately, they are indeed not separate, but interactive components in the totality of the human person. Each component is a system in itself whose smooth functioning is necessary for the ongoing complex interactions between the systems. The complexity and beauty of God's creative work in human beings, male and female, is expressed well by the psalmist when he says, "I am fearfully and wonderfully made" (Ps. 139:14).

MOVEMENTS IN THINKING

As the thinking of young adolescents begins to shift from the concrete operations of childhood to the formal operations of adulthood, there are implications for a wide range of attitudes and behaviors. The change happens slowly, with some shifting back and forth before it is firmly established. As has been indicated in the chapter on Piaget, adolescents become able to conceptualize and to think about their own thinking. This moment enables them to accept the contrary-to-fact condition as a purely logical proposition that can be reasoned about regardless of its factual truth (Elkind, 1984). They can deal with possibilities. They can imagine the ideal world, family, and parents, and thus their own parents and family may find themselves being criticized in comparison. When this happens, it appears as an abrupt change from the pleasant, accepting attitude of the older elementary child. While this movement indicates growth for the adolescent, it is not likely to be experienced as such by parents, teachers, and youth leaders! They also experience new argumentativeness as youth create a case for their positions.

David Elkind presents helpful information regarding the egocentrism of adolescent thought. It continues as a lack of differentiation, but in different ways than in children. Adolescents have difficulty differentiating between that which is transient and that which is abiding. Thus a young adolescent can assume that a moment of personal failure or embarrassment continues to live on in other people's minds, while in fact it is usually transitory. "I'll just die, if I see him again!" It is painful for the young person when he or she thinks the experience remains as vivid to others as it does to him or her (Elkind, 1978a).

A second lack of differentiation is between the objective and the subjective in the realm of thought.

> Because they cannot yet differentiate between the subjective content of their own thoughts and the objective content of the thoughts of others, they assume that others are as interested and observant of them as they are of themselves. Hence the self-consciousness of early adolescence. (Elkind, 1978a, p. 122)

Elkind suggests that, because of this, young adolescents construct an "imaginary audience" that constantly observes both their behaviors and their appearance. This motivates behaviors in part to get response or reaction of the audience. Elkind supports the importance of this "imaginary audience" to provide the approval and affirmation needed at a time when there are limited past experiences to provide it. The negative influence of the "audience" can come as adolescents find pleasure in imagining the grieving or angry responses of people in response to their suicide or vandalism (Elkind, 1978a). While the concept of "imaginary audience" is modified through life experience, it may reoccur in adults during periods of strong emotion.

The third failure of differentiation concerns the universal and the particular. This is the inability to differentiate between what is unique to him or herself and what is common to everyone. Therefore a new experience or an especially deep desire is unique only to them. No one else has ever felt this way before. The positive side of this "personal fable" is that the adolescent feels special and valuable. The negative consequences of this sense of uniqueness "may give rise to recklessness if it is thought of as 'others will get hurt and die but not me' " (Elkind, 1978a, p. 127). Thus, while others might get hooked on drugs, he will not. Other teenagers may become pregnant, but she will not. Elkind is clear in stating there are other negatives involved in this kind of behavior besides the "personal fable." This pattern of thought also is found in adulthood, and Elkind calls it "a healthy defense against the inevitable emotional and physical disappointment of life" (Elkind, 1978a, p. 128). It loses value only when taken too seriously.

Being sensitive to the movements in adolescent thinking can help the adult who interacts with youth respond with grace and patience. This helps keep the lines of communication open so that adolescents experience in human form the acceptance and care of a loving God. To the "trapeze artists," it says someone is there on the adult side who values them and reaches out to assist them on their journey toward adulthood.

PHYSICAL GROWTH: SPURTS AND PUBERTAL CHANGES

The variability in physical development during adolescent years is phenomenal. One adolescent may complete physical development before another one has even begun the sequence. This makes life very different for the two persons. The beginning of the growth spurt for girls is eleven or twelve, while the average boy begins at thirteen. The change of the body in size, shape, and sexual characteristics affects the adolescent's sense of identity. Often youth are critical of the changes they perceive in themselves. As they compare themselves with peers and with the idealized norm portrayed by the media, it is easy to perceive themselves as less attractive than they would wish, and their self-concept suffers (Coleman, 1980). Appearance is an all-important question for adolescents.

The girl who develops before her peers faces the problem of appearing mature while not yet being prepared for the social pressures or the accompanying expectations. Boys who develop early are put in an advantageous position with girls of their own age, but may also face expectations of responsibility for which they are unprepared.

Sexual development reaches maturity during the high school years. One of the tasks of adolescence is the acceptance of one's own body in the overall quest for identity. Sexuality can be an area of struggle for self-acceptance and peer recognition. In the context of disintegrating moral standards in this society, it is also an area of experimentation as youth copy models of adult behavior in society. The resulting teenage pregnancies and abortions create additional anxiety and pain for adolescent girls and their families.

Physical development also brings satisfaction and joys to adolescents as they test out new strengths and abilities. Young men in late adolescence discover they can now surpass their fathers in a variety of sports. They are often taller. Girls are blossoming into the beauty of young womanhood while their middle-aged mothers may sense decline. In the swing between struggle and satisfaction in physical development, adolescents need affirmation of their physical identity. The body is a marvelous creation. Sexuality is a gift to be enjoyed, but temptation to abuse it is rampant. As such, it calls for special care so that the Creator God may be honored in its use. With this perspective, the swing of the adolescent trapeze artist steadies as it moves toward adulthood.

ADOLESCENT DEVELOPMENT

PSYCHOSOCIAL DEVELOPMENT:
THE MELODY AND THE HARMONY OF IDENTITY

The major task of adolescents is to take all the segments of their lives and arrange them "into some meaningful, workable whole" that they can own as their identity and with which they are relatively comfortable (Elkind, 1978b, p. 153).

> In a sense, the personal identity that the adolescent must construct is built out of a host of separate identities: sexual, familial, racial, religious, ethnic, peer, student, and so on. It is only during adolescence that, for the first time, the young person becomes aware of how many different roles he plays. His job is to integrate these into a sense of "they are all me." (Elkind, 1978b, p. 153)

It is the task of adolescents to work with their several roles in various areas of life to bring them into harmony so that the melody of their own identity becomes clear. When the various roles conflict and are not drawn together in harmony, the clear melody of identity is not perceived. There is, instead, confusion and dissonance. Erik Erikson uses the terms "coherent identity" versus "identity diffusion" (Coleman, 1980, p. 51). The coherent identity "develops out of a gradual integration of all identifications" (Erikson, 1980, p. 95).

Adolescents viewing life with all its variety of conflicting possibilities and choices experience stress. To manage this time they "temporarily overidentify to the point of apparent complete loss of identity, with the heroes of cliques and crowds" (Erikson, 1980, p. 97). The adolescent clique becomes a safety net providing a safe place just to be, as youth dream about and discuss the possibilities and choices offered them. As they make decisions about themselves and their relationships to others, they integrate the disparate facets of their lives into a sense of wholeness. This in turn gives them confidence in handling new stress situations.

Elkind uses the term "patchwork" self in commenting about those youth who are unable to integrate attitudes, values, and habits into a connected whole. This is growth by substitution rather than integration. The inner conflict and unsettledness results in a variety of unstable behaviors in stress situations such as anxiety and physical complaints, boredom and fatigue, conforming to the peer group, self-punishing behavior, unhealthy competition, anger, and fear (Elkind, 1984). These youth are vulnerable in today's society.

James Marcia, in interviews with older adolescents in college, identified four stages in identity development: (1) identity diffusion, in which youth have made no commitment to a set of beliefs or vocation; (2) identity foreclosure, in which youths' commitments to goals and beliefs are the result of choices by others; (3) moratorium, in which youth are actively searching through options to arrive at identity; (4) identity achievement, in which youth have resolved the current identity crisis and have made commitments to a set of beliefs or occupation (Coleman, 1980).

John Coleman, in discussing research in identity crises, states that the most likely time for adolescents to experience identity problems is in early adolescence, and that most adolescents adapt gradually over the years to the changes in identity.

> There is simply no evidence to suggest that the great majority of adolescents experience a serious crisis of identity, and most studies seem to conclude that only 25-35 percent of the total population of teenagers at any age level could be said to have a disturbance in this area. (Coleman, 1980, p. 56)

Coleman, while acknowledging stress and change in the life of adolescents, believes that the majority cope with the problems successfully. It is that successful negotiation of identity formation which supports a second task in older adolescence, that of developing intimate and life-sustaining relationships. Youth who are unsure of their identities will have difficulty entering intimate interpersonal relationships and will tend to isolate themselves either through more formal relationships or through repeated attempts at intimacy which result in failure (Erikson, 1980).

MORAL REASONING AND BEHAVIOR

Childhood's hierarchical and concrete stage of moral reasoning begins to shift in adolescence to one more influenced by peers.

While parents continue to be a resource in their moral development, adolescents tend to conform to the expectations of their group of peers and of other significant adults in their lives. Their approval now rivals that of parents. Socialized into the norm of society, "rules" continue to be given from the outside. Conflicts will arise for youth as they experience discrepancies between values of their peer groups and their parents. They will also note differences in values among parents of their peers and use them in arguing for a desired privilege (Mattheson, 1975).

As young adolescents increasingly gain new abilities to think beyond the concrete, the motivations behind behavior and idealism become factors in moral reasoning and judgment. Their idealism expressed in words is often not carried into action. Elkind calls this "apparent hypocrisy," as, in their expression of a value, they consider themselves working toward it. When it does not come into being, adults may well be criticized for their hypocrisy. As youth become involved in working toward a particular cause, the differentiation is made between experience and realization of an ideal (Elkind, 1984).

As older adolescents begin to move out of the conventional levels, where their reasoning and behavior have rooted out of expectations of family, peers, and society, some of them will begin to think through the concept of broader human rights. Right action now is concerned with the greatest good for all people. Definition of the greatest good is not arrived at easily. In their broadening world, older adolescents encounter more and more diverse viewpoints, making moral decisions more complex. In a society moving away from absolute truth, the adolescent's own subjective experience takes on greater significance in the deliberations.

William Perry (1970) identified three basic levels in the intellectual and ethical development of college students: dualism, relativism, and commitment. The positions are variable in duration, represent a "central tendency," and represent "points of outlook" through which persons look at their world. The movement in positions involves "the reorganization of major personal investments" (p. 48).

In the three positions of "dualism," college students are engaged in modifying a simplistic right-and-wrong, authority-oriented structure of belief. The next three positions fall under "relativism," as students increasingly become aware of a multiplicity of views and of how positions might change, depending on context. At first, relativism applies only to certain categories of problems, but progresses to include all of thinking. This creates a change in relationship to authorities, who are now perceived to be also grasping for truth. Perry states that this position represents the "critical division between 'belief' and the possibility of 'faith' " (1970, p. 131), for it is here that the older adolescent invests him- or herself in doubting beliefs and in searching for personal faith. This is a move toward commitment.

The level of "commitment" is one that develops qualitatively around the area of responsibility. The person risks some definition of his or her own position and what the implications might be. The choosing of responsible action leads to an owning of the position. Perry states that it is at this point that the older adolescent "discovers that he has undertaken not a finite set of decisions but a way of life" (1970, p. 153).

The process of development can be short-circuited by an adolescent who, being threatened by the multiplicity of beliefs, retreats into the absolute and dualistic structures of early positions. Continued development during relativism may be deflected by persons who escape from responsibility by becoming either passive or alienated in the uncertainty of pluralism. Development can also be delayed by "temporizing," defined as the hesitancy to take further steps toward commitment at any position. This may be for shorter or longer periods, sometimes a year (Perry, 1970). While every study has boundaries, there are strong implications for ministry in Perry's research if adolescents are to have a thinking faith.

FAITH DEVELOPMENT:
"GO DOWN TO THE POTTER'S HOUSE . . ."

Jeremiah went to the potter's house and watched him working at the wheel. "But the pot he was shaping from the clay was marred in his hands; so the potter formed it into another pot, shaping it as seemed best to him" (Jer. 18:4).

ADOLESCENT DEVELOPMENT

Human beings in their life of faith have to be refashioned again and again. Unlike clay, people exercise their wills and are often responsible for the rough places that necessitate their being refashioned. In the lifelong process of being conformed to the image of Christ (Rom. 8:29), there are many starts and stops and periods of uneven growth. There are moments of transformation and periods of formation as God, like a potter, works in the lives of His people.

Faith development overlaps with the life issues being worked on by adolescents in their other developmental areas. It can bring meaning and coherence to all of life. While some aspects of faith development can be charted in levels or stages, the area of saving faith in Jesus Christ is the realm of the Holy Spirit, who works in His own way and time. However, God's creation has order and sequence, and a certain order can be perceived in the development and growth of faith.

In John Westerhoff's description of four styles of faith, two tend to be dominant in adolescence: "affiliative faith" and "searching faith." Affiliative faith includes the foundation of the experienced faith of childhood. It is characterized by a sense of belonging to the community of faith, the dominance of "religious affections" or emotions, and "a sense of authority" gained from the affirmation of the Christian story by the church and its life (1976, pp. 94–95).

In searching faith, mid or late adolescents begin to move toward a faith that is their own. In this movement, they question the faith they have claimed from the church. While this may not feel like growth to parents and the church, adolescents need their supportive affirmation. During this searching time, faith is subjected to critical judgment, and youth may decide to explore alternatives. In this process, the intense emotions of teenage faith start to be balanced by deeper understanding. This is facilitated as the faith community continues to meet the needs of experienced and affiliative faith (Westerhoff, 1976).

James Fowler (1981) describes the first stage of adolescent faith as both "conventional" and "synthetic." It is conventional in that it is the faith of the church community, but it is synthetic in that it is unexamined. While unexamined, it is still entirely personal with deep emotional involvement. Authority is still located outside the self, residing in the "they" of the significant youth subculture and an institutional authority.

Older adolescents may experience contradictions between rejected authorities, and in this process they may be moved to reflect on the values involved. If so, they could begin the transition into individuative reflective faith. Here they reflectively sort out their own beliefs and assume the responsibility of integrating them into attitudes and lifestyles. It is a further definition of the self as adolescents align the heart and will with their beliefs. This is a process well represented by the picture of the trapeze artist swinging back and forth, this time on the adult side. It is facilitated by caring adults/mentors who affirm them in their journey.

Adolescence is a special time in God's plan of human development, punctuated by much change with the potential for pain and joy in the youth themselves, in families, and for society.

FOR FURTHER READING

Cinger, J., & Peterson, A.C. (1984). *Adolescence and youth: Psychological development in a changing world* (3rd ed.). New York: Harper & Row.

Coleman, J. (1980). *The nature of adolescence.* New York: Methuen & Co.

Dragastin, S., & Elder, G., Jr. (Eds.) (1975). *Adolescence in the life cycle, psychological change and social context.* Washington, DC: Hemisphere.

Elkind, D. (1984). *All grown up and no place to go.* Reading, MS: Addison-Wesley.

Hill, J. (1980). *Understanding early adolescence: A framework.* Carrboro, NC: Center for Early Adolescence.

Perry, W., Jr. (1968). *Forms of intellectual and ethical development in the college years.* New York: Holt, Rinehart and Winston.

Shelton, C. (1983). *Adolescent spirituality, pastoral ministry for high school and college youth.* Chicago: Loyola University Press.

10

Adult Development

Fred Wilson

Lobsters and soft-shelled crabs outgrow their shells and become more vulnerable as they wait for the new shell to develop. Adults also seem to outgrow their "shells" and have periods of vulnerability as they change from one era of life to another. Some of these transitions are expected to occur at certain ages and include things such as high school graduation, marriage, children, grandparenting, and retirement. There are also some transitions that are unique to an individual and that are not socially expected at a certain age, such as divorce, early death of a spouse or child, or the loss of a job. Some transitions occur primarily by internal causes, such as menopause, romantic love, chronic disease, or mental disease. Others are primarily caused by external events, such as winning a lottery or experiencing a war.

Adult development is commonly divided into three time periods or eras: early, middle, and older adulthood. Each of these eras has its own biological, psychological, and sociocultural character, and each adds a distinctive influence to the whole. At any one time an adult faces certain issues, tasks, and life events very common to other adults living in the same era. This chapter explores the major adult eras and transition periods based on the research of Levinson (1977, 1990; Levinson et al., 1978) as summarized in Table 1.

Table 1
Levinson's Developmental Eras and Transitions of Adulthood

17 to 40   **Early Adulthood**

	17 to 22	Early Adult Transition
	22 to 28	Entering the Adult World
	28 to 33	Age 30 Transition
	33 to 40	Settling Down

40 to 60   **Middle Adulthood**

	40 to 45	Mid-life Transition
	45 to 50	Entering Middle Adulthood
	50 to 60	Culmination of Middle Adulthood

60 to 80   **Late Adulthood**

	60 to 65	Late Adult Transition
	65 to 80	Late Adulthood

DEVELOPING A LIFE STRUCTURE

As adults experience each era, their "life structures" change. Levinson (1990) defines life structure as the underlying pattern or design of a person's life at any given time. It describes how a person has related external and internal roles and issues together. The external aspect focuses on one's relationship to society through social and cultural roles affecting work, marriage, family, and religious faith. The internal meanings of these roles tend to evolve as if attached to a time clock announcing that one's perceptions are due for a change at each era in the life cycle. Levinson writes:

> The concept of life structure requires us to examine the nature and patterning of a person's relationships with all significant others and the evolution of these relationships over the years. . . . At any given time, a life struc-

ture may have many and diverse components. . . . Most often, marriage-family and occupation are the central components of a person's life. . . . (1990, p. 42)

Levinson et al. (1978) view the adult life structure as a boundary that mediates and governs the relationship between the individual and the environment. This life structure is both a cause and effect of the relationship of the self in the world. Its intrinsic ingredients are aspects of the self and aspects of the world, and its evolution is influenced by factors in both realms. Thus, life structure requires a person to think conjointly about the self and world rather than making one primary and the other secondary or derivative.

While admitting that there is no age-linked stage for personality development, social roles, or the sequence of major life events, Levinson argues that there is "an underlying order in the human life course, an order shaped by eras and by the periods in life structure development" (1990, p. 43). He believes personality, social structure, culture, gender, social roles, major life events, biology, and other influences exert a powerful effect on the actual development of the individual life structure at any given time and on its development during adulthood.

Working with Transitions

A transition period serves to terminate an existing life structure and creates the possibility for a new one to be formed. The transition period has three major roles: to reevaluate the existing life structure; to explore potential areas of change in the self and how one deals with the world; and to commit to making significant choices that assist in the formation of a new or transformed life structure in the new era (Levinson, 1990). Levinson (1990; Levinson et al., 1978) theorizes that a specific life structure is not permanent. Rather, it needs to change as an adult grows across the life cycle. This combination of eras and transition periods provides the foundation for the flow of the adult life cycle, while allowing freedom for a variety of individual expression and development.

While some stage theories argue that development involves movement from worse to better, or less mature to mature,

Levinson explicitly rejects this idea. He argues that developmental tasks of adults are not automatic:

> The tasks of one period are not better or more advanced than those of another, except in the general sense that each period builds upon the work of the earlier ones and represents a later phase in the life cycle. There are losses as well as gains in the shift from every period or era to the next. (Levinson et al., 1978, p. 320)

Using Life Structure and Transitions as Part of Ministry

Life structure and transition periods may be helpful constructs for those ministering to adults. First, they remind us that humanity is continually conceptualizing answers to the existential question, *What is my life like now?* This suggests other related questions: *What are the most important areas of my life and how are they interrelated? Where do I invest most of my time and energy? Are there things not in my life or relationships to God, spouse, children, family, career, leisure, and faith that I would like to make more satisfying or meaningful or change?* There is a significant niche for educational ministry in the church to play in assisting this ongoing life structure development.

Second, they raise the possibility that adults may be more open to change during transition periods. They will be looking for alternatives to what they now have in their lives. This happens without assuming the view that things will necessarily improve or people will become more mature. This allows for significant biblical doctrines related to humanity to be maintained: the sinfulness of humanity, freedom of choice, variety of responses, and the need for critical self-reflection.

Third, they remind us of the importance relationships have to adults. They open the possibility that the church may be a safe environment where adults in groups can examine their current life structure and adapt it in light of Scripture as guided by the Holy Spirit.

Levinson identifies four eras in the human life cycle with three transition periods. This chapter primarily explores the last three eras, which focus on adult development. For Levinson (1990), the preadulthood era covers birth to age twenty-two. These are the formative years, during which the individual grows from being highly dependent and undifferentiated to the beginnings of a more independent, responsible adult life. This era marks the most rapid biological and psychological growth. (Please see the previous two chapters for details on childhood and adolescent development.)

EARLY ADULT TRANSITION

The years from about seventeen to twenty-two are called the "early adult transition." This is a developmental period when "preadulthood" disappears into the era of "early adulthood." During this transition, the person starts a new period of individuation by modifying his or her relationships with family and society so as to take a place in the adult world (Levinson et al., 1978). Thus, childhood and adolescence provide a starting point from which to begin the adult era.

The developmental task is to leave the preadult world and establish oneself as capable of financial and psychological independence. Most often this is accomplished with minimum conflict with parents by the young adult moving into an apartment or moving geographically to attend college, start a job, or join the military.

The developmental goal of separating from parents is not to end the family relationship altogether (Levinson, 1990). Because one is developing a life structure, it is important to reject certain aspects of the parent-child relationship (e.g., all-controlling parents in relation to a submissive or rebellious child). Also, it is necessary to sustain some prior aspects while adding new qualities to the parent-child relationship. This might include mutual respect between both parents and child as they begin to see each other as distinctive adult individuals with both shared and distinct interests.

Because the parents are at least forty or older, they also have very specific developmental tasks of their own. Table 2 outlines the various areas where the two different eras of adults are changing. Parents must move past the dependency of the small child on them for every need to the realization that the early adult is not only able to be independent and separate from them, but that another stage of relationship is also available:

mutual interdependence. For the early adult, however, the relationship to parents is but one aspect of developing the initial life structure that includes the influence of career, friends, lovers, politics, religious life, and cultural perspective. In this tran-

Table 2
Summary of Areas of Adult Development from 18 to 80

Area	Early Adulthood	Middle Adulthood	Late Adulthood
Physical Change	Apex of most physical functioning Best time for childbearing	Beginning signs of decline in strength, elasticity of tissues, height, heart	Significant decline in most areas (speed, strength, work capacity, elasticity & system functioning
Cognitive Change	High skill on most measures	Some loss of skill on fluid time, unexercised skills High cognitive investment	Progressive decline in crystalized intelligence & large loss of fluid skills
Family & Sex Roles	Major role acquisition Forming of marriage & family roles Clear gender separation Family role gradually dominates with women doing most family & house work	Launching of children Empty nest adjustment Care for elderly parents starts Possibility of some sex role crossover	Grandparent role dominates Family and sex roles increasingly less dominant
Relationships	Emphasis on forming of friendships/ partnership High marital satisfaction until first child Gradual decrease of marital satisfaction & contact with friends	Increase or drop in marital satisfaction Possible increase in importance of friends Rediscover self	Experience high marital satisfaction Possible increase in importance of friends and siblings
Work Roles	Choose career with several possible job changes Start low but increasing work satisfaction Increasing focus on career success Find a mentor	Plateau on career steps Experience higher work satisfaction Become a mentor	Retirement & leisure Work role becomes less important Decrease of self-esteem

Major Tasks	Separate from birth family Form partnership Begin & raise family Find job Create life structure Strive for career success	Launch family Redefine self & life goals outside of family & work Care for aging parents Reevaluate life structure	Cope with retirement Cope with decline in body and mind Redefine sense of self Reset life goals/ structure Accept fact of death Cope with illness
False Assumptions to Overcome	I'll always belong to my parents & believe in their world. Doing things my parents' way will bring results. Life is simple/ controllable. There are no significant coexisting contradictory forces in me.	There is no evil or death in the world. Safety can last forever. Death doesn't happen to me or my family members. It is impossible to live without a protector (for women).	Retirement is a vacation. Life is over at sixty. My body will never grow old. I have nothing to give or contribute to the lives of others.

Sources: Gould (1975, 1978), Levinson et al. (1978), Lowenthal et al. (1974), Sell (1985), Sheehy (1976), and Vaillant (1978)

sition, many relationships will be weighed, tested, experimented with, and incorporated into an initial life structure.

Formulating the Dream

The formulation of a "Dream" related to one's future life and work is an important aspect of this transition according to Levinson (1977, 1990; Levinson et al., 1978). While research shows that most adults at least have a general vision of what the good life would be, the Dream is initially an undefined wish or hope of what one desires to accomplish in life. It ranges from fantasy such as winning a Nobel prize to the practicalities of exploring a particular career. Some males have Dreams that are more tied into their ideal of a home or family as opposed to a career. This tends to influence where these men settle down in the future and sets limits on their willingness to move for the sake of an occupation. Many women tend to focus on the importance of family and community life rather than on an occupation-related Dream.

Early Adulthood Era

The second era covers the years from seventeen to about forty or forty-five and is known as "early adulthood." This era is the time of greatest energy and excitement while also being the time of greatest contradictions and stress. The twenties and thirties are a time of peak biological strength and performance. This is a season for developing and fulfilling goals, building a place in society, getting married, raising a family, and advancing to a more "senior" position in the adult world as the era comes to a close. This era holds the potential of great satisfaction in terms of intimacy, sexuality, family life, career advancement, creativity, and fulfillment of life goals. But it also carries the crushing stresses of initiating parenthood while starting a career, taking on heavy financial responsibilities when income is relatively low, making crucial choices relating to marriage, family, career, and lifestyle before having a great amount of life experience or maturity. Early adulthood is the primary era when external and internal forces are in strongest competition.

Forming an Adult Identity

In their twenties, early adults form and test a preliminary adult identity or life structure. They make initial choices related to marriage, career, housing, and lifestyle. During this period, many couples may live together, marry and raise children, form a family, and become part of the larger community. Thus, early adults start as "novice" adults and move through several intermediate steps to becoming more established or "senior" in their positions at work, in the family, and in the community. This process develops gradually, often with pain, as the adult grows in understanding and ability to handle responsibility.

Exploring Options

The initial tension of this era is to explore the options available as an adult but to commit to some specific aspects of a new life structure. In studies of women, the process of establishing a career and marriage were extended over the full era rather than occurring primarily at the beginning of the period as in the case of men (Roberts & Newton, 1987). Vaillant (1978) found that men in this period focused on "making the grade" in their careers through competition with others in their fields.

Working with a Mentor

Two primary relationships are important for men and women at this time. First, there tends to be a special relationship with an experienced person in the chosen career, often older, who serves as a support person or sponsor—a mentor. The mentor helps the young adult begin to fulfill his career, family, or community Dream. The mentor may come from a broad range: from a boss, to a teacher, departmental administrator, or supervisor.

Levinson (in press) found women to have more difficulty than men in identifying a mentor because there are fewer women to function in this capacity. He also found cross-gender mentoring was limited by the complications of sexual issues in the relationship. Unfortunately, older men have tended to ignore and question the seriousness of the intentions of younger women in mentoring situations (Roberts and Newton, 1987).

Finding a "Special" Woman or Man

The second important relationship Levinson identifies focuses on the role of a "special" woman or man. For males, the special woman is not only a sexual intimate but also part of achieving his Dream in a manner similar to the mentor. She provides guidance, offers financial support, and nourishes his hopes. In a marital relationship, the marriage tends to flourish if each is able to nourish the other person's Dream. Where this is not the case, the result is marital strain and possible divorce by midlife. Marriages tend to be influenced primarily by external forces, since most couples are unaware of the inner needs and life of their mates. Part of the goal of the twenties is attempting to develop marriage stability (Sheehy, 1976).

Age Thirty Transition

Levinson (1990) identified a transition at between twenty-eight and thirty-three which he calls the "age thirty transition." Most of the men in his sample reworked parts of their life structure that had been tentatively developed at the early adult transition. The cause of this transition seems to stem from a sense of feeling that time is running out and that change must be made soon if commitments are to be terminated or made.

Sheehy (1976) argues further that adults in this period feel restricted by choices made in the twenties. She found many adults to be terrified by the many options and decisions made in the twenties. Adults seem to have difficulty realizing that change is inevitable during this time. Inner aspects of their lives were set aside then, due to the desire to meet other people's expectations and the busyness of life. Gould (1978) found his sample of adults to be opening up to what is inside, as well. He calls it a time of rediscovering feelings, interests, talents, and goals that have been ignored because they interfered with goals or beliefs, suppressed because they caused conflict, or hidden while trying to find a mate and enter the job market in the twenties. Resolution brings a realistic understanding of one's strengths and abilities as well as a more complete philosophy of life.

In the thirties, Levinson's sample of men (1978) tended to settle for fewer of their major goals and build their life structures around those central choices made during the age thirty transition. This transition seems to be a midcourse correction time for most men, while it is a major time of overhauling and developing a new life structure for others. After the age thirty transition period, most of the men focus on the two tasks of establishing their own niche and working at advancement in their occupations. Most men find it a time of relative stability.

On the other hand, the age thirty transition for women tends to be dominated by the priority of finding and developing a career. Among women, the relative importance of family and career becomes reversed from the twenties, so that those who focused on family in the twenties focus on careers in the thirties, and vice versa (Adams, 1983). The rest of the thirties do not evidence the stability identified by men. This seems to be a prolonged period of instability as women wrestle with the additional pressures of careers and family (Roberts and Newton, 1987).

MIDLIFE TRANSITION

From roughly forty to forty-five, the "midlife transition" period brings early adulthood to a conclusion while initiating middle adulthood. Research (Gould, 1978; Levinson et al., 1978; Sheehy, 1976) indicates that there are appreciable changes between these two eras. One developmental task of this transition period is to develop another step in individuation (Levinson et al., 1978). Change here may lead to becoming more compassionate, reflective, and judicious, as opposed to being tyrannized by inner conflict and external demands. Without significant change, a person's life may become more trivial or stagnant.

Measuring One's Success

This is a time when an adult weighs the relative success or lack of it in obtaining self-selected goals that indicate he or she has "become one's own man or woman." Success is seen as achieved when: (1) One's work has flourished; (2) One has risen up the career ladder to a certain position; (3) One has become recognized as an influence in one's career and/or social world; (4) One has obtained some sense of seniority in terms of responsibilities and rewards (Levinson, 1990).

Midlife "crisis" normally comes from a strong feeling that the male will not achieve his "culminating event" that marks the accomplishment of his Dream. His promotion up the ladder is blocked; he has no realistic hope of obtaining the recognition, position, and perks he desires; his current way of viewing his life structure is perceived as hindering his progress. About 8 percent of Levinson's sample of forty men reported they experienced difficult struggles within themselves and their worlds (1978).

Levinson (1990) identifies three major tasks at this transition time: terminate early adulthood, initiate middle adulthood, and grapple with polarities of one's life. These will be explored in more detail below.

Terminating Early Adulthood

First, the individual terminates the early adult era by reviewing and reappraising what has been accomplished. This is spurred on by the recognition of the person's own mortality and a desire to use the remaining time of life wisely. The adult asks: *What have I done with my life? What do I really get from and give to my wife/husband, family, friends, community, and self? What do I want for myself and others? What are my central values and how are they reflected in my life? What have I done with my early Dream and what do I do with it now? How satisfactory is my current life structure and how shall I change it to provide a better foundation for the future?* The individual experiences a time of de-illusionment. Levinson et al. defines this as "a reduction of illusions, a recognition that long-held assumptions and beliefs about self and world are not true" (1978, p. 192).

Initiating Middle Adulthood

Second, the adult initiates the first steps toward middle adulthood. The person identifies and begins to modify negative areas of one's present life structure, continues acceptable areas, and tests new options. Some people make radical external changes including divorce, remarriage, major shifts in occupation and lifestyle, marked decline in the level of functioning, and notable progress in creativity or social mobility. Internally, a person grapples with personal values, social outlook, personal contributions to the world, and what she wants for herself.

Wrestling with Polarities

Third, individuals begin to deal with several competing polarities that are sources of deep division in one's life. During this time of midlife individuation, four areas of polar opposites are reintegrated into an adult's life structure: young/old, destruction/creation, masculine/feminine, and attachment/separateness (Levinson, 1978 & 1990).

Thus, adults in this transition wrestle with questions such as: *How do I deal with my biological changes that say I'm older and not younger? What legacy will I pass on to the next generation — raising my children, maintaining family continuity, career contributions, early retirement, mentoring younger adults? How can my destructive activities toward others and myself coexist with my desire to be more creative in my influence on life? How can masculine traits (thinking, doing, making, having) be integrated with feminine qualities (feeling, submissiveness, admitting weaknesses) or vice versa, that I now desire for myself? How do I balance my desire to be more attached to others while I also desire significant times of separateness?*

Revisiting the Dream

Three additional areas of the adult's life structure are normally modified during the midlife transition period: the Dream, mentoring early adults, and marriage. Part of reappraising one's life is to understand and evaluate the role of the Dream developed and modified in early adulthood. While most men and women in Levinson's study had a discernible Dream, those Dreams played a variety of roles. The Dream was anything from a burning passion to a quiet force, very modest to ambitious, fairly vague or very specific, an inspiration or a source of conflict. While the Dream grows out of a "sense of self-in-world" (Levinson et al., 1978, p. 245), it identifies meanings for the person's existence in the world. While the Dream serves to motivate, it can also be illusory. Some Dreams are impossible to obtain and lead one to a sense of failure. Part of the developmental process of adulthood is to bring the Dream more into line with reality as opposed to continuing the illusion of omnipotence and perfection. Part of the process of adult development is accepting one's own contradictions, limitations, and failures as balanced with the possible.

Revisiting Mentoring

One way an adult confronts these illusions is to accept responsibility for the next generation of early adults. While no longer a full peer with those in the twenties and thirties, an adult at midlife has greater maturity and insight that can be passed on as a mentor. The satisfaction of mentoring seems to lie in furthering the development of young women and men, assisting them in forming and living out their Dreams. While mentoring builds off of the parental impulse, Levinson claims it is more complex and requires at least the initial reviewing of one's life structure. In addition, mentoring offers a person the opportunity to maintain contact with youthful energy, as well as make positive use of one's knowledge and skills at middle-age. Several hazards for mentors, however, should be dealt with biblically: the temptations to dictate another person's life, to exploit the relationship for selfish reasons, and, to the other extreme, the excessive giving of self to the protégé's needs while overlooking one's personal needs.

Revisiting Marriage

A third aspect of reevaluating an adult's life structure relates to marriage. The reasons for marriage, the quality of the marital relationship, and the differences of life experiences may all contribute to a middle adult becoming aware of dissatisfaction with marriage. During the "becoming one's own man" period, the man often blames the woman for the problems. However, during the midlife transition, males are often able to recognize their own weaknesses, admit their own contributions to marital problems, and deal with past images and assumptions they brought into the marriage. Or it may be the wife who takes the initiative in reevaluating the marriage. Observing these possibilities, Levinson writes:

> Being more free of familial responsibilities in her late thirties or early forties, she seeks to expand her own horizons and start new enterprises outside the home. She becomes the voice of development and change. Through the "division of labor" that often occurs in a marriage, the husband may then become the voice of the status quo. Moreover, a man who feels that his own youthfulness is in jeopardy may be more threatened than pleased by this wife's invitation to modify their lives. If he can accept her liberation from a primarily domestic role, the partners can work together toward a new and more intimate relationship, sharing well what they have in common and pursuing their separate interests on a more autonomous basis (1978, p. 257).

Adjustments may lead to various changes, from separation and divorce to reworking and improving the marriage. At times it becomes obvious that the two have developed at different rates and in different directions. Often, after years of denial and maintaining the status quo, the marital strains come to a head during the midlife transition period. At times one or both seek outside companionship. Extramarital relationships may reflect the adult's struggle with the young/old or feminine/ masculine polarities. Nevertheless, both spouses have to make new choices as each reexamines the level of commitment to the marriage.

ADULT DEVELOPMENT

MIDDLE ADULTHOOD ERA

"Middle adulthood" lasts from about forty to sixty-five. During this third era, a person's biological capacities decrease but are sufficient for a valuable life. People become "senior members" of their particular worlds. The dual responsibility for one's own work and perhaps the work of others is balanced with the development of the next generation of early adults that will eventually lead the next generation.

Levinson et al. (1978) found men in his study between forty-five and forty-seven moving into a period he called "entering middle adulthood." The primary task accomplished during this period is the making of crucial choices, providing meaning and commitment to these choices, and constructing a life structure around these choices. Several patterns of entering middle adulthood were identified.

However, only a small group of the men tended to make revised choices, were ready to commit to them, and began developing a new life structure during the transition period. For this group, the midlife transition period served to reaffirm and sharpen their choices made in earlier periods of life. In many of the other cases, Levinson found the men were unable to form a stable life structure and needed this entire period to build the new life structure. Some of the negative things that occurred at this time included marital separation, quitting a job, terminating a significant relationship (friend, mentor, lover), moving to another location, breaking away from the early adulthood model. Each of these served to give the man space to test and reconstruct a new life structure. They needed time to explore options, test preliminary choices, and overcome disappointments. The period did not end until the task changed and a new transition period started.

While men struggle to accept their limitations related to death, it seems women have a greater concern to set out on their own, to challenge the assumption that they need to be protected, and expand their lives in new directions (Levinson, in press). Some women return to work in hopes of realizing their own Dreams or to assert their sense of independence. A majority of women make qualitative revisions in their life structures and feel better about themselves than those who do not make changes. Only women who had lived extremely family-oriented life structures were critically affected by the leaving of children from home (Roberts & Newton, 1987). Menopause for women, as well as sex hormone changes for men at this time, did not appear to be a critical aspect of midlife.

LATE ADULT TRANSITION AND LATE ADULTHOOD

The last era, "late adulthood," starts at about sixty. This period is initiated by the "late adult transition," which lasts roughly from sixty to sixty-five. In the early sixties, middle adulthood normally ends. The character of living is altered by many fundamental biological, psychological, and social changes. The period of late adulthood may last to eighty-five. No one major marker event highlights this period, according to Levinson et al. (1978).

Around sixty comes a new awareness of bodily decline and experience of limitations. Aches and pains are more frequent. Medical warnings remind one to take certain precautions or face more severe consequences in regard to heart disease, cancer, endocrine dysfunction, defective hearing and eyesight, depression or other emotional disorders (Kimmel, 1989). There is also an increased frequency of death and serious illness of friends and colleagues. All of these combine to intensify a sense of aging and mortality.

In addition, Western culture defines a change of generation in the sixties connected closely to retirement. Words such as "elderly," "golden age," and "senior citizen" have given a negative tone to this time period. During the "late adult transition," age begins to dominate over youth in the adult's mind. A person fears that youth within is dying and that the old indicates an empty, dry structure devoid of energy, interests or inner resources. The task of this period, according to Levinson (1990), is to maintain one's youthfulness in a form appropriate to late adulthood. This means ending and modifying one's earlier life structure.

Responsibilities tend to decrease significantly. The older adult becomes a source of modest assistance and moral support for children and grandchildren. There are adjustments to retirement and a decreased sense of esteem, influence, and power (Santrock, 1985). If leisure has been treated as a lifelong component of one's personal life, the older adult will have a head start in attaining a sense of productivity and fulfillment during retirement (Okun, 1984).

Financial and social security tend to become the primary determinates of a freedom of choice on where to live and how to spend the retirement years (Levinson et al., 1978). Thus, a further developmental task of this time period is to form a new balance between involvement with society in general and with one's self (Okun, 1984). This can become a time where talents are fully realized, as in Picasso, or leadership is exerted, as in Churchill, Gandhi, and Rockefeller. However, most adults tend to believe they have completed the major portion of their contributions to life. As the older adult appraises his or her life, the person begins to gain a sense of integrity for the contribution of that life as a whole. By finding meaning and value in one's life, however incomplete and full of weaknesses, the older adult begins to come to terms with the approach of death (Kimmel, 1989). This developmental perspective of retirement and post-retirement life requires sensitivity to the environmental realities as well as changing personal (health and aging) constraints if older adults are to continue to feel useful as productive and contributing members of society.

CONCLUSION

For too long, the church has operated on the myth that to be adult is to be finished. First, the myth is based on a false three-stage concept of life: childhood, youth, and adulthood. In this myth, adulthood seems to be the end of growth or development rather than an ongoing interaction between the adult's internal self and external world. Second, the use of "finished" suggests that the only change to be expected in adult life is deterioration. Unless the church can break out of this combination of outdated expectations, ministry to adults will continue to have destructive effects.

One destructive effect of this myth is that it suggests a negative imagery for growth, change, adaptation, and maturity:

getting old. This can lead to depression and despair. Another negative effect is that it may block realistic reflection and the making of choices. Adults will continue to believe their decisions must last a lifetime and feel trapped by life. As a result, alternatives and options may be prematurely closed down at any time in adulthood.

But because adults outgrow their "shells," have periods of vulnerability, and change from one era of adulthood to another, the church must take adults much more seriously. The contexts in which adults live (marriage, home, work, leisure) carry ministry significance. Predictable life events, transition periods, and crises may provide adults and those who minister to them with a framework in which to evaluate options and make choices that will influence their lives and walks with God.

FOR FURTHER READING

Egan, G. & Cowan, M. (1980). *Moving into adulthood: Themes and variations in self-directed development for effective living.* Monterey, CA: Brooks/Cole.

Levinson, D., Darrow, C., Klein, E., Levinson, M., & McKee, B. (1978). *The seasons of a man's life.* New York: Knopf.

Sell, C. (1985). *Transition: The stages of adult life.* Chicago: Moody Press.

Sheehy, G. (1976). *Passages: Predictable crises of adult life.* New York: Dutton.

Smith, R. (1990). *Learning to learn across the life span.* San Francisco: Jossey-Bass.

11

Development in the Family

Donald M. Joy

Families are always in transition. Couples turn into parents. Infants become toddlers. Middle-school kids ripen into emerging, hormone-driven teens and then young adults. The original pair imagine themselves still to be "kids" among their peers until, perhaps, their fifties. Playful impulses deceive them into believing that they are still young and vital, only trapped in bodies with thinning shock cushions in their joints, bulging waistlines, and waning sexual powers. Then come grandchildren, retirement decisions, illnesses and deaths of lifelong age-mates, and other signals that development is continuing to carry them along the stream of life.

A Henry Martin cartoon summarizes the developmental nature of life. In it, two middle-school boys toting book packs are ambling out of a suburban residential neighborhood. One is musing to the other: "You want to know what life is all about? I'll tell you what life is all about. Life is about day-care centers, nursery school, kindergarten, elementary school, middle school, high school, college, grad school, night school, adult school, continuing education school, alumni college, and elderhostels. That's what life is all about."

In this chapter we will examine developmental aspects of the historic family in which one adult female and one adult male provide long-term parenting and care for children born to their intimate union. Cross-cultural studies of families would need to look at issues involving polygyny and polyandry and implications across the decades of a family's experience. In North America today, Koons and Anthony (1991) report that, whereas only 3 or 4 percent of adults were single in the 1800s, and that married adults hit an all time high of 98 percent following World War II, today's adults are almost an even split between marrieds (52%) and singles (48%). This means that many adults are never married, but many more are previously married. The largest status change between 1960 and 1987 according to the *Families in the Nineties Project* (National Research Foundation, 1988) is the "never married" single mother category, jumping from 4.2 percent of single parents in 1960 to 28.5 percent in 1987. The same data display a virtual doubling of divorced single parents (from 23% to 40.7% of all single parents) and a halving of the other side of the distress: married with spouse absent dropped from 46.3 percent to 24.7 percent of all single-parent households, suggesting a rise in no-fault and other divorce provisions to terminate an otherwise dead marriage.

Single parenting family development follows most of the family development dynamics presented here, though they are not explicitly addressed. And blended families in which survivors of previous marriages combine children and strive for positive family relationships constitute still another version of family much more complicated than the household and family development addressed here.

FAMILY LIFE CYCLE

K. Edwin Graham guided the late William Cessna and me (Joy and Cessna, 1974) as we developed a family financial planning curriculum targeting clergy in training. The Institute of Life Insurance had invested heavily in training teachers in public schools in principles of family finance, only to discover that teachers do not have access to families in ways to enhance their financial management. So the Institute funded Graham's efforts to bring pastors' skills on line for family ministry in financial matters.

In that context, we examined the seasons of a family's life. As we identified the changing urgent agendas within a family's life cycle, we noted emerging family needs that might present opportunities for ministry intervention and support as well as needs which might not always show up in traditional pastoral and congregational ministry agendas. We presented these visually in a full circle to suggest that each marriage that aspires to becoming a family — two becoming one, then three-in-one in the image of the Trinity, which includes the Holy Spirit as the spirit of the Father and of the Son — is replicating itself and that the circle of family life is a continuous fabric across the generations.

1. Marriage and Family Establishment

This "start up" point in the family life cycle begins, of course, with the awakening of the need for intimacy that drives the establishment of a new household and potential family. By most measures of marital satisfaction, these "honeymoon years" will mark the highest scores across the lifetime of the couple, rising again after low points dipping through the child-centered and teen decades, but never to the heights that characterized the early marriage.

The years in which the young ripen, seek intimacy, and marry are the special focus of the church's ministry. Education, special events, pastoral care, and counseling enrich the resources our young enjoy as they move toward marriage and establishing a home. The "bride and groom" are central figures in the faith community. Courtship coaching, engagement training, premarriage counseling, gift showers, weddings, and post-marriage counseling describe the myriad services we focus on in the launching of a new household.

The parent households, as well, come in for special needs and attention as the wedding bells take away a son and a daughter, leaving significant transition work for families of origin.

2. Child-Centered Decades

These are the "workhorse years" of the marriage, in which responsibility, duty, and postponed desires characterize the couple. In a culture that has made the two-income household essential for maintaining a comfortable standard of living, the child-bearing years tend to be the lean years, economically. And with the substantial developmental needs of the first year of life, the child deserves enormous investment of time with both parents. So, in the family of two, three, or four or more children, a year's full-time investment of one parent's attention is likely to take most of one decade for birth and early parenting tasks.

Both parents may and many must be in the workplace to feed, clothe, and fund the school and college years of their children. The needs and stresses of the family reach their peak during these decades. It is little wonder that such families are the heart of any congregation. Parents are at their peak of physical energy and often volunteer to staff programs in which their children are or soon will be participants. Families sense that they need a support network larger than themselves and find that pooling their energy and their children creates a community in which everybody wins.

These are the decades of an unending parade of rituals, graduations, promotions, awards, public appearances, dedications, conversions, baptisms, and crises. Congregations that consider these lean years for parents will schedule special retreats, encounters, and enrichments to nurture the strength of the marital bond of the parents of these all-star children. And the very programs the congregation has created for children will serve as the long-term investment that attaches children to the church as adults.

3. Empty Nest and Second Honeymoon

Sooner or later, the nest is empty and Dad and Mom are alone again. If their family was complete by the parents' mid-twenties, the event tends to occur in their mid-forties. Postpone parenting and you simply add twenty years to the last child's birth date, yielding the probable date the nest will be empty again.

Looking at each other across the breakfast table, parents always wonder what they have left "after children." Nicely bonded children leave home best and write or call least—adding to the pain of this transition. The silence around the house and across the table can be deafening. If they are lucky, Mom and Dad have kept in touch through the bearing, training, and launching years. But a worst-case scenario is of a man and a woman who barely know each other when there is not a kid between them who needs their full attention.

Now in their midlife agenda, both parents are likely to be stretching to embrace new or advancing careers. They tend to resign the volunteer positions and other elected ones at church, no longer attached by the sense of duty to keep the children's programs up and going. Instead of four to six hours each week in church life, they may revert to fewer than two, and drift into a fairly anonymous status while they are on the church turf.

If they succeed in grasping their "after-forty" dream with its "now or never" gasp motored by new reflections on their own mortality, they will tend to thrive, maintaining their energy and production capacities. But Levinson (1976) found that, if they do not make the promotion or find they have to settle for a smaller piece of the corporate pie than they dreamed, they may fall prey to depression, toxic symptoms, and failure to thrive.

Congregations rarely sense and therefore do not flex to meet the needs of the mid-career set who have mounted their career stallions for one final ride for the gold. While they are counted on to oversubscribe the budget and to finance the latest church expansion or relocation project, their needs come last and professional staff are least equipped to read their needs or to design helpful interventions. Like volunteers everywhere, they need celebration, appreciation, and affirmation. Since they have unlimited time to spare from their career fast tracks, these ministries need to be built into special occasions that merit their participation, and into the most public and visible parts of congregational life — the morning worship service.

These midlifers not only are the prime financial foundation of the church, they continue to be the financial base for launching households that have spun out of their now-empty nest. Somehow they manage to juggle assets to underwrite new lines of credit for their recently launched sons and daughters, and still fully fund their own retirements and begin to plan how to endow a significant program or institution. They supplement their own burial insurance with substantial term policies to offset their many liabilities as they tiptoe through this final honey-moon of theirs.

4. Surviving Spouse

Dreamed-of family reunions that never quite happened now occur at the funeral of a lost parent. In best-case scenarios, life itself was the party and everybody's business is up to date, so the funeral is a celebration—even if untimely. "See that the entire family is hosted at the Marriott for a dinner after the funeral!" was the surprisingly predictable cover sheet on one last will and testament. His family honored him with nearly an hour of remembered best and most energizing memories of the husband and father whose death was the occasion of their first real "family reunion."

In worst-case scenarios, shame issues drive hostility and vio-lence, and funerals are disaster zones. Jealousies drive post-funeral arguments and quick moves are calculated to compensate for old grievances. In such a family war zone the surviving spouse is the lightning rod for toxic energy left over from past abuse or rivalries. The will is read as a final sentencing, and every line interpreted as an extension of injustices felt from childhood.

Congregations know all too well the encroaching needs of the final decades of the survivors. Their new loneliness is often compounded by virtual isolation from family members who are now far away and at urgent points in their own careers.

These aging survivors must have abundant needs monitored: nutrition, mobility, competency to manage personal affairs, fi-nancial advice and eventually management, extended care, and intensive care. They will continue to participate in traditional services and many will be enriched by special programs and events for the leisure-time crowd. But eventually they will re-ceive institutional care and will need the church to "come to them" if they are to experience the community of faith at work in any personal way.

AS THE HELIX TURNS

Turn now, to look at the family as a system of unfolding life cycles. Developmentally we will want to see the parents' cycle of needs and agendas in the light of that of their children's. A larger look would include the previous generation, as well, since today many of us find ourselves for more than two decades in the "in-between" generation where the launching of children is balanced out on a daily basis with the protecting and nurturing of our aging parents.

The Family Life Cycle diagram below serves well as a flat, two-dimensional picture of a family's career. But the time line it images misses the oscillating movement of the adults' search for meaning and developing orientation and perspectives on the moral and spiritual domains as they interface with each other and with the helixes of each child.

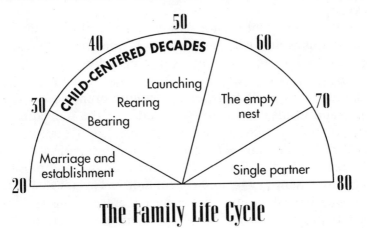

The Family Life Cycle

John Westerhoff (1976) offered a correction to conceptions about development as "stair steps," the common error in imaging developmental stages. He urged us to consider the integrating rings of a tree as we x-ray a cross-section of development, noting that the earlier structures are essential for later developing circles of growth. I spun out Westerhoff's image in actual diagrams (1983) demonstrating numerous expanding perceptions, including progressions from fear to respect, from terror to reverence, and from taboos through laws to principles and to pure essence. I diagrammed Piaget's findings about the development of the idea of justice, Gilligan's expanding and encompassing attachment, and the idea of God's incarnation in Jesus reaching back across developmental layers to evoke "meaning making" at all developmental stages and levels. I even offered a developmental speculation about ways of viewing the authority of inspired Scripture.

Noted writer Walter Wangerin (1986) spins a complicated and sometimes painful fictional model of adult wrestling with faith and life issues laid over the Orpheus myth. If individuals ripen in their ways of solving moral and spiritual problems as Piaget (1965) and Kohlberg (1981) suggest, and if faith unfolds in a predictable sequence of ways of expressing that faith as Fowler (1974, 1984, 1987) contends, then the several developmental journeys of parents and children deserve a theoretical model we could call the family's seasons of faith and moral reasoning.

In the absence of such a data-based model of family development, this is an invitation to provide your own ethnographic stories to fill in the content of a Kegan-like master "helix" (Kegan, 1982) within which to lift multiple "coiled spring" helixes. One or two will represent the adult-parent developmental cycles, and inside, more tightly coiled, are the individual helix portrayals of each child across the years.

Consider the simplest developmental evaluation we might make on any family. Piaget's stages of cognitive and moral reasoning are essentially limited to childhood. This means, theoretically, that typical parents should have a grasp of "formal operational thought" and use the process spontaneously in solving most daily questions and making decisions. Their children may experience the same crisis and may see the parent decide and act in a certain way, but conclude that the problem should be solved in a way consistent with concrete and objective reasoning. So, the question of which child should be reprimanded the most is answered by the child under the age of ten by a simple formula: the one who did the most harm. The young child does not ask whether the child in question intended to do damage or whether it was purely accidental. While a parent who takes time to think through the episode will tend to ask questions to determine the child's intent, many times parents make moral decisions without collecting the evidence. So we tend to confirm the young child's wrong conclusion about who gets the stiffer reprimand.

DEVELOPMENT as "HOLDING ON" AND "LETTING GO"

In the developmental design of families, the long infancy and childhood of humans underscores the deep need for long-term formation of the young. In the best of families, security and trust are the gifts of adults who have passed from desperate insecurities, have their trust and intimacy needs met, and hence are ready to lay down their lives and set aside their needs to provide continuous care for the newborn. Magid and McKelvey (1987) stress the urgency of providing a predictable and need-meeting first year of life. The authors demonstrate how pathologies abound if adults are "not there" physically or emotionally for the young child.

CHILDREN'S TRIGGERS FOR ADULT DEVELOPMENT ISSUES

Virtually unexamined is the visible pattern in which children's development triggers parent response. On the most positive note, the pregnancy months tend to prepare both the mother and the father for receiving the child. Fetal movement is evidently a strong bonding source, but parents who have not intended to produce a given child tend to respond by embracing a state of readiness that appears to be rooted in the pregnancy itself.

Negative responses tend to show up when a child's emergence to an age or a physical development status is a reminder of the parent's unresolved childhood grief or abuse. So parents may find themselves showing symptoms of depression and anxiety rooted in memories of their own abuse at precisely the time represented by their child's development.

DEVELOPING FAMILY STRENGTH

Relationships in the family predict the quality of relationships established beyond the family and into the next generation. Bradshaw (1988) describes how bonding to violence acts as a super-attachment by which the generations stick close, return home to live next door, and perpetuate the violence and abuse. In contrast, family bonding that establishes a strong orientation to trust actually empowers children to grow up and to leave home for faraway missions, certain that the security and safety of the early years is going to surround them anywhere on earth.

Stinnett and Defrain (1985) identified six characteristics that are associated with homes whose children enter into adult productive lives in a smooth progression from childhood to adulthood. The "strong families" demonstrated high degrees of commitment, appreciation, communication, time for each other, spiritual wellness, and coping ability.

Sheldon and Eleanor Glueck (1950) provided a "prediction scale" based on the home's social characteristics. In their study, 500 felony-level juvenile boy delinquents were compared to a sample of nondelinquents. Out of 400 items, three were shown to be most significant: discipline, supervision, and cohesiveness of the family, represented by daily meals together and holidays celebrated as a family. When Maude Craig and Selma Glick (1964) designed and completed a ten-year study of more than 300 boys in single parent homes in a New York City high crime neighborhood, those three social factors accurately predicted nondelinquency in 97.1 percent of the cases.

W. Robert Beavers (1974) cautions against intentionally designing one's family along the lines of the high stress "neurotic" family with its priority on making a good appearance outside the family and its authority center limited to one Lone-Ranger parent. Following a consulting stint with the Department of Health and Human Services during which I evaluated family systems research as a means of identifying positive interventions to offer families to reduce the risk of their teens becoming prematurely sexually active, I offered (1993) four "windows" of opportunity for families to check their "systems." By rating two variables as low or high, there are four combinations: the intimate family—high distribution of responsibility and high value of every person; the competing family—low and low; the chaotic family—low value but defaulted responsibility to a survival mode; and the showcase family—high value, but monarchical, hierarchical control. The systems studies corroborated what Scriptures had laid bare as my wife and I (1987) revealed our earlier report on our lifelong search for truly biblical relationships between men and women.

THE PERSISTING FAMILY

Will pain and trouble abolish the family? Did atheism and materialistic communism destroy hunger for truth, for faith, and for God?

Family development issues are the central fabric of human history. The meek—those tamed and gentle by virtue of suffering—are the ones who inherit the earth. David Cohen (1991) has put together a pictoral and narrative overview of family development and ritual in *The Circle of Life.* The circle, reminiscent of our own Family Life Cycle, moves from birth and childhood through initiation and adolescence, through marriage and adulthood to death and remembrance.

It turns out that the family's transition points are not only occasions for celebration and ritual, but that they always are marked, as well, by a certain level of pain and often evoke tears. Pain, here as most everywhere, tends to be a part of the glue that endears family members across the generations.

FOR FURTHER READING

Bradshaw, J. (1988). *Bradshaw on the family.* Deerfield Beach, FL: Health Communications.

Craig, M., & Glick, S. (1964). *A manual of procedures for application of the Glueck prediction table.* New York: New York City Youth Board.

Joy, D. (1983). *Moral development foundations: Judeo-Christian alternatives to Piaget/Kohlberg.* Nashville: Abingdon.

Joy, D. (1993). *Risk-proofing your family.* Pasadena, CA: U.S. Center for World Mission. See also video-assisted *For parents only: risk-proofing your family* (1990). Muncie, IN: Bristol House, Ltd.

Magid, K., & McKelvey, C. (1987). *High risk: Children without a conscience.* New York: Bantam.

Section 3

Applying Developmentalism to Christian Nurture

12

Developmental Discussion

Jim B. Parsons

Teachers who study the teaching methods of Jesus know that Jesus loved discussion groups. Of course, Jesus also lectured. And, there are biblical examples of Jesus using group work and individualized instruction. Jesus was like all good teachers. He used teaching methods based on circumstances and needs.

Discussion is a wonderfully rich and exciting way to teach. But it is not the only way to teach. The teacher's first task is to accurately assess the demands of the environment, the nature of the content being taught, and the particular needs of his or her students. A Christian teacher may choose from a rich variety of teaching methodologies. This chapter focuses on the nature and the purposes of developmental discussion.

PART I:
BASIC ASSUMPTIONS OF DEVELOPMENTAL DISCUSSION

**Developmental Discussion Is Not a Teaching Technique;
It Is a Teaching Attitude**

Once you decide that developmental discussion is an appropriate teaching methodology, where do you find the recipe for discussing? You don't. There is no "right way" to conduct a discussion. Discussion is more a way of thinking about teaching than it is a teaching recipe. Discussion always works best when the teacher and the students have a good relationship. The first task of the discussion leader is to establish a good relationship with the students.

Discussion is based on the belief that each student has knowledge that can benefit the whole group. Biblical authority for this belief can be found in verses like 1 Corinthians 14:26. This verse outlines how worship should be ordered in the church. It states that God has given different members of the church body different insights that they are encouraged to share with their brothers and sisters in Christ. The verse also sets an evaluation criterion for a developmental discussion by stating that all things "must be done for the strengthening of the church." If sharing does not build the body, it should be silenced.

Developmental discussion gives voice to all participants. In doing so, it eradicates the line between expert (teacher) and novice (student). Instead of a metaphor of power and control, developmental discussion is based on a metaphor of edification.

Developmental Discussion Does Not Just Happen; It Takes Preparation

Talking about the weather over coffee is not developmental discussion. There is a content to Christian education, and teachers must prepare by studying the content. Part of the discussion leader's task is the presentation of the biblical Gospel. A teacher who utilizes developmental discussion must not forget the biblical mandate to proclaim the Gospel of Jesus Christ. It is wrong-minded to believe that in a discussion anything goes.

Developmental Discussion Is Based on Fundamental Beliefs about Christian Education

Belief 1: People are able to understand the Bible
To use developmental discussion, you must believe that God has given people the ability to understand His Word. How we teach shows what we believe about people's capabilities. If we

do not believe that people can understand the Gospel, we have no alternative. We must sit them down, shut them up, and pour the content into their empty heads. However, if we believe that people can think and learn on their own, we will create experiences and opportunities where they experience the kind of tension and exercise that helps them grow.

Belief 2: People want to learn and understand the Bible

Many teachers fear discussion because implicitly they believe that students and teachers are in conflict. Hence, they fear that students will seize opportunities to revolt and turn the classroom into chaos. They see the desires and natures of their students standing against their goals as teachers. To overcome the problem, they treat students like enemies. They work to "keep the lid on" their classes.

But developmental discussion cannot thrive in such an atmosphere. Instead, a teacher who uses developmental discussion must choose to believe that people want to learn—that the Holy Spirit moves within them, even without their knowing, to create a deep yearning for truth. Teachers make this choice both because it is true and because believing that students and teachers can work together creates the only environment where true discussion can take place. Teachers will use developmental discussion only when they believe their students want to learn.

Belief 3: People like to talk with one another

Most people like to talk with each other. They enjoy the social aspect of community and of feeling "at home." At home, people share themselves, revealing more as they feel the comfort to do so. Community is a powerful motivating force. Developmental discussion is based on the biblical idea that people within the church share a mutual responsibility for each other. The pedagogical implication of these beliefs is that we must allow people to share with each other when they come together in a Christian community.

Belief 4: People do not want to be embarrassed or to seem strange

Churches are both places of worship and places of socialization. The relationship between people is important in setting an environment where discussion can flourish. Often teachers believe they are discussing when they allow others to speak during class. But, unfortunately, sometimes teachers already have "the" correct answer in mind. They dutifully give the student voice, pleasantly and without interruption. Then, after the student has finished speaking, the teacher gives "the" correct answer to the class.

Certainly, some answers are neither correct nor biblical. However, developmental discussion celebrates the different insights which siblings in Christ are given. When teachers sweep up after their students by giving "the" correct answer, students do not miss the implication. Many simply clam up. What is the sense of speaking if someone will "correct them" by giving the right answer later. The pedagogical foundation of developmental discussion is not talk; it is shared relationship. Developmental discussion honors the insights of students by making them feel accepted.

Belief 5: People tend to trust human authority and status too much
Human authority must constantly be critiqued and questioned. Often, teaching in Christian education sees disagreement as discord or nastiness. In discussion, teachers and students should be able to disagree in a spirit of mutual celebration and love. Teachers and students both must realize that the position of teacher is held tenuously—by the grace of God, with a responsibility to prepare and an attitude of holy rigor. The teacher must not encourage the students to believe that he or she always has the answer. If this happens, the students will not grow and the teacher will be pulled away from the central point of the task.

Belief 6: Humans respond to love and caring
It may be more blessed to give than to receive, but people must have the opportunity to give. People need to be loved, that goes without saying; but what often goes unsaid is that people need to experience giving love, too. During a developmental discussion the teacher can be still, listen, and assess what is happening. It is hard to talk and think at the same time. Developmental discussion, more than any other teaching methodology, allows a

teacher to make little plans to show acceptance and consideration and bestow worth on the ideas and thoughts of others.

Belief 7: People usually can smell a scam
The first task in loving someone is to love him. It is hard to fake caring. There are two ways to look at people; either they are worthy of love or they are not. God didn't hate sinners, He loved them. The little things, both for good and bad, that a teacher says, stay with students for a long time.

If you, as a teacher, are going to choose developmental discussion as a teaching methodology, it is important to see your students as worthy of love. Regardless of your teaching methods, how you choose to see people is the first step in becoming a Christian educator. Students know when the teacher cares. It would be almost impossible to teach using discussion if you do not love your students.

Belief 8: Human life tends to be simple, not complex
Teachers who use developmental discussion remember that students need (a) identity (to believe they are special); (b) freedom from fear (to be comfortable in the knowledge that things will work out, that one does not have to be "on guard" all the time); (c) to belong (to love and be loved); (d) to work (to develop and use personal talents); (e) to grow (to know that they are progressing toward a goal, regardless of how hard that progress may be); and (f) to be a decision-maker (to know that what you think counts and that you make a difference in the world).

PART II: HOW TO DISCUSS (COMPLETING SEVEN TASKS)

The most important thing to remember about using discussion in your class is not to learn the right recipe but to build the right attitude. In discussion, many paths lead to the same goal. But only one attitude will work. This section offers suggestions about how to set up a classroom where developmental discussion can flourish. From the eight beliefs listed above, it is possible to build seven tasks a discussion leader must work to complete. These are:

Work to Build Relationships

Management or discipline in teaching is not based on status or power. Instead, teaching is, at its most basic level, a relation developed between a teacher and a student.

Arrange the Physical and Emotional Classroom Environment

Good discussion leaders do not manipulate student behavior. Instead, they create an environment where learning happens easily. This environment includes both the physical layout and the psychological or emotional climate.

Set Out the Task or Project Clearly

Open discussion does not mean a lack of structure. Good discussion leaders know that most students, regardless of age, struggle without clear directions. The good discussion leader lays out the task clearly. Students may then propose changes; however, it is easier to add choice to structure than to structure confusion.

Give Students Time for Consideration

Research suggests that thoughtful responses do not happen quickly. Instead, students need time to consider alternatives and weigh the implications of their choices. Developmental discussion works best when time to consider is built into the methodology.

Reaffirm the Basic Task of Discussion and Listen for the Voices of the Students to Emerge

Good discussion leaders encourage students to respond by creating an atmosphere of openness and comfort and by reassuring students that responses and ideas, but not people, may be criticized. Then, as the voices and ideas of students begin to come forth (not all voices will speak confidently at first), the discussion leader supports and magnifies the ideas of the speakers.

Ask the Right Kinds of Questions

The best way to encourage developmental discussion is to ask questions. But not all questions are created equal. Some questions encourage expansive thought and consideration; some questions discourage thought. For example, discussion leaders may only ask questions about what they stated in a lecture. Such questions encourage rote memorization and tend to reinforce the power and status of the teacher, at the expense of the growth of the students' power and status. The good discussion leader works to help students grow more able and less dependent on the leader — not more dependent on the leader.

Expect and Prepare for Initial Resistance from Students
If you are a teacher who wants to use developmental discussion, you should expect that it might take your class time to grow comfortable with the methodology. Your students may not be comfortable with discussion, for reasons mentioned earlier in the chapter. In fact, you may sometimes even sense resentment for what you are doing.

I encourage discussion leaders not to give up too soon. Always listen to what people say, but do not quit too quickly. Your students may not be used to discussion as a teaching methodology. Most did not experience it in school, even in university classrooms. Developmental discussion is not common in evangelical teaching. As a result, it takes time to help students feel comfortable with the classroom equality that developmental discussion encourages. While it is important to honor knowledge, throughout Christian education there is too much emphasis on the power of the expert. That emphasis is sometimes hard to break down.

PART III: HELPING STUDENTS READ

Recently, a senior elder in my church said to me, "You know, Jim, I just finished a remedial reading course. It was very helpful. My problem was that I relied on hearing the Bible and had never learned how to learn." This elder's point is instructive. Christian teachers must help their students "learn how to learn."

In a Bible-centered classroom, students must read and study the Bible. Without this biblical "meat," discussion is not filling. But for many people like my friend who took the remedial reading course, reading the Bible is not easy. Teachers can help their students learn how to read so that they can discuss more fully. When constructing reading tasks, a number of learning principles should not be ignored. My own teaching experience and reading the body of research suggest a short list:

Give Students a Purpose for Reading
If students know why they are reading, they will be better able to focus their attention on the task.

Provide a Directed Reading Activity
That Will Help Focus Their Reading
A project (something to do), even a simple one, helps.

Help Students Get Started
For example, a teacher who begins by setting the scene well or giving the background with fluency and emotion helps make the reading easier for the students.

Look for and Eliminate Barriers
to Understanding Before Reading
For example, if there are words that students may not know, define them. Students, particularly those with reading problems (and adults are included here, too), might come to a word or idea they don't understand, throw up their hands, and psycho-logically quit—"Here's something else I can't understand."

Provide Bite-size Chunks
Reading and discussion, like other activities, is best done in moderation. It is always best to quit before the task becomes BORING.

PART IV: ASKING POWERFUL DISCUSSION QUESTIONS

Teachers often forget how powerful the human activity of asking a question and receiving an answer can be. But a study of the life of Christ highlights how often Christ uses questioning techniques.

My primary goal for my students is to help them grow to see the power of the Scriptures in the reality of their own lives. I also want them to understand and reconcile their lives in the world in the light of the Gospel message and to encourage them to take responsibility for what they learn as they live their lives. Specifically, I want them to understand that they must be "doers of the Word and not hearers only." To help accomplish these goals, I have developed a typology of questions that address these particular needs I wish to attend to. My purpose in asking these types of questions is to help students draw human life into the discussion of the Gospel.

Question Typology

Focusing questions
A focusing question helps people find out more about the section of the Bible being studied.

For example, these questions are drawn from the story of the Good Samaritan.

Jesus shows that a number of people pass by the wounded man. Who are these people? Why do you think He uses these as examples?

Layering questions
Layering questions ask people to go past the section of the Bible being studied and consider other circumstances that are similar to those in the "story." Think again of the story of the Good Samaritan.

Things have changed since this story was told; still, many groups remain in the same conflict situation as the Jews and the Samaritans. If you were going to retell the story in a modern setting, what groups could you use to make the meaning of the story just as authentic? What groups in your own community (define community broadly) might be in conflict?

Extending questions
Extending questions push past situations in the Bible right into the students' own lives. They are much more personal than layering questions.

Again consider the story of the Good Samaritan.

Be honest. Is there a person or group of people for you that might fit into the same category as the Samaritans fit into in the eyes of the Jews of Jesus' day? Rewrite the story of the Good Samaritan, substituting the name of the person or group that you choose into the role of the Samaritan. What meaning does the story have for you? Could it be true?

Deciding questions
Deciding questions ask students to make decisions, evaluate, and make commitments to act on things they've learned.

What wounded people do you know? What can you do to "help bind their wounds"? What long-haul commitment can you make to someone that would really be a help to him or her? Are you willing?

SUMMARY

I hope that readers who read this chapter looking for a specific recipe for conducting a discussion are not too disappointed. My teaching experience and my reading of research suggest that conducting a strong, developmental discussion relies less on a precise format than it does on the development of a way of living together as a group of learners. Certainly, skills like helping students learn to read more easily and thoroughly and asking thought-provoking questions help encourage a more focused and powerful discussion. However, these skills are no more important than working from a set of basic beliefs about (1) teaching and learning and (2) the power of the Bible to help shape human lives.

If developmental discussion is to work well, teachers must prepare. But their preparation is less one of learning the right steps than it is one of building personal relationships, working consistently from a clear set of beliefs, and preparing the environment so that learning can happen. Last, the good discussion leader must seek ways to become smaller in status and power as the students become larger. These are not easy tasks, but the end result is a powerful developmental discussion — a wonderful way to teach and learn.

DEVELOPMENTAL DISCUSSION

FOR FURTHER READING

Baloche, L. (1994). Breaking down the walls: Integrating creative questioning and cooperative learning into the social studies. *Social Studies, 85*(1), 25–30.

Beauchamp, L., & Parsons, J. (1992). *Teaching from the inside out*. Edmonton: Les Editions Duval.

Eble, K. (1976). *The craft of teaching: A guideline to mastering the professor's art*. San Francisco: Jossey-Bass.

Gangel, K. (1974). *Twenty-four ways to improve your teaching*. Wheaton, IL: Victor Books.

Holden, J., & Bunte, K. (1995). Activating student voices: The Paideia seminar in the social studies classroom. *Social Education, 59*(1), 8–10.

Kazemek, F., & Rigg, P. (1985). Tithes: Poetry and Old People. *Lifelong Learning, 4,* 4–8.

Martin, C. (1988). Action first—understanding follows: An expansion of skills-based training using action method. *Journal of European Industrial Training, 12*(2), 17–19.

Oliver, L. (1995). Is the United States ready for a study circle movement? *Adult Learning, 6*(4), 14–16, 19.

Wooden, S., et al. (1994). ORIDING: An adult teaching-learning technique. *Adult Learning, 5*(6), 18–19.

13

The Developmental Use of Lecturing

Ronald T. Habermas

The lecture method has fallen on hard times; at least some would like to think so. Naysayers philosophically range from existentialists to progressivists. Even cartoonists have gotten into the fray. Gary Larson (of "Far Side" fame) created a sarcastic cartoon of a father scolding his son for throwing a ball through a window. In the illustration, the father stands behind his overhead projector diagramming the recent catastrophe to the boy, seated before him. The caption reads: "Eventually, Billy came to dread his father's lectures over all other forms of punishment."

Indeed, lecture-bashing has reached a new high, or low, depending on one's perspective. The irony is that most of these attacks are perpetrated through one method—more lectures. Like the angry mob who blindly hangs the wrong person in its zealous quest for justice, more often than not the lecture method has been falsely accused and condemned. This reality leads to the thesis of the chapter: *There is no such thing as bad lectures, only bad lecturers.* Christian educators must inquire, "What does a good lecture sound like?" and "How can this method advance developmentally balanced learning?" In short,

"What must be known about the design of an effective lecture?" As we analyze this area, at least six categories of knowledge or truth emerge.

Truth #1
Effective Lecturers Exhibit a Thorough Knowledge of Their Subject

Whether it is called a sermon, a presentation, a speech, a demonstration, or a lecture, speakers must know what it is they are talking about. To some, this first category of knowledge might appear obvious. But those who have sat through addresses espousing error or ignorance would rebut that claim as presumptuous. Moreover, such experiences in miseducation have caused lecture to be cynically defined as "material that proceeds from the notebook of the teacher to the notebook of the student, without going through the head of either one!"

Wlodkowski (1985) states that three basic skills converge within all noteworthy instruction. The premier skill centers on the need for teachers to know their topic (the *what*). Wlodkowski then cites four subpoints. First, good teachers are able to explain their knowledge of the subject in easy-to-understand terms. The mark of a skillful lecturer is turning complex concepts into simple (versus simplistic) ones, not the reverse. Second, good orators, like good sculptors, shape their presentations with helpful examples, jokes, or analogies. Third, model teachers should have such a complete grasp of their material that it produces "relaxed familiarity" with the subject. They are not tied down to their notes. Fourth, Wlodkowski claims that good lecturers know their limits. They recognize the boundaries of their knowledge.

Truth #2
Effective Lecturers Embrace the Intimate Knowledge of Their Learners and Their Learning Environment

The story is told of a professor who, on the first day of the semester, walked to the front of the lecture hall, adjusted the cassette recorder, and—without ever saying a word—left the room with the taped lecture running. Day after day this event was repeated; students heard only the recorded monologue. Finally, by the start of the second week, the smarter students emulated their prof. They brought their cassette recorders to class. And, with uniformed precision, when their teacher left the room, they each pressed the "record" buttons on their machines. They exited as well.

Lecturers who are insensitive to their learners and to their setting run the risk of similar consequences: producing uninterested, unmotivated students. The second of three basic skills identified by Wlodkowski is empathy (the *who*). Empathy is expressed by understanding the learners' needs and expectations, by adapting to the learners' experiences and skills, and by adjusting to the learners' perspectives and age-appropriateness.

Jesus Christ, the Master Teacher, epitomized sensitivity toward His hearers. In particular, He meticulously observed people whom He served in order to customize His instruction. The Lord's purposeful examination of the widow who gave her small offering (Mark 12:41-44) reveals one well-known example. But many other explicit illustrations of observation surface in Scripture, including Christ's compassion for the crowd, following rejection by His hometown (Matt. 9:36); Christ's care for the 5,000, which led to the miraculous feeding (Matt. 14:14); and the Lord's concern for the widow in her loss (Luke 7:13). Chase Collins (1992), an accomplished storyteller, explains how important it is to develop skills of observation, challenging teachers to "cultivate an attitude of seeing" (p. 166) the world around them. "When I keep my eyes open for glimpses of people and what they are doing, it feeds me with the energy, curiosity, and compassion I need for stories and just plain living" (p. 172).

Besides understanding the learners, teachers must also observe their particular environmental settings. Paul's intentional research of the Athenian culture, just prior to his address at the Areopagus, enabled him to testify that he had consciously "walked around and looked carefully at" their objects of worship (Acts 17:23). He had systematically analyzed his surroundings.

TRUTH #3
EFFECTIVE LECTURERS ENGAGE THE SYNTHESIZED KNOWLEDGE OF BOTH THEIR SUBJECT AND ENVIRONMENT

It's a false notion to believe that if an instructor accomplishes the first two skills in an independent fashion, then the benefit of these combined skills will be automatic. That is, some good teachers hold an acceptable level of subject knowledge; other good teachers understand the people and the place where they teach. But only great teachers do both, without compromise. This third skill is what Wlodkowski described as demonstrating clarity of presentation as well as showing enthusiasm (the *how*).

Years ago, as a college student at a church social, I witnessed how a talented professor demonstrated this synthesized knowledge. Following the exhausting and chaotic activities of a hayride, this young man had the unenviable task of giving a devotional to three dozen youth in the hayloft! Without a doubt, this professor knew his material, the first skill of teaching. This instructor likewise knew his audience: his message was relevant to the youth, concise, and punctuated with appropriate illustrations. But the thing I recall most about this man was his ability to fuse these two skills into one. In part, this skill was accomplished because he was prepared for the unexpected. In the hayloft that night, no electrical power was available; the speaker was left without any light. "How would the professor read his selected verses and notes?" I asked myself anxiously, since I was the one who formally invited him to come. But my worry was short-lived. As he began, he deftly shifted his small Testament and clipped notes to his left hand, removing a small flashlight from the right pocket of his coat. That night I learned a few things from the professor's devotional; but I learned a more potent lesson about the value of synthesized knowledge between topic and environment.

The Lord displayed this complementary skill in Mark 4:33-34: "With many parables Jesus spoke the word to them, as much as they could understand. He did not say anything to them without using a parable. But when He was alone with His own disciples, He explained everything." Christ's method of imparting knowledge of the subject (i.e., via parables) was shaped by his learners' capabilities (i.e., Jesus taught them to the extent that "they could understand"). Furthermore, Jesus was aware of His environment, since when He was "alone" with His close followers (versus the crowd) He made the extra effort to interpret His parables.

TRUTH #4
EFFECTIVE LECTURERS EXAMINE THE TECHNICAL KNOWLEDGE OF THEIR DELIVERY

Space does not permit a detailed look at this complex issue, but several principles will be highlighted within two broad categories. The first category represents technical features about the lecture itself. Howe (1966) differentiates between the "method" and the "principle" of oral addresses. He states that lectures and sermons—though monological in their method—should be dialogical in their essence, drawing hearers into the communication process. We have all heard presentations where the speaker consistently answers questions that we ponder to ourselves. Howe calls this implicit dialogue. And he concludes that this feature of lecture is essential to responsible Christian education.

Lowman (1990) contends that the lecture requires definitive boundaries: an engaging introduction (perhaps using a statement of paradox) as well as a convincing conclusion. The body of the presentation must reflect careful preparation, too. With this in mind, Eble (1976, p. 52) aptly describes what needs to be done by suggesting what the contents of a poor lecture consist of, including lack of references to the audience's present context; failure to respect the hearers' knowledge or interests; displays of false modesty about oneself or the subject; insensitivity to time; use of arcane terms; excessive appeals to expert authority or to qualification of terms; and repeated use of multiple quotations.

The second category of technical knowledge identifies particular dimensions about the teacher. Here, Farrah (1991) notes the significance of nonverbal communication, including diction, inflection, intentional pauses and silence, rate of speech, awareness of time, and listener feedback. She cites research that points out two primary deficits within the ineffective teacher that negatively affect delivery: insufficient preparation and lack of self-confidence.

TRUTH #5
EFFECTIVE LECTURERS EVIDENCE THE COMPREHENSIVE KNOWLEDGE OF THE LEARNING PROCESS

As Peter reached the end of his convicting sermon on the Day of Pentecost, Luke summarized: "When the people heard this, they were cut to the heart and said to Peter and the other apostles, 'Brothers, what shall we do?' " (Acts 2:37) All skillful teachers recognize the broad domains of learning within this verse: the cognitive, affective, and behavioral features, respectively. For example, Lowman (1990) suggests that lecturers teach critical thinking skills, not only by giving adult learners valuable insights but also by telling them how those insights were reached. Lowman concludes that "students will think more critically about a subject if an instructor exhibits a healthy skepticism at times about the field's assumptions and methods" (p. 106).

Besides sensitivity to human domains, comprehensive knowledge of the learning process includes understanding diverse learning modes. Mark Twain once quipped that he had received public schooling as a child but he never let it interfere with his education. Twain was referring to formal, nonformal, and informal education. In brief, good lecturers value the importance of pertinent theories, realizing how they pertain to developmental concerns and types of learning.

TRUTH #6
EFFECTIVE LECTURERS EMPLOY THE COMPLEMENTARY KNOWLEDGE OF OTHER TEACHING METHODS

No method is ever singled out for use all by itself; several methods are combined throughout wholesome instruction. This is the case with exemplary lectures, too.

Consider the Master Teacher's example. One glance at a

red-letter edition of the New Testament shows that Christ's first-recorded oration was the Sermon on the Mount in Matthew 5 through 7. Notice the complementary fabrics of instruction that were woven into this sermon: (1) the poetry of the Beatitudes (5:1-12); (2) the metaphors of salt and light (5:13-16); (3) a series of six contrasts: "You have heard that it was said . . . But I tell you . . ."; (4) a half-dozen relevant topics, like murder and divorce (5:17-48); (5) a structured sample of model prayer (6:9-13); (6) object lessons of birds and lilies (6:25-33); (7) proverbs (7:6); and (8) visual imagery using earthly and heavenly comparisons (7:7-27).

Likewise, stressing this feature of complementary methods, Lowman (1990) explains eight helpful forms of the lecture method, ranging from lesser to greater student involvement. The "formal oral essay" represents the most structured approach to monologue, since a large body of information is presented, often written out and read to students. Some say this approach to lecture is most accurate, for the term "lecture" originates from the Latin word *legere*, meaning "to read." In the "expository lecture," the most common type of college lecture, the teacher still occupies the majority of the time, but some questions are raised by bolder students.

"Provocative lectures" challenge students to reassess their knowledge and values. This procedure is often followed at the end of a semester, after a common set of knowledge has been studied. Questions (even rhetorical ones) and reflective exercises provoke evaluation of student understanding. At a more sophisticated level, modern-day parables provide the necessary jolt to challenge learners, as LeFever (1985) suggests: "Perhaps, along with the familiar Biblical parables, we need to shock with contemporary parables that contain spiritual truth. We can stretch people's thinking by using the same literary style Jesus was so fond of" (p. 212). LeFever then produces several parables in detail. One specific example comes from the ingenious mind of the late Joseph Bayly. His book *The Gospel Blimp and Other Stories* (1983) contains several contemporary stories that I have used to prompt learner reflection.

"Lecture-demonstration," the fourth lecture variant offered by Lowman, provides helpful sensory input for verbalized messages within a broad subject range.

"Question-lecture" offers a different twist to presentations, for the teacher answers inquiries previously prepared by students.

This instruction is less direct than "lecture-discussion," where the teacher provides more spontaneous interaction with learners. In this latter case, discussion is interlaced with the lecture. Many pastors use this approach in a modified way. After the morning sermon, they explain details and implications of the message, in a classroom setting, following a dialogical format.

The seventh variation is the "lecture-recitation." Here, the speech is occasionally interrupted for students to share their prepared responses to assigned questions, when a particular piece of literature is read, or drama is performed. I have found that reading Jon Scieszka's *The True Story of the Three Little Pigs* (1989) to my class encourages students to gain helpful new perspectives. This creative text is based on the familiar fairy tale, retold by the wolf, who thinks he was falsely accused.

The eighth and final variation is the "lecture-laboratory." Representing the most experimental version of monologue, this method (interspersed by short lectures) elicits student responses through personal observations, experiments, or other forms of independent work.

CONCLUSION

Unless we broaden our views about lecture and upgrade our respective skills, we Christian educators will continue to be haunted by the reality of Larson's earlier-cited cartoon. That is, we will minister to students who, like Billy, dread our lectures over all other forms of punishment — or any other teaching method. The best prescription for this malaise requires emulating those who are healthy; modeling noteworthy lecturers. It is at this juncture that we must contrast ineffective with effective lecturers; for the latter group, we realize, has something to say, something worthwhile. In the final analysis, good lecturers motivate. They call for responsible action. They get their message out and they get it right. They say just enough — nothing more, nothing less, nothing else.

For Further Reading

Bayly, J. (1983). *The Gospel blimp and other stories.* Elgin, IL: David C. Cook.

Brown, G. (1978). *Lecturing and explaining.* London: Methuen.

Eble, K. (1976). *The craft of teaching: A guideline to mastering the professor's art.* San Francisco: Jossey-Bass.

Gangel, K. (1974). *Twenty-four ways to improve your teaching.* Wheaton, IL: Victor Books.

Horne, H. (1971). *Teaching techniques of Jesus.* Grand Rapids: Kregel.

Joyce, B., Weil, M., & Showers, B. (1992). *Models of teaching* (4th ed.). Boston: Allyn and Bacon.

Taylor, C. (1988). *The art and science of lecture demonstration.* Philadelphia: Adam Hilger.

Weimer, M. (Ed.). (1987). *Teaching large classes well.* San Francisco: Jossey-Bass.

14

The Developmental Use of Mentoring

Robert Drovdahl

Development and discipleship/mentoring[1] share both long histories and recently resurgent popularity. Their histories date to the classical Greek world. Greek philosophers described development as a person's moral and spiritual growth from beginning to perfection (Talbert, 1985). Homer's *The Odyssey* provides the etymological roots of mentoring. Prior to departing for Troy, Odysseus sought a guardian for his son, Telemachus. The person who served for ten years as Telemachus' teacher and guide was named Mentor (Murray, 1991).

Development and discipleship also played important roles in the New Testament world. Both helped describe Christian living and Christian self-understanding for Jesus' early followers. For example, New Testament writers often identify the goal of Christian living as developing maturity (Eph. 4:11-16; Phil. 3:12-16; Col. 1:28-29; Heb. 5:11–6:3; 1 Peter 2:1-2). Even Jesus' life is portrayed by two writers, Luke and the author of Hebrews, as one of developing maturity (Luke 2:41-52; Heb. 2:10; 5:7-10). Though the specific term *disciple* fades from use outside the Gospels and Acts, the New Testament writers clearly see Christian living as discipleship—following and imitating Jesus (following — Matt. 19:27-28; Mark 9:38; Luke 6:39-40; John 8:12; imitating — Rom. 8:29; 1 Cor. 11:12; 1 Thes. 1:6; 1 Peter 2:21). In Luke's Gospel, development and discipleship are intimately linked and figure prominently in the narrative structure.

Discipleship in Lukan perspective is constituted primarily in terms of *followership.* The calling of the first disciples, Peter, James, and John, ends with all three leaving everything and following Jesus (Luke 5:11). Jesus links Peter's confession of Jesus as "the Christ of God" with Jesus' challenge: "If anyone would come after Me, he must deny himself and take up his cross daily and follow Me" (Luke 9:23). In all three interactions with would-be disciples in Luke 9:57-62, the operative word is "follow." The theme of following is so strong that, as Talbert (1985) notes, Luke adapts his Marcan source so that Simon of Cyrene carries the cross *behind* Jesus (Luke 23:26).

The idea of development, though not as pervasive as discipleship, is also prominent in Luke and provides a controlling structure for Luke's narrative. Thus Luke sets the stage for describing Jesus' life in developmental perspective by stating at the outset, "Jesus grew in wisdom and stature, and in favor with God and man" (Luke 2:52). The Greek term for "grew" was commonly used to describe the path a person follows from beginning to maturity (Talbert, 1985).

A standard approach to the biographies of philosophical-school founders in ancient Greece was to describe the life and teachings of the founder and then show how the founder's life and teachings were reproduced in the lives of the founder's disciples. Talbert (1985) holds that Luke's Gospel follows this pattern, a conclusion clearly supported by Luke's inclusion of Jesus' observation, "A student is not above his teacher, but everyone who is fully trained will be like his teacher" (Luke 6:40). For Talbert, the shape of Luke's narrative suggests that being a disciple of Jesus means to develop as Jesus developed. Discipleship serves as a time-honored means of development.

Despite linked histories, discipleship and development have followed different paths in the twentieth century. The resurgent interest and popularity in both stem from better understanding the dynamics of development and discipleship. However, with the notable exception of James Fowler, developmental theorists' research has not been primarily in service to Christian discipleship. Likewise, research on Christian discipleship has been more focused on spiritual disciplines rather than spiritual development.

This chapter aims to renew the conversation and connection between development and discipleship, so each may benefit from the other's labor. We activate the conversation by posing two questions:

- What contributions might discipleship make to a person's development?
- What perspectives does developmental theory offer for the task of making disciples?
- By reconnecting these two concepts we seek new light for the design of educational ministry.

DISCIPLESHIP FOR THE SAKE OF DEVELOPMENT

Particular insights of developmental theory have been carefully addressed in the previous two sections of this volume. Before considering discipleship's contribution to developmental Christian education, we must first briefly sketch our understanding of discipleship. The image of discipleship dominant today offers a fairly restricted picture of discipleship's setting, content, and relationships. The setting is one-on-one with regular meetings between discipler and disciple. The content is programmed instruction in the spiritual life, often combined with instruction in the basic beliefs of the faith. The relationship is highly directive, with the mature believer guiding the less mature believer.

While some prefer a more narrow, highly structured definition of discipleship (Hadidian, 1987) that offers the advantage of precision, we will employ a broader, more inclusive understanding (Coleman, 1987; Hull, 1990). The broader understanding emphasizes the discipleship relationship as the critical factor and deemphasizes the external conditions and characteristics of the discipler/disciple or the discipleship program. Hull (1990) identifies three qualities of a discipling relationship: intentionality, accountability, and caring. Where these qualities are present among persons who are following Jesus, discipleship is in process. If we wish to include discipleship in our design for educational ministry, relationships with these qualities must be encouraged. We now consider the value these qualities have for a person's development.

Intentionality and Development

Since development is not automatic, it is particularly important to focus the intentionality in a discipling relationship on personal development. Development is more than accumulated experience, so we must "discriminate between experiences which are educative and those which are mis-educative" (Dewey, 1938, p. 37). Dewey suggests two criteria for educative (development enhancing) experience: the principles of continuity and interaction.

Since "every experience is a moving force" (Dewey, 1938, p. 38), the principle of *continuity* asks, "Is this experience leading to greater or lesser maturity?" Intentional discipling relationships pay attention to the direction of one's experience. For example, a friend recently described a spiritual formation group he meets with weekly. Each week they trace the footprint of God in their lives by asking questions such as: *How have you experienced God's love this last week? What has God taught you this week about holiness of heart and life? Have you sensed any influence or work of the Spirit this week?*

In addition, they anticipate God's work by asking, *How do you hope to grow in your love for God this week?* When discipleship explores the continuity and direction of people's lives, development is more likely to result.

The principle of *interaction* acknowledges that educative experiences result from a good match between external event and internal readiness. Few, if any, events can be described as inherently good. This truth holds for spiritual events as well. As the author of Hebrews reminded his readers, "You are not ready for solid food"! (Heb. 5:12) Development brings great advances in understanding readiness and, therefore, great advantages for discipleship. When are followers ready to struggle with vocational questions? When are followers ready to explore the relationship between law and love? Developmental theory's tendency is to outline the next step in human growth. Discipleship's tendency is to say, "Take it!"

The principles of continuity and interaction highlight the importance of readiness. Peter's experience in Acts 10 illustrates these principles in action and demonstrates a point of growth in his life. How does Peter travel from his strict background, forbidding association with Gentiles, to the Gospel proclaiming that in Christ there is neither Jew nor Greek? He does so by traveling through an intermediate experience, a vision where God commands him to eat unclean animals and birds. Peter's encounter with Cornelius' servants is positive because external event and internal readiness are matched. Admittedly, visions do not constitute developmental markers, but the concept is applicable when readiness is seen in developmental categories. Consider how the external event of call to "full-time" Christian ministry has been managed by the church. What constitutes internal readiness for this call? What experiences need to precede this call and what experiences need to follow for there to be continuity and positive interaction with the call? This question cannot be answered without considering the person's cognitive, psychosocial, moral, and faith developmental standing.

The principles of continuity and interaction serve as reminders that no experience is inherently good; not a mission trip, not a Bible study, not an evangelistic outreach effort. Each must be evaluated in light of a person's readiness, and development is a critical factor in determining readiness.

Accountability and Development

In *After Christendom?*, Hauerwas (1991) suggests that, in a voluntary, consumer-oriented society, it is nearly impossible for the church to be a disciplined community because people resist the essential ingredient for a disciplined community: willingness to open one's whole life to the discipline of others. This is the heart of accountability. Hauerwas likens accountable growth as a disciple to learning a trade such as bricklaying. The analogy highlights the importance of practicing the disciplines of Christian living resulting in transformation "like that of making oneself an apprentice to a master of a craft" (p. 103). Critical to effective apprenticeship is willingly accepting the authority of teachers who "derive their authority from a conception of perfected work that serves as the telos of that craft" (p. 105).

While the above analogy has strong affinity with discipleship envisioned as disciplined habits, it also offers insight to the relationship between accountability, habits, and development. Dewey (1938) provides the connection: "the basic characteristic of a habit is that every experience enacted and undergone modifies the one who acts and undergoes . . . [and] the quality of subsequent experiences" (p. 35). Not only do we possess habits; habits possess us.

When discipling relationships provide accountability for the habits of one's life, conditions for development exist. Christian discipleship has long touted the value of spiritual disciplines in service of transformed living. The value of a developmental theory for the practice of spiritual disciplines is twofold: first, helping identify developmentally appropriate habits to practice; and second, broadening the circle of appropriate habits. As Hull (1990) argues, "We must stop thinking that only Bible teaching, sharing your faith, memorizing Bible verses, and teaching ministry skills are discipling" (p. 36).

Caring and Development

Most who research or write about discipleship/mentoring position the discipling/mentoring relationship as unique among the formal and informal relationships in our lives. Levinson et al. (1978) suggest a mentor is typically one-half generation older than the protégé. Thus, the mentor is neither friend nor parent, but a unique blend of both. Bey and Holmes (1992) suggest that two criteria, degree of commitment and comprehensiveness of influence, differentiate between a coach, role model, and mentor. However the role is positioned relative to other relationships, two "caring" qualities are essential in discipling relationships: support and challenge.

Daloz (1986) identified support and challenge as two of three primary functions of a mentor. We support others when we *listen* carefully to what life feels like from their perspective; *provide structure* for stability in times of stress or anxiety; *express positive expectations* regarding their ability to succeed; *share ourselves* as honestly as possible; and *make the relationship special.* We challenge others when we *set tasks* before them; engage in discussion that *expands awareness* and perspective; *hold high standards* for their performance; and *heat up dichotomies* by opening points of dissonance in their lives.

Support is like "apples of gold in settings of silver" (Prov. 25:11). Challenge is like "iron sharpening iron" (Prov. 27:17). When both are present in a relationship the optimum environment for development is present. Support without challenge may leave a person in a status quo state. Challenge without support may paralyze a person.

When discipleship has development in view, care will be taken to provide both support and challenge. The Jesus whose messianic call is portrayed as so supportive that He would not break a bruised reed or quench a smoldering wick (Matt. 12:20), challenged a Syro-phoenician woman regarding her worthiness to receive God's mercy (Matt. 15:21-28) and decidedly rejected the offer made by a teacher of the law to "follow . . . wherever you go" (Matt. 8:19).

DEVELOPMENT FOR THE SAKE OF DISCIPLESHIP

Discipleship provides the relational energy for development in Christian faith. Intentional, accountable, caring interaction with fellow disciples contributes to a person's development. We now turn to the question of developmental theory's contribution to an understanding of discipleship. We suggest a developmental perspective will guard against the tendency to distort discipleship in three ways: (1) to overemphasize hierarchy; (2) to hurry discipleship; and (3) to spiritualize discipleship. *Developmental perspective requires a discipleship of mutuality.*

The first distortion results in one-dimensional, one-directional discipleship: the process whereby one mature Christian supervises an immature Christian's life. When developmental theory informs discipleship it controls the twin conditions which create a strong sense of hierarchy: one-directional authority and one-directional service.

One-directional authority vests all authority in the discipler and calls for total submission from the disciple. The shepherding movement, which peaked in the mid-1980s, was a relatively high-profile example of distorted, hierarchical discipleship

(Digitale, 1990). The Burks (1992) document the personal damage that resulted from placing authority for every area of their lives into the hands of a supposedly spiritually mature shepherd.

One-directional service implies that one person gives while the other receives; one person is needy and one meets needs. Several years ago I joined a group of men meeting weekly for Bible reading and prayer. One week we were asked what we hoped and expected from our time together. We were all surprised when one person announced, "I'm not here to receive anything. I'm here to give." When pressed, he added that his spiritual needs were met by Christ alone.

Authoritarian hierarchy in a discipling relationship distorts the overall picture of how Jesus' followers discipled one another. While a few particular New Testament relationships might be described this way, the pervasive theme is mutuality in discipleship, Christians working out their followership in multilayered and multifaceted relationships. Development reminds us that Christian formation is a lifelong process, that the journey is the destination. When development informs discipleship, the tone is "doing with" not "doing to" or "for."

Developmental Perspective Requires "Leisurely" Discipleship
It is said that when Jean Piaget first brought his theory of cognitive development to America, he found audiences typically asked what he eventually labeled the American question: "How can we speed up the process?" This desire to reach a destination quickly points to the second tempting distortion of discipleship—packaging it into a predetermined, scheduled program. Six weeks. Twelve weeks. A year at the most. When discipleship becomes a program, the emphasis falls on production, moving people through, and getting people out.

A developmental perspective demands that we never see people being through with discipleship. High school students whose discipleship has been forged within the framework of synthetic-conventional faith are not automatically prepared to manage their discipleship through the developmental tasks of young adulthood. And young adults whose discipleship has been forged within the framework of individuative-reflective faith are not automatically prepared to manage their discipleship through the developmental tasks of middle adulthood. When development informs discipleship, it will look more like running a marathon than the 100 meters.

Richard Edwards (1985) notes that "unfinished discipleship" may have canonized status in Matthew's portrayal of the disciples. The disciples play a prominent role in Matthew's narrative. They are both commended for their faith and followership and criticized for their failures and lack of faith. The portrayal begins favorably. Peter, Andrew, James, and John respond to Jesus' call by immediately leaving everything to follow Him. This picture of perfect discipleship soon fades into a more complex image. Before there is even a story to offer evidence, Jesus foreshadows the unfinished character of their lives by calling them men of little faith (Matt. 6:30). Four more times the disciples are described as having little faith (8:26; 14:31— Peter only; 17:20; and 21:20). Matthew concludes his Gospel by describing the mountain scene where the disciples receive the Great Commission. When the disciples see Jesus, Matthew says they worshiped Him but also doubted.[2]

Developmental Perspective Requires Holistic Discipleship

Developmentalism generated its theoretical power in part by sorting human experience into tracks: cognitive development, psychosocial development, moral development, faith development, and other tracks. Yet developmentalism has also noted the interdependency between these tracks. While development across tracks is not uniform, it is roughly coordinated.

Discipleship aimed at spiritual maturity must also aim at human maturity. We cannot expect people to commit their vocational selves in a particular Christian direction if they do not have the requisite human maturity. Steele (1991) describes the goal as holy wholeness: "Must one be holy to be whole? Must one be whole to be holy? . . . Optimal human development is the correlation of holiness and wholeness" (p. 106).

SUMMARY

Developmental theory offers significant benefits to those who incorporate discipling/mentoring into their design for educational ministry. It brings the *telos* of discipleship into focus.

Discipleship can guide people toward healthy development — as whole and holy persons who follow Jesus.

Development can guide people toward healthy discipleship — as Christians linked in mutual care through intentional accountable relationships.

FOR FURTHER READING

Daloz, L. (1986). *Effective teaching and mentoring.* San Francisco: Jossey-Bass.

Fowler, J. (1984). *Becoming adult, becoming Christian: Adult development and Christian faith.* San Francisco: Harper & Row.

Hull, B. (1990). *The disciple-making church.* Grand Rapids: Baker.

Segovia, F. (Ed.) (1985). *Discipleship in the New Testament.* Philadelphia: Fortress Press.

Steele, L. (1991). *On the way: A practical theology of Christian formation.* Grand Rapids: Baker.

NOTES

1. In this article, *mentoring* and *discipleship* are used synonymously. Mentoring and its related terms have greater currency in the secular arena; discipleship is used more often in Christian circles. Yet both have similar relationships in view.

2. The NIV translates Matthew 28:17 "they worshiped Him; but some doubted," thus implying perhaps that some believed and some doubted. Although this is a fair rendering of an ambiguous phrase in Greek, Edwards (1985) argues that a better translation would be "they worshiped Him but were not sure" (p. 59). This would be more consistent with the late manuscript ending of Mark's Gospel, where Jesus rebukes the disciples for their lack of faith (Mark 16:14).

15

Developmentalism and Groups

Julie A. Gorman

One of my favorite "Hagar" comic strips shows the cartoon character seated for what is obviously an optometrist eye examination. The hooded doctor points to the random letters of the eye chart. To the implied question of ability, the patient replies, "Yes, I can read it—but it's boring and I can't follow the story!" Some people are always trying to read more into something than exists.

Can developmentalists be accused of "seeing a prince in every frog?" Are we straining when we look at small group structures and see developmentalism? Or is developmentalism inherent in effective small groups? When we examine groups through the filter of developmental theory, what factors appear significant? What developmental processes necessitate careful implementation? What theoretical and practical insights are revealed?

The small group is a popular methodological tool for learning. For the most part, it is perceived as a nonthreatening, easily doable way of helping persons grow and change.

With all the major methodologies available to Him, Jesus chose the small group community of the disciples to present and process the Good News of the King and the kingdom. With this group, He spent most of His time and shared the bulk of His teaching.

There is a direction and a sequence of levels moving in that direction in groups. That direction believers call "maturity," and the process of movement is labeled "Christian formation." All of life is Christian formation. Everything we are becoming and doing is for the purpose of forming us in Christ. All of life moves us toward this goal or away from this goal. Groups do this in unique ways. While developmentalism often focuses on the specific individualized growth of the person, biblical developmentalism (growth that is ultimately shaped by the Word of God) stipulates that it is impossible to mature alone. We are continually affected by and, in turn, actively affect the community of Christ in which we dwell. The community we label "group" is a necessary component for our development in Christ. We cannot fully develop without it. Individualized development is always in light of the body's development.

"We will in all things grow up into Him who is the Head, that is, Christ. From Him the whole body, joined and held together by every supporting ligament, grows and builds itself up in love, as each part does its work" (Eph. 4:15-16).

It is as we join together, each supplying, that we grow up into Him. Small groups never become ends unto themselves. They are for the purpose of helping the believers "grow up" in the direction of the Head.

How do small groups reflect their developmental nature? The following five areas depict the essence of developmentalism.

PURPOSE:
THE HIGH VALIDITY OF
DIRECTIONAL MOVEMENT IN GROUPS

Effective small groups have a direction in mind and cultivate growth toward that end. The more clearly that purpose is understood and embraced by members, the more satisfactory is their group experience both in fulfilling the persons and the task of the group. Groups lacking purpose usually end up disbanding. As long as persons see groups making progress toward that desirable end, they will remain in the group.

Groups that function effectively place high value on the growth of persons both as individuals and as a unit in the direction of the goals. This means they are never satisfied with just information. Data, content, and communication is given for the purpose of moving the persons in the group into the next stage of being and thinking. This is developmentalism. In terms of the group, there is a constant dual focus: How does the development of the individual affect the group? How does the development of the group affect the individual? In addition, we face the implications of how the development of both of these impacts leading and learning in a group setting.

Looking at groups in this developmental way suggests several implications for ministry. First, can we justify that this group impels the persons involved in the direction of more fully carrying out that purpose for which God designed them (maturity)? Having this as a clear-cut overall purpose helps to define Christian groups. How does the personal growth of individual members play a part in the group's passage to maturity? Secondly, is there an expectation and an evaluation of moving in the direction of this purpose and the goals of the group? Do we go to a group session with this holy expectation of transformation in mind? Do we reflect on and confront one another with standards of growth? Continual change is at the heart of development. It is a sign of life.

PERSONS:
HIGH VALUE OF MEMBERS AS PERSONS

Persons bring to a group factors that are greater than the group setting and that will affect the group in its setting. Members are not just parts of a whole, but valued structural engineers who determine what learning and transformation will take place. The developmental level of persons in a group will condition what goes on in that group, what objectives we can expect to reach, and how to reach them. When we take seriously the developmental observation that persons control what will be learned by them, we spend more effort on motivation and on discovering what it is they want to learn. When we realize that their level of development will determine what they receive and integrate, we will give more attention to discovering what that level is and how to work with it. We will refrain from delivering content regardless of appropriateness, readiness, and conditioning. We will match groups to learners and learners to groups. This matching includes selection of content and how it is taught, level of cognitive ability with what is communicated, and level of challenge with degree of faith development.

Each person brings to the group a holistic system of being. Each has an album of previous experiences with resulting framework of operations. Each comes with current life issues, dilemmas, frontiers of development that condition the next step of learning and growth.

Developmentalism helps us see the potential in knowing well the participants and their life issues as well as the group culture and level of growth in such areas as commitment to one another, security and trust, openness to change, group expectations and practices, acceptance of persons and responsibility. This high view of persons is reflective of our being made in the image of God. Groups who grasp this, respect persons as responsible, influential catalysts of their own development, both individually and as a group.

Coupled with this high value of persons is a realistic view of them as marred by sin, which can cause "blind spots" in their insight and blockage in their carrying out God's will even when it is desired. Persons can prevent themselves from learning, can hinder a group from growing, and can distort truth to their own ends. Being Christian developmentalists means that we hold in high regard God's created persons as image reflectors and we come under the authority of the Person of the Holy Spirit, who can penetrate hardened wills, shape desires and motivations, reveal truth and wisdom, and reframe existing conditions. It means that when two or three who know Christ as Lord are gathered together, the group is inhabited by the Divine Enabler who causes us to know faith over fact, hope over despair, wisdom over confusion, and power over weakness. We freely confess that God is greater than theory, though He may choose to operate according to the principles of that theory on a regular basis so we can embrace it as trustworthy as far as it goes.

PROCESS:
HIGH VALUE OF GROUP MEMBER INVOLVEMENT
AND PROCESSING

This value encompasses five facets of developmentalism.

The Validity of Active Engagement in Groups

Groups offer many opportunities for the participants to be involved. Because of this "hands-on" nature of learning in a small group, it is almost impossible not to learn. The processes of discussing, reflecting, sharing, all contribute to the involvement of the learner. When participants must wrestle with "how a subject fits my life," they are likely to be transformed.

Content is important in a small group. The more it overlaps and is shown to be relevant to the lives of the learners, the more energetic is their involvement. Small group communities have a way of allowing persons to "try on" ideas and talk about implications. They are laboratories for faith formation as persons construct beliefs and own commitments to them in the course of stating what they think. When the learning process is one-way (from tellers to receivers), it is easier for the student to remain unmarked while the teller talks on. But two- or more-way interactions are like a teeter-totter — the movement of one causes reciprocation in the other.

The Validity of Group Interaction for Disequilibration

The relational nature of active small groups sets up social interactions between members that often result in the learner's normal operational procedures becoming imbalanced, a condition which often leads to further enlarged insight. The frequent conversational interchanges that occur provide a barrage of ideas and conditions with which a person must cope. The personal voicing of values that are different from those by which one has operated sets off a chain reaction of having to rethink and defend with greater conviction those one holds, or having to work on a new set of operational patterns because of the realization that the old ones are inadequate.

Because groups often allow members to wrestle with biblical truths, their meaning in context and in life, and their application to personal values and lifestyle, they promote a personal handling of truth that stretches the boundaries of our reality. Such mind-bending truth calls for soul-searching response, and this often leads the learner into uncharted territory. Being confronted with new principles of operation that call for more widespread practice may not fit with "how I've always thought or behaved." Scripture is meant to be formational—which means causing disequilibrium to the ways we have previously found comfortable. It is a catalyst for growth as group members encounter it for themselves as it relates to their lives, and join others in discussing its meaning for daily living. Groups are a climate where this can happen at its best.

Being with others in small interactive units also presents challenge in how we feel and act toward others. Research has shown that there is an impact exercised by the group itself on the individual within the group. Group climate can cause people to refrain from their usual negative behaviors or can give them a sense of safety and belonging that nurtures them into being open to examine issues avoided or never explored. Feedback, which is a natural component of groups, makes a person aware of inappropriate or individualistic behaviors exhibited, and this becomes the beginning of critical viewing of heretofore accepted ways of thinking and acting. Knowing you are loved and accepted can produce a disequilibrating emotional release that frees persons to become more honest and accepting. Groups have many ways of creating dissonance within a person.

The Validity of Groups in Resolution —
New Construction of Reality

Although the dynamics of group processing may be the "great provoker," they are also the great enabler of new meaning-making. Because group members are seen as responsible, they must work through this "new development" and come to new insights and enlarged perspective if they are to continue to function as members of the group community.

· Constant group interactions reveal inconsistencies and disequilibration. The stimulating climate of the group with its varied personalities and interactive display of values urges participants to assimilate or accommodate the new group data and come to terms with what is believed and become again a congruent member of the group. Groups urge transformation.

In a group setting, persons reveal this condition of being in transition, moving back and forth between new and old ways of thinking and acting. This reality construction "birth room" is an exciting and safe place to integrate new insights and bring forth "new persons." The sense of belonging and being an acceptable part of something larger than the individualistic self ushers persons into tackling resolution of incongruencies in their thinking and being. Thus the person who has learned to act in a certain way observes and becomes positively acquainted with another member who responds differently. The relationship and close interaction with that member leads to honest questioning and active hearing with the encouragement to take steps in new directions.

Being with Christ's body in groups allows for seeing Him lived out in various personalities and through numerous life-oriented settings. Such reality exposures lead to awareness and movement in the direction of likeness. As we encounter His glory reflected in one another, we grasp more of transformation. "And we, beholding as in a mirror, are being transformed into His likeness from glory to glory" (2 Cor. 3:18). Groups can allow us to get close enough to people to catch more of the "glory" and want it in our life. Many a group has become "Christ" to a hurting, struggling member who was transformed by being in their midst and seeing Jesus.

The Value of All of Group Life in Promoting Learning

Developmentalism does not limit the instruments or settings of learning. Being transformed does not require textbooks, and teacher, and classroom setting. Rather, developmentalism sees all of life as prompting learning. Small groups naturally do this. Casual conversations, topics of study, illustrations of participants, questions raised, applications attempted, encouragement given, helpfulness (giftedness) affirmed, trying out of convictions, shared emotions, caring acts, challenges to thinking and evaluation, friendly reception, hesitant probing—everything teaches. The group is alive with stimulation on all levels—emotional, relational, valuation, faith development, conceptional, existential expectations.

The small group makes it virtually impossible to remain passive or to ignore the new data and experiences that are before the group. In the group process, members are confronted with data and experiences that require action: either assimilation or accommodation. They cannot disregard them. (Dettoni, 1993, p. 30)

The Value of Form Following Function

The methods found in a developmental group systemically grow out of all of the above developmental aspects. The purpose will determine which methods are used to accomplish movement in that direction. The high value of persons will condition which methods are to be used based on the level of understanding found in receivers. And knowing that transformation is accomplished by disequilibration prompting adaptation suggests the process that methodology must follow. Thus the function is to accomplish the large purpose of transforming the person by presenting and processing truth on his or her level, intended to stimulate and confront in such a provocative way as to cause new meaning, feeling, acting, and being to occur.

Therefore, effective small groups are not locked into certain methodology but, when aimed at transformation of members, methods are chosen for their capacity to actively involve persons in being directly involved in constructing and reconstructing their own inner realities. This means that they will read the Scripture themselves. They will utilize forms of meaning-making that maximize their involvement. They will confront arguments, raise questions, interview, test themselves, paraphrase, present conclusions, compare opposing views, research meaning, design plans, carry out simulations, practice truth, and evaluate results. There is no way that group times can be limited to "discussion only." For transformation to occur, the whole person must be involved. Groups that are simply small lecture units are unlikely to promote change.

POWER:
THE HIGH VALUE OF EMPOWERING LEADERSHIP

With participants recognized as responsible for their own learning and change, what role does the group leader perform? Usually the small group leader has some position power (appointed to lead) and some referent power (earned respect of participants). But in a developmental small group the leader's primary function is to motivate, structure for active involvement, and urge personal application. An empowering leader longs for people to fulfill their God-given potential as new creations in Christ Jesus. The Apostle Paul exclaims, "My dear children, for whom I am again in the pains of childbirth until Christ is formed in you" (Gal. 4:19). There is an urging, a commitment to making aware of what God's will is as declared by Scripture and as reflected in life. "Since the day we heard about you, we have not stopped praying for you and asking God to fill you with the knowledge of His will through all spiritual wisdom and understanding" (Col. 1:9).

This empowerment to act on known truth comes from God at work in the group members, turning understood truth into reality of life and growth. Paul reminded the Corinthians that we are "only servants, through whom you came to believe—as the Lord has assigned to each his task. I planted the seed, Apollos watered it, but God made it grow. So neither he who plants nor he who waters is anything, but only God, who makes things grow" (1 Cor. 3:5-7).

How do group leaders empower? (1) They know their participants so they can present content for their appropriate level of development. (2) They facilitate open sharing of truth so members may hear and be enlightened or confronted by truth in others. (3) They set the tone so it is safe to grow and question and test out preliminary steps in new directions. (4) They provide or do not prohibit encounters with content and experiences that are outside the member's present level of comfort and comprehension. (5) They continually pursue laying truth over life. "In what way will we be different if we take seriously this principle and operate out of it in our everyday lives this week?" (6) They encourage and provide for reflection so members can get in touch with their ways of thinking and operating, and with issues that arise when these ways are challenged by new insight. (7) They provide support and encourage group solidarity for those going through disequilibration and adaptation. "Let's share some of the fears that arise as we think of putting into practice this calling of God. What makes it hard to want to obey this command?" "Find a partner who will support you with a phone call and prayer this week as you seek to carry out this promise made to God." (8) The leader empowers by selecting methods that allow the participants to take active responsibility for being open to transformation in their minds, attitudes, and lifestyles.

Such leadership does not build a base of power for the leader, but calls members to actively participate in exploring their own growth and in serving as catalysts for the group and others' growth.

Passages of the Group:
The High Value of Maintaining a Developmental Perspective on the Growth of the Group as a Whole

The Group Itself Grows in Developmental Sequence

There are several descriptive models of group progress. In each, the group moves through one stage to another toward completing the task and maintaining good group relationships. In true developmental fashion,

> the linear movement suggests steps in a given order with resolution of one phase . . . prerequisite to the solving of the next stage of dilemmas. . . . As the classic children's "Bear Hunt" suggests, "Can't go under it. Can't go over it. Gotta go through it." (Gorman, 1993, p. 220)

These stages are descriptively labeled "forming," beginning and dependence; "storming," testing and conflict; "norming," unifying and setting boundaries; "performing," harmonizing and producing (Johnson & Johnson, 1991). M. Scott Peck describes progression from Pseudocommunity to Chaos to Emptiness to Community (Peck, 1987). In each case, disequilibrating forces in individuals caused by being in a group propel the group forward in a herky-jerky fashion. Their active involvement in initiating and responding enable the working-through to a new stage of development. Groups may move more quickly through one stage than another, but each is seen as essential in the movement toward functionality and fulfillment.

A Developing Group Is Active, Not Stuck

The very dynamics of movement within a group ensure its developmental nature. Smith and Berg (1987) have explored this movement within groups and the causes of "stuckness." In a way that is reminiscent of the active processing within a person when imbalance causes reconstruction, groups move when paradoxes of group life present contradictory extremes that require effort to incorporate each extreme as it becomes evident. Much like a hot air balloon, groups move first in one direction and then in another as imbalances become conscious needs. The incorporation of one realization unveils the need for the opposite and creates movement again in the growth of the group.

What are these paradoxical extremes that release energy?

There are opposing factors in preserving one's identity as an individual and developing one's identity with the group, in remaining independent, free and isolated or in developing interdependence, being obligated and knowing intimacy. We vacillate between self-disclosing vulnerability and self-protecting withholding. Between wanting authority and not wanting it. Between being distant and uninvolved and intensely involved. (Gorman, 1993, p. 231)

The extremes in exposure are illustrated in "If they really knew me, would they like me?" and "Can they like me unless they really know me?"

"Stuckness" in group development is the group's refusal to respond to these extremes. Fearing "rocking the boat" and eventual capsizing of the group, members shut down movement in three different ways. (1) They look for compromise and use up group energy trying to maintain balance by including elements from each perspective. On the surface, harmony exists, but resolution has been denied and new frustrations occur. (2) They try to eliminate one side through show of force or vote. But in defeat, the opposing ideas become even more appealing as the organism struggles to grow. Shutting down opposing needs temporarily shuts down development. (3) Some groups try to ignore or put aside their differences in order to get on with the "business of the group." This results in an underground "stand-off" with each polarized segment doing its own thing. The group development is neutralized even though they may continue to grow on the surface (Smith & Berg, 1987). Movement grows out of living within the paradox.

> In moving toward the paradox, not away from it, by immersing oneself in both of the contradictory forces, it is possible to gain insight into what links them together and thus be released to explore new territory. Movement means exploration of new paradigms — new "framing" for ideas and concepts being discussed. (Gorman, 1993, p. 233)

The Value of the Deviant

In a group, the deviant is the person who chooses to live outside the norms observed by the group. The deviant, by actions, is saying that there is something within the existing group structures that is not being addressed and needs to be considered, evaluated, and accommodated. In developmental terms, the deviant is a positive prompter to the group that it needs to enter disequilibration and reconstruct its reality. Often disdained and shut down, the deviant usually drops out of a group and the group fails to grow in that realm of concern. The stage of differentiation begins with someone suggesting, "Do we always have to be in the same roles? Operate the same way? Follow the same format? Be the same kind of group?" This is a moment of transformation, or ossification if the interrupter is silenced. The deviant is a reminder that life means continual development, and zest for life comes from risk and change.

GROUP MINISTRY WITHIN A CHURCH REFLECTS DEVELOPMENTALISM

Utilizing the developmental stages that a group passes through in its life span, Gareth Icenogle has designed a series of stages that a church moves through in the birth, expansion, proliferation, demise, death, burial, and eventual rebirth of small group ministry. This developmental model suggests adaptation and accommodation at each stage by those who seek to promote and produce transformation within small groups. It is a sequential model that sees each stage as beneficial and natural for the church who embraces small groups (Gorman, 1993).

True community is developmental to the core. Small groups incorporate and reflect the principles of developmentalism. The person working with them must be acquainted with basic human development. Christian group community suggests three developmentalism principles that enhance and enrich the theory.

One of these principles, inherent in God's plan for our development in His likeness, is the absolute necessity of corporate development along with individual development. Piaget's emphasis on individualistic, personal growth must be matched with a realization that God made us and evaluates us within a corporate framework. It is never enough for a Christian to say, "I grew," without corresponding focus on, "What am I contributing to the growth of the body?"

Secondly, Christian group development reminds us that together we reflect the image of Christ, and as we are together, He is in our midst. That encounter with the living Christ prompts growth. It is God who causes development. We cannot grow "by pulling ourselves up by our own spiritual bootstraps."

Thirdly, faith supersedes cognitive, affective, social, and valuative boundaries. By the mystery of faith a person can be transformed without understanding completely, can be changed in will without having to work through a series of attitudinal changes. Theories give us limited grasp of partial truth, but are marred by our human inadequacies and prejudicial views. Blind spots are inevitable. But we "press on, grasping ever more firmly that purpose for which Christ grasped us," knowing that someday our development shall be complete "for we together shall see Him as He is and corporately and individually we shall be like Him."

FOR FURTHER READING

Arnold, J. (1992). *The big book on small groups.* Downers Grove, IL: InterVarsity Press.

Gorman, J. (1993). *Community that is Christian.* Wheaton, IL: Victor Books.

Griffin, E. (1982). *Getting together: A guide for good groups.* Downers Grove, IL: InterVarsity Press.

Napier, R.W., & Gershenfeld, M.K. (1989). *Groups: Theory and experience* (4th ed.). Boston: Houghton Mifflin.

Smith, K., & Berg, D. (1987). *Paradoxes of group life.* San Francisco: Jossey-Bass.

16

On Being a Developmental Teacher

John M. Dettoni

Being is not the same as doing, feeling, or thinking. Most of us have grown up with thinking. We have gone through years of schooling that emphasized untold amounts of data acquisition for recitation or repetition to our teachers and professors through various tests and papers. If you grew up in a local church, you were given heavy doses of material to memorize (to know).

For most teachers in the church and in our Christian schools at any level, the issue should not be what a person knows cognitively. God is not going to ask us to pass a written or oral exam on the Bible in order to receive eternal life with Him. Scripture was not given as a means to impress people with our voluminous knowledge of biblical data; nor is Scripture for winning Bible Trivia. Rather, the written Word of God was given to us that we might come to know intimately and personally the Lord Jesus Christ, the living Word of God. In becoming intimately related to Christ, we do need to acquire a good deal of biblical material cognitively. But it is also necessary to receive it affectively and practice it behaviorally. Thinking, feeling, and doing, however, are not the ends of knowledge. The end of knowledge is to BE someone transformed by the written Word, to become more like the living Word.

Take this book, for example. If you have persevered so far, you have been exposed to numerous ideas about the interface of developmentalism and the teaching/communicating processes within the church and in various other forms of Christian education. If all you do is memorize some pertinent data from one of these relevant chapters, you will not have achieved much. If you like what you have read and that is all, you have not been changed. Even if you begin to do some things differently in your teaching, you still may be short of the mark. We all need to think, feel, and do things differently because of our exposure to the data of this book. Ultimately, however, we need to be new creatures, changed from within. In a word, we need to be *transformed* that we might be developmental teachers and communicators. Hence, we call this final chapter "On Being a Developmental Teacher" in order to signal that we are talking about the need to be a different person.

Becoming that different person is a process, not a crisis experience. If what the many knowledgeable authors have written in this volume is a reflection of truth to the degree that we can discover it empirically and theologically, then those who read this book need to begin to be different people in the actual execution of their teaching. The preceding chapters all have direct implications to the practice of being a developmental teacher. Some chapters actually suggest definite changes and implications for our teaching. In this chapter, I will not repeat unnecessarily what has been said already. I will, however, seek to draw out some additional implications. The actual applications of these implications will differ from teacher to teacher and from situation to situation. It is my intention, however, that people will not read this book without at least being challenged to begin to be different teachers than they were before.

SCRIPTURAL FOUNDATIONS FOR DEVELOPMENTAL TEACHING

Psalm 119

Aside from being the longest chapter in the Bible, Psalm 119 is also a primary source that indicates the roles of learners and teachers and the purpose of teaching and learning. Before you read more of this chapter, I encourage you to read Psalm 119, looking for answers to the following questions:

1. Who is active in the teaching/learning processes?
2. Who is the teacher?
3. What are the actions of the teacher?
4. What are the actions of the learners?
5. What are some of the reasons the learners learn?

In Psalm 119 you will find that both learners and teacher are highly active in the whole process of learning. The teacher is God, who reveals His law, precepts, commandments, word, decrees to the learners. Note well that the psalmist does not limit God's revelations to just the Decalogue or Old Testament Law. Rather, the psalmist has in mind the whole of God's revelation to us in Scripture.

Learners are also active—even more so than the teacher. Almost every verse shows that the learners are doing something with what the teacher has revealed. Nowhere is there any suggestion that learners are simply sitting passively, taking notes on their tablets or papyri; nor are they merely memorizing the teacher's lectures for regurgitation on a test. They are not "Hiding God's Word in their hearts to get a star on their charts." Far from it. They are learning actively in order that they might not sin against God (v. 11). Learners are becoming different people, people who are not sinners.

A number of verbs describe the learners' activity in the teaching/learning processes. Some of these are to *seek* God, *recount* or *restate* God's laws, *follow* His statutes, *meditate, delight, see* (metaphorically). As you read and reread Psalm 119, in some way mark in your biblical text the actions of the learners as they are involved in the learning processes.

Note that the learners are different because of the combination of the teacher's actions and their own active involvement in the learning situation. Some of the outcomes of the teaching/learning processes are as follows: walk according to the law of the Lord, do nothing wrong, fully obey God's precepts, obey His decrees, praise Him with an upright heart, live according to God's ways. Notice that all of these actions come from having internalized God's revelation. Nowhere is mere factual knowledge the goal of teaching and learning. Rather, the goal is to help the learners to be transformed into different people because they have encountered God's revelation, have responded positively to it, and have taken action in order that they might be changed in their inner selves (vv. 9, 11, 45, 77, 93, 105, 112, 130, 133, 165, 169-176).

Psalm 119, therefore, suggests a developmental learning paradigm in which teachers help learners to be active in the entire learning process, as opposed to the "acquisition-of-data" process. Learners are actively receiving the teaching, using it, and being changed by it. These actions are the basics that could be expected in any developmental learning experience.

1 Corinthians 3:1-9

The role of teachers
These verses show the roles of developmental teachers as they relate to learners. Verse 1 suggests that teachers must distinguish between the mature and immature, that is, make a developmental distinction among learners based on their levels of development. This implies that teachers must discern the development of the learners. Teachers must know their learners in order to teach them developmentally. Personal relationships with learners are necessary in order for a teacher to know his or her learners well enough to distinguish between the less and more mature. While relationships take time, they also pay off in effective teaching. Jesus modeled the developmental teacher as He went about teaching His disciples over a three-year period of time. He knew them quite well, as even a cursory reading of the Gospels demonstrates.

Verse 2 suggests that it is the teacher's responsibility to provide food appropriate for learners' development. This implies that teachers must know their learners' needs and levels/stages of development in order to provide the input appropriate. One of the roles of a teacher must be to determine the level/stage of development of the learners and their readiness to learn. We court disaster in our teaching if we treat all learners alike. This is especially the case when the group members whom we are teaching vary in their levels of development. Therefore, it is incumbent on teachers to know human development, understand how that development impacts the teaching/learning process, work with those developmental levels of the learners, and encourage continued growth and development to higher levels of maturity.

Verses 6 through 9 suggest several additional insights into teaching developmentally. One is that all teachers can—and undoubtedly do—contribute to the development of learners. Some, as other parts of Scripture suggest, contribute negatively; they hinder growth or cause a regression into the old ways (see Gal. 3:1; 5:7-12). This implies that the teacher's responsibility is to provide the best nurturing environment for learners. Teachers, like good farmers, must prepare the soil, sow good seed, cultivate, nurture, and wait patiently while the plant/learner grows.

Nurturing is probably one of the greatest needs in the church, and the least observed action. There are all sorts of discipleship materials and courses from a host of church and parachurch organizations that all purport to enable a person to be a discipler. It is strange that there is so much available and seemingly still so few people who are completely following Christ in a sane and holistic fashion.

Growth from within

Second, these verses suggest that development and growth, and therefore learning, come from within, not from externals. Learning, like the physical growth of a plant or a person, in the end is not controlled by environment. Environment, however, can foster or hinder growth. Ultimately, God is the one who gives the results. It is required of teachers to be found faithful (Matt. 24:45-51) and not to hinder or frustrate the work of the Holy Spirit (Eph. 4:30). Learning, however, comes from within the learner and is assisted and facilitated by teachers and the learning environment that the teachers and learners provide. Learning itself comes from the inner actions of persons in their relationships with God, mediated by human teachers' various teaching/learning strategies, methods, and materials.

Teachers need to choose developmentally appropriate teaching/learning strategies, methods, and materials that engage learners at their levels of development and interests. Merely lecturing or delivering information to students, regardless of their developmental ability to interact with that content, is potentially full of negative consequences. It is negative because people will not learn when material is developmentally inappropriate, especially if it is more than one stage below or above their modal or usual stage of being. If the material is too immature and simple, people will get bored. If it is too mature, the people will misunderstand the material, consider it irrelevant, discard it, or do all of these. Regardless, the results are about the same: communication of spiritual truth flounders on the rocks of developmental error. Teachers need to be able to steer their ship of teaching so that learners do not flounder.

Partners with God
Third, teachers are coworkers with God. Therefore they must do their part to help make learning more effective. They must work with God, not against Him and the workings of His Holy Spirit in the lives of learners. Thus, all teachers — pastors, parents, professors, Sunday School teachers, youth workers, adult Bible study teachers, peers — have God-given roles to play in order to foster learners' growth and maturity in Jesus Christ. As coworkers with God, all teachers help to nurture the learners' development into increasing Christlikeness. The issue is whether or not we work with God or against His plan of development for humanity.

WHAT IS A DEVELOPMENTAL TEACHER?

There is no human being who meets all the characteristics of a perfect developmental teacher. We each live with various limitations that are characteristic of being both human and sinful. However, we need to become aware of our lack of perfection, beginning and continuing to make progress, with God's help, to reduce our imperfections and to become what we know we should be. We can strive with all the power that Christ so mightily gives us to be the teachers that He wants us to be. With this in mind, a committed developmental teacher has the following characteristics:

Holistic Teaching

One, a developmental teacher teaches for the development of the whole person. For the Christian teacher (professor, parent, pastor, peer, professional counselor) this means a special emphasis on faith and spiritual development. Too often, teachers seem to forget that humans are not just minds to be taught cognitive materials nor just some disembodied souls to be saved. Humans are composed of physical, cognitive, social, affective, moral, and spiritual/faith development aspects or domains of development. People do not develop in one domain apart from the others. Human beings are integrated wholes and, as such, development in one area affects development in other areas, too.

Teachers, therefore, need to keep in mind that spiritual truth must be addressed to the mind, emotions, moral thinking, and behavior as well as to the spiritual/faith domain. Teachers also must remember that learners' physical conditions and environmental factors, such as a comfortable setting, sufficient lighting, proper ventilation, and appropriate seating need to be considered in the teaching plan. All these elements are crucial to the learning process. We teach for the whole person, not just for the spiritual.

Developmental Appropriateness

Two, an effective developmental teacher teaches on the developmental stages/levels of learners. It is axiomatic in developmentalism that learners cannot comprehend much of any teaching that is more than one stage above their modal stage. Nor will learners respond positively if teaching is more than one stage below them. They will consider that communication as simplistic and an insult to the level of development that they have already achieved.

Considering learners' developmental stages/levels is more than just giving rote recognition of learners' describable developmental stages. Effective developmental teaching means, instead, that teachers construct their individual lessons and the teaching/learning environment to strategically teach on the level of the learners or no more than one level above their modal stage.

Felt Needs

Three, effective developmental teachers "scratch where learners itch." That is, teachers teach to the developmental needs and existential concerns, needs, and personal interests of the learners. Developmental teachers teach as Jesus did with the Samaritan woman at the well (John 4:4-42). Jesus "scratched" the woman's felt need. This is also the approach that Philip used in teaching the Ethiopian eunuch (Acts 8:26-40).

People have needs that they already know. Often, teachers start not with the learners' agendas but with their own content-driven agendas. Instead, developmental teachers start where people already have a felt need. Then they help them move to a deeper, but perhaps not recognized, need that the teacher knows or senses. When teachers begin with content or their own agendas, the learners are left to wonder where the teaching/learning experience is going and how it relates to their own realities.

It is contrary to the nature of God to merely dump content on people regardless of their felt needs and their developmental stages. It would almost be like God dropping an eternal version of John Calvin's *Institutes of the Christian Faith* on the world, but written from God's perspective. Probably no one would understand it. Likewise, if we teach beyond the developmental ability of learners to comprehend, we will not be effective teachers.

Anticipated Outcomes

Four, effective developmental teachers have definite but flexible anticipated outcomes for their lessons and for their courses. Teachers teach for change in knowledge, feeling, doing, and being. These outcomes are stated by the teacher in his or her lesson preparation based on knowledge and experience with the learners and within the spectrum of the content area and curricular goals. Even if a teacher has never seen the class ahead of time, he or she will need to make some assumptions about the developmental levels/stages of the learners and what their needs are. Based on these tentative assumptions, outcomes can be stated by the teachers in order to help them plan and strategize their lessons. If anticipated outcomes are stated, the lesson plans can be developed more readily in light of those outcomes desired. If no outcomes are stated, teachers could do almost anything and never have to worry about achieving anything.

Maturing Teachers

Five, effective developmental teachers are themselves maturing and developing as whole persons. All effective teachers are learners, too. Not one of us has "arrived" at perfection. Instead, like Paul, we "press on toward the goal" (Phil. 3:14). Teachers must not be like the proverbial bald-headed barber selling hair grower. Instead, teachers should demonstrate in both their teaching and daily living that they are continually growing. Nothing is as inconsistent as a teacher who has become stultified or, worse yet, ossified. Teachers show that they are developing by sharing their own growing edges, new insights, and their very selves with their learners. It often seems that learners are taught more from the person of the teacher than from the lesson of the teacher.

Person Orientation

Six, effective developmental teachers are person-oriented rather than content-oriented. Such an orientation shows itself in the following qualities:

- Empathy—the ability to place oneself as teacher in the roles of the learners, thereby feeling some of the emotions that the learners are having during the teaching experiences.

- Trusting of learners—believing that they want to learn; that they will make reasonably good choices to enhance their education; that they can and will control their own learning; that they will not need to be forced to learn by rewards and threats of punishment.

- Fairness and justice—being impartial; not playing favorites or picking on any particular students or groups of students, recognizing that all learners are made in the image of God and should be treated with dignity and justice.

- Relationality—being personal and not merely objectively professional; treating learners as human beings, not just as an organized body into which cognitive data are poured.

- Informality—creating a relaxed, learner-centered educational environment in which both teacher and learners can maintain progress toward achieving learning outcomes, while providing an environment of care and interest in learners as whole people.

- Formality—providing an orderly arrangement and presentation of content that is coordinated with all of the teaching/learning experiences—content that is systematic and logical, though not necessarily organized in a lock-step fashion, lesson plans that are designed in detail, and executed for the development of learners as whole people. Effective developmental teachers have a well-developed plan for their teaching.

- Flexibility—open to change during the lesson; having the ability to make changes in methods, outcomes, and to a degree the content; dependent on the transactions with the learners and their needs, concerns, and interests. Effective developmental teachers modify their plans depending on the responses of the learners during the lesson. Lesson plans are not a legal requirement. Plans are often modified in the middle of the dynamic of the teaching/learning process.

- Tolerance—accepting differences of opinion, open to free discussion and challenges of each other within a context of inquiry, not of inquisition.

- Non-judgmentalism—refusing to make negative judgments about the worth of those who disagree with the positions of teachers, school, or church; providing experiences by which learners can explore for themselves—with direction from the teacher—areas of interests, needs, and concerns, within the curricular guidelines of the course.

- Openness, Transparency, Vulnerability—being able to be a person, not just a professional teacher, nor simply one of the magisterium or masters of the school; communicating one's own weakness, questions, and problem-solving procedures, thereby enabling learners to understand how the teacher came to his or her conclusions. Effective developmental teachers are those who share of themselves in their teaching. They show their humanness and do not function as merely a human computer spitting out data.

- Discernment of learners' needs—being careful that what is taught meets felt and real needs of learners and does not simply satisfy the curricular requirements of one's institution or the content requirements of one's discipline.

Effective Instruction

Seven, effective developmental teachers ARE teachers; they do not just know how to teach. They demonstrate this in the exercise of their teaching through several indicators:

- A mastery of developmental stages/levels in order that they might understand their learners. This is demonstrated by lessons that are developmentally appropriate and on the actual developmental stages of the learners.

- A mastery of the content to be taught. This is demonstrated by teaching appropriate, meaningful, and important content in its breadth and length, not superficially.

- A mastery of design, development, and execution of their lessons, choosing appropriate desired outcomes. This entails the appropriate use of methods, materials, and strategies, demonstrated by actively involving learners both in the learning environment and extending that learning environment outside of the classroom.

- Coming prepared to the learning environment to teach in order that learning might occur. This is demonstrated by teachers' having their materials prepared, their lesson plans well in hand, and the learning setting prepared for the teaching/learning encounters.

Active Learning

Eight, effective developmental teachers constantly seek to provide experiences and data for learners that will enable and facilitate their active involvement in their own learning. Teachers must engage learners in the active pursuit of learning through the learners' engagement with the content within their own context and environment. Teachers, therefore, need to be environmentally sensitive. That is, they need to be aware of the sociocultural, geographic, economic, and ethnic issues that are being faced by their learners, along with, of course, learners' stages/levels of development.

Evaluation

Nine, effective developmental teachers seek to evaluate the teaching/learning process in which they are involved in order to make appropriate corrections. No one except God is perfect. This means that all teachers need improvement. Even someone considered to be a model teacher needs to make constructive changes.

Prayer

Ten, effective developmental teachers pray much for their learners and for themselves. Prayer for both learners and self is an admission that ultimately teachers are not in control of learning, that we are coworkers with God in teaching. All teachers need God's help to make lessons vital in the lives of their learners, and teachers recognize that they teach best when they are filled with the power of the Holy Spirit rather than only their own excitement (see Eph. 5:18).

ROLES OF TEACHERS AND LEARNERS

Generally, the role of a developmental teacher is to engage learners in asking "why?" types of questions about their environment, history, the biblical text, and so on. Teachers engage learners in the active pursuit of data by engaging in dialogue, asking probing questions, presenting problems to solve, and constructing real and contrived experiences to encounter. They help learners examine issues, problems, interests, and concerns that relate to the learners and their past, present, and future environments. Teachers need to facilitate the gathering of information and data with which learners can actively engage in dialogue with themselves, teachers, and fellow learners. Teachers must help learners to explore the issues and face the realities. They provide input through content presentation, questions, and exposure to new experiences and sources of information. Teachers engage learners in active pursuit of truth. Above all, teachers need to continually share themselves, encouraging learners through the difficult tasks of actively learning, offering corrections, and waiting while learners process their engagement with content and experiences.

Learners, on the other hand, need to come to a teaching/ learning experience with a mind-set to become engaged in the pursuit of learning. They need to remove barriers and other hindrances to learning. They must be alert and prepared to actively pursue data, other content experiences, and meaning for themselves. If they come disequilibrated, they will learn because they will be motivated to achieve equilibrium through the active quest of learning. Learners must seek information, experiences, and transactions that will enable them to learn. Under the guidance and facilitation of teachers, they can search for truth and rejoice in the finding and sharing of that truth with others who are also engaged in that quest. Learners must do more than acquire information; they must receive and digest it for themselves so that it becomes part of their feelings, behavior, and very beings, integrating it into their personhood because they have become what they know, feel, and do.

SUMMARY

In sum, an effective developmental teacher teaches for the growth and development of the learners, not merely for data acquisition, nor for indoctrination of dogma in a mindless fashion to satisfy some authorities' dictates, nor for the manipulation of learners to authorities' purposes. Rather, effective developmental teaching that is biblical and Christlike helps learners to be formed in Christ and to grow up into Him in every way (Gal. 4:19; Eph. 4:13; Col. 1:28). Teaching is not for transmission of information alone, but for transformation of the person. We teach for growth, maturity, and development of learners, not so that they can merely pass a test nor to satisfy some administrative body that oversees the school. We teach that people will become mature and complete, being transformed more and more into Christ's likeness (Eph. 4:13; Col. 1:28-29; 2 Cor. 3:18).

Learning is not always easy. Teachers sometimes face seemingly insurmountable obstacles of culture, language, history, and physical environment. Yet teachers are asked to be faithful to their calling to act as a mother nursing a baby, as those who share their very lives, who live exemplary lives before the learners, who encourage, comfort, and urge their learners (1 Thes. 2:7-13). Teachers see their learners as Paul saw the Thessalonians, as "our glory and joy" (1 Thes. 2:19-20).

The final evaluation of effective developmental teachers is well summed up by Paul, "For now we really live, since you are standing firm in the Lord. How can we thank God enough for you in return for all the joy we have in the presence of our God because of you?" (1 Thes. 3:8-9)

CONCLUSION

This book has begun to expose readers to basic concepts of developmentalism, showing some basic relationships between developmentalism and Christian thought. It has outlined briefly major developmental theories, focused on age-groups from a developmental perspective, and provided implications for various aspects of teaching. Now this final chapter has sought to refocus the intent of this book and its many contributors to the one critical area that will make or break the church at the turn of this century. That issue is the ability to be a developmental teacher. This is not a teacher who gives lip service to developmentalism but actually treats people like rats, mice, pigeons, and other animals. Rather, it is a teacher who treats people as those made in the image of God, carrying the divine imprint on them, and therefore deserving of respect, encouragement, and help to develop into all that God is calling them to be.

Each of us as teachers has within our power to work with the Holy Spirit in His divine work as the Teacher of human beings. It is our decision either to work with Him or to make His work more difficult. The ultimate goal in our teaching is that people's lives will be transformed because they have met personally the Living Word of God through the written Word which we have taught.

FOR FURTHER READING

Hendricks, H. (1987). *Teaching to change lives.* Portland, OR: Multnomah.

Issler, K., & Habermas, R. (1994). *How we learn.* Grand Rapids: Baker.

Kuhmerker, L. (1991). *The Kohlberg legacy for the helping professions.* Birmingham, AL: Religious Education Press.

Piaget, J. (1970). *Science of education and the psychology of the child.* New York: Viking Press.

Reference List

Adams, D. (1983). *The psychosocial development of professional black women's lives and the consequences of career for their personal happiness.* Unpublished doctoral dissertation, Wright Institute.

Angelo, T. (1993). A "teacher's dozen": Fourteen general, research-based principles for improving higher learning in our classrooms. *American Association of Higher Education Bulletin, 45,* 3–13.

Ashton, P. (1975). Cross-cultural Piagetian research: An experimental perspective. *Harvard Educational Review, 45*(4), 475–506.

Bayly, J. (1983). *The Gospel blimp and other stories.* Elgin, IL: David C. Cook.

Beadle, M. (1970). *A child's mind.* Garden City, NJ: Doubleday.

Beavers, W. (1974). The application of family systems theory to crisis intervention. In D. Switzer (Ed.), *The minister as crisis counselor* (pp. 181–210). Nashville: Abingdon.

Beavers, W., & Hampson, R. (1993). Measuring family competence: The Beavers systems model. In F. Walsh (Ed.), *Normal family processes* (2nd ed.). New York: Guilford Press.

Beilin, H. (1992). Piaget's enduring contribution to developmental psychology. *Developmental Psychology, 28*(2), 191–204.

Belenky, M., Clinchy, B., Goldberger, N., & Tarule, J. (1986). *Women's ways of knowing: The development of self, voice, and mind.* New York: Basic Books.

Benson, C. (1943). *A popular history of Christian education.* Chicago: Moody Press.

Berger, K. (1993). *The developing person through the life span* (3rd ed.). New York: Worth.

Bey, T., & Holmes, C. (Eds.). (1992). *Mentoring: Contemporary principles and issues.* Reston, VA: Association of Teacher Educators.

Bloesch, D. (1978). *Essentials of evangelical theology.* New York: Harper & Row.

Boehlke, R. (1962). *Theories of learning in Christian education.* Philadelphia: Westminister.

Bradshaw, J. (1988). *Bradshaw on the family.* Deerfield Beach, FL: Health Communications.

Bronfenbrenner, U. (1979). *The ecology of human development.* Cambridge, MA: Harvard University Press.

Bruner, J. (1983). *Child's talk: Learning to use language.* New York: Norton.

Buchanan, T. (1991). *Age-related differences in the relation between moral cognition and moral action: A meta-analytic review.* Durhan, NH: University of New Hampshire.

Burgess, H. (1975). *An invitation to religious education.* Birmingham: Religious Education Press.

Burks, R., & Burks, V. (1992). *Damaged disciples.* Grand Rapids: Zondervan.

Butman, R. (1993). The "critical years" of young adulthood. In K. Gangel & J. Wilhoit (Eds.), *The Christian educator's handbook on adult education* (pp. 247–61). Wheaton, IL: Victor Books.

Capps, D. (1983). *Life cycle theory and pastoral care.* Philadelphia: Fortress.

———. (1987). *Deadly sins and saving virtues.* Philadelphia: Fortress.

Cohen, D. (Ed.). (1991). *The circle of life.* San Francisco: Harper.

Coleman, J. (1980). *The nature of adolescence.* New York: Methuen.

Coleman, R. (1987). *The master plan of discipleship.* Old Tappan, NJ: Fleming H. Revell.

Coles, R., & Coles, J. (1980). *Women of crisis II: Lives of work and dreams.* New York: Addison-Wesley.

Collins, C. (1992). *Tell me a story: Creating bedtime stories your children will dream on.* Boston: Houghton Mifflin.

Craig, M., & Glick, S. (1964). *A manual of procedures for application of the Glueck prediction table.* New York: New York City Youth Board.

Cully, I. (1979). *Christian child development.* New York: Harper & Row.

Daloz, L. (1986). *Effective teaching and mentoring.* San Francisco: Jossey-Bass.

Damon, W. (1988). *Moral child: Nurturing a child's natural moral soul.* New York: The Free Press.

Dasen, P. (Ed.). (1976). *Piagetian psychology: Cross-cultural contributions.* New York: John Wiley.

Dettoni, J. (1993). Small groups and developmentalism. *Christian Education Journal, 13*(3), 29–38.

Dewey, J. (1938). *Experience and education.* New York: Macmillan.

Diaz, R., Neal, C., & Amaya-Williams, M. (1990). The social origins of self-regulation. In L. Moll (Ed.), *Vygotsky and education* (pp. 127–54). Cambridge, MA: Cambridge University Press.

Digitale, R. (1990, March 19). An idea whose time has gone? *Christianity Today,* pp. 38–42.

Dolezal, J. (1984). *A summary and systematization of Jean Piaget's position on affectivity.* Master's thesis, Wheaton College, Wheaton, IL.

Downs, P. (1994). *Teaching for spiritual growth: An introduction to Christian education.* Grand Rapids: Zondervan.

Duska, R., & Whelan, M. (1975). *Moral development: A guide to Piaget and Kohlberg.* New York: Paulist Press.

Eble, K. (1976). *The craft of teaching: A guideline to mastering the professor's art.* San Francisco: Jossey-Bass.

Edwards, R. (1985). Uncertain faith: Matthew's portrait of the disciples. In F. Segovia (Ed.), *Discipleship in the New Testament* (pp. 47–61). Philadelphia: Fortress Press.

Elkind, D. (1984). *All grown up and no place to go.* Reading, MS: Addison-Wesley.

―――. (1979). *The child and society.* New York: Oxford University Press.

―――. (1978). *The child's reality: Three developmental theories.* Hillsdale, NJ: Lawrence Erlbaum Associates.

―――. (1978). *A sympathetic understanding of the child, birth to sixteen.* Boston: Allyn & Bacon.

Erikson, E. (1950). *Childhood and society.* New York: Norton.

―――. (1969). *Gandhi's truth.* New York: Norton.

―――. (1980). *Identity and the life cycle.* New York: Norton.

―――. (1968). *Identity: Youth and crisis.* New York: Norton.

―――. (1958). *Young man Luther: A study in psychoanalysis and history.* New York: Norton.

Farrah, S. (1991). Lecture. In M. Galbraith (Ed.), *Adult learning methods* (pp. 161–86). Malabar, FL: Krieger.

Foster, R. (1978). *Celebration of discipline.* San Francisco: Harper and Row.

Fowler, J. (1984). *Becoming adult, becoming Christian: Adult development and Christian faith.* San Francisco: Harper & Row.

―――. (1987). *Faith development and pastoral care.* Philadelphia: Fortress Press.

―――. (1981). *Stages of faith: The psychology of human development and the quest for meaning.* San Francisco: Harper & Row.

―――. (1974). *To see the kingdom: The theological vision of H. Richard Niebuhr.* Nashville: Abingdon.

Fowler, J., Nipkow, K., & Schweitzer, F. (Eds.). (1991). *Stages of faith and religious development: Implications for church, education, and society.* New York: Crossroad Publishing Company.

Gainsburg, H., & Opper, S. (1988). *Piaget's theory of intellectual development* (3rd ed.). Englewood Cliffs, NJ: Prentice-Hall.

Gardner, H. (1981). *The quest for mind: Piaget, Levi-Strauss, and the stucturalist movement* (2nd ed.). Chicago: University of Chicago Press.

Gielen, U., & Lei, T. (1991). The measuring of moral reasoning. In L. Kuhmerker, with U. Gielen, & R. Hayes (Eds.), *The Kohlberg legacy for the helping professions* (pp. 61–81). Birmingham, AL: Religious Education Press.

Gillespie, V. (1991). *Religious conversion and personal identity.* Birmingham, AL: Religious Education Press.

Gilligan, C. (1982). *In a different voice: Psychological theory and women's development.* Cambridge, MA: Harvard University Press.

Gilligan, C., Murphy, J., & Tappan, M. (1990). Moral development beyond adolescence. In C. Alexander & E. Langer (Eds.), *Higher stages of human development: Perspectives on adult growth* (pp. 208–225). New York: Oxford University Press.

Gleason, J. (1975). *Growing up to God: Eight stages of religious development.* Nashville: Abingdon.

Glueck, S., & Glueck, E. (1950). *Unravelling juvenile delinquency.* Cambridge, MA: Harvard University Press.

Goldman, R. (1964). *Religious thinking from childhood to adolescence.* New York: Seabury Press.

Gorman, J. (1993). *Community that is Christian.* Wheaton, IL: Victor.

Gould, R. (1975, August). Adult life stages: Growth towards self tolerance. *Psychology Today,* p. 78.

_____. (1978). *Transformations: Growth and change in adult life.* New York: Simon & Schuster.

Hadidian, A. (1987). *Discipleship.* Chicago: Moody Press.

Hample, S., & Marshall, E. (1991). *Children's letters to God.* New York: Workman.

Hartshorne, H., & May M. (1975). *Studies in deceit: Book one, general methods and results.* New York: Arno Press.

Hauerwas, S. (1991). *After Christendom?* Nashville: Abingdon.

Havighurst, R. (1965). *The educational mission of the church.* Philadelphia: Westminster.

Holmes, A. (1983). *Contours of world view.* Grand Rapids: Eerdmans.

Howe, R. (1966). The dialogical foundations for Christian education. In M. Taylor (Ed.), *An introduction to Christian education* (pp. 85–93). Nashville: Abingdon.

Hull, B. (1990). *The disciple-making church*. Grand Rapids: Baker.

Johnson, D., & Johnson, F. (1991). *Joining together: Group theory and group skills* (4th ed.). Englewood Cliffs, NJ: Prentice Hall.

Jones, S. & Butman, R. (1991). *Modern psychotherapies*. Downers Grove, IL: InterVarsity Press.

Joy, D. (1983). *Moral development foundations: Judeo-Christian alternatives to Piaget/Kohlberg*. Nashville: Abingdon.

————. (1993). *Risk-proofing your family*. Pasadena, CA: U.S. Center for World Mission. See also video-assisted (1990), *For parents only: risk-proofing your family*. Muncie, IN: Bristol House, Ltd.

Joy, D., & Cessna, W. (1974). *Family financial planning seminar*. Wilmore, KY: Center for the Study of the Family.

Joy, D., & Joy, R. (1987). *Lovers: What ever happened to Eden?* Dallas: Word.

Kegan, R. (1982). *The evolving self: Problem and process in human development*. Cambridge, MA: Harvard University Press.

Kimmel, D. (1989). *Adulthood and aging: An interdisciplinary, developmental view*. New York: John Wiley and Sons.

Kohlberg, L. (1980). Educating for a just society: An update and revised statement. In B. Munsey (Ed.), *Moral development, moral education, and Kohlberg* (pp. 455–70). Birmingham, AL: Religious Education Press.

————. (1991). My personal search for universal morality. In L. Kuhmerker, with U. Gielen, & R. Hayes (Eds.), *The Kohlberg legacy for the helping professions* (pp. 11–17). Birmingham, AL: Religious Education Press.

————. (1981). *The philosophy of moral development: Moral stages and the idea of justice*. San Francisco: Harper & Row.

————. (1984). *The psychology of moral development: The nature and validity of moral stages*. San Francisco: Harper & Row.

————. (1969). Stage and sequence: The cognitive-developmental approach to socialization. In D. Goslin (Ed.), *Handbook of socialization theory and research* (pp. 347–480). Chicago: Rand McNally.

Kohlberg, L., with Candee, D. (1984). The relationship of moral judgment to moral action. In L. Kohlberg, *The psychology of moral development: The nature and validity of moral stages* (pp. 498–581). San Francisco: Harper and Row.

Kohlberg, L., with Higgins, A. (1984). Continuities and Discontinuities in Childhood and Adult Development Revisited — Again. In L. Kohlberg, *The psychology of moral development: The nature and validity of moral stages* (pp. 426–497). San Francisco: Harper and Row.

Kohlberg, L., with Levine, C., & Hewer, A. (1984). The Current Formulation of the Theory. In L. Kohlberg, *The psychology of moral development: The nature and validity of moral stages* (pp. 212–315). San Francisco: Harper and Row.

Kohlberg, L., with Powers, C. (1981). Moral Development, Religious Thinking, and the Question of a Seventh Stage. In L. Kohlberg, *The philosophy of moral development: Moral stages and the idea of justice.* (pp. 311–372). San Francisco: Harper and Row.

Koons, C., & Anthony, M. (1991). *Single adult passages: Uncharted territories.* Grand Rapids: Baker.

Kuhmerker, L. (1991). Fostering moral development through dilemma discussions. In L. Kuhmerker, with U. Gielen, & R. Hayes (Eds.), *The Kohlberg legacy for the helping professions* (pp. 91–102). Birmingham, AL: Religious Education Press.

LeBar, L. (1958). *Education that is Christian.* Old Tappan, NJ: Revell.

LeBar, L., & Plueddemann, J. (1989). *Education that is Christian.* Wheaton, IL: Victor Books.

LeFever, M. (1985). *Creative teaching methods.* Elgin, IL: David C. Cook.

Levinson, D. (1977). The midlife transition. *Psychiatry. 20*(2), 99–112.

Levinson, D. (1990). A theory of life structure development in adulthood. In C. Alexander & E. Langer (Eds.), *Higher stages of human development: Perspectives on adult development* (pp. 35–53). New York: Oxford University Press.

Levinson, D., Darrow, C., Klein, E., Levinson, M., & McKee, B. (1978). *The seasons of a man's life.* New York: Knopf.

Liddell, H., & Scott, R. (Eds.). (1974). *A lexicon: Abridged from Liddell and Scott's Greek-English lexicon.* Oxford, NY: Clarendon Press.

Lowenthal, M., Thurnher, M., & Chiriboga, D. (1974). *Four stages of life.* San Francisco: Jossey-Bass.

Lowman, J. (1990). *Mastering the techniques of teaching.* San Francisco: Jossey-Bass.

Magid, K., & McKelvey, C. (1987). *High risk: Children without a conscience.* New York: Bantam.

Mattheson, D. (1975). *Adolescence today: Sex roles and the search for identity.* Homewood, IL: Dorsey Press.

Moll, L. (Ed.). (1990). *Vygotsky and education.* Cambridge, MA: Cambridge University Press.

Moore, W. (1982). *William Perry's cognitive-developmental theory: A review of the model and related research.* Olympia, WA: Center for the Study of Intellectual Development.

Mouw, R. (1992). *Uncommon decency: Being civil in an uncivil world.* Downers Grove, IL: InterVarsity Press.

Murray, M. (1991). *Beyond the myths and magic of mentoring.* San Francisco: Jossey-Bass.

National Research Foundation (1988). Families in the nineties project. U.S. Department of Commerce; Bureau of the Census.

Neal, C. (1990). Training high-risk parents to be teachers of their own children. In paper presented at *Society for Research in Child Development.* Seattle, WA.

Neal, C., & Diaz, R. (1989). Teaching for self-regulation: A comparison of low and high risk mothers. In paper presented at *Biannual meeting of the Society for Research in Child Development.* Kansas City, MO.

Okun, B. (1984). *Working with adults: Individual, family, and career development.* Pacific Grove, CA: Brooks/Cole.

Palmer, P. (1983). *To know as we are known: A spirituality of education.* San Francisco: Harper & Row.

Parks, S. (1986). *The critical years: The young adult search for a faith to live by.* San Francisco: Harper & Row.

Pascarella, E., & Terenzini, P. (1991). *How college affects students.* San Francisco: Jossey-Bass.

Peck, S. (1987). *The different drum.* New York: Simon & Schuster.

Perry, W. (1981). Cognitive and ethical growth: The making of meaning. In A. Chickering (Ed.), *The modern American college* (pp. 76–116). San Francisco: Jossey-Bass.

_____. (1977). Comments, appreciative and cautionary. *The Counseling Psychologist, 6*(4), 51–52.

_____. (1970). *Forms of intellectual and ethical development in the college years.* New York: Holt, Rinehart and Winston.

Piaget, J. (1965). *The moral judgment of the child.* New York: The Free Press.

_____. (1973). *To understand is to invent.* New York: Grossman.

Plueddemann, J., & Plueddemann, C. (1990). *Pilgrims in progress.* Wheaton, IL: Shaw.

Price-Williams, D. (1981). Concrete and formal operations. In R. Monroe, R. Monroe, & B. Whiting (Eds.), *Handbook of cross-cultural human development* (pp. 403–22). New York: Garland STMP Press.

Ratner, C. (1991). *Vygotsky's sociohistorical psychology and its contemporary applications.* New York: Plenum Press.

Regas, G. (1987). *Kiss yourself and hug the world: Keys to authentic and vital living.* Waco, TX: Word.

Richards, L. (1975). *A theology of Christian education.* Grand Rapids: Zondervan Publishing House.

Richards, L. (1983). *A theology of children's ministry.* Grand Rapids: Zondervan.

Roberts, P., & Newton, P. (1987). Levinsonian studies of women's adult development. *Psychology and Aging, 2,* 154–63.

Rogoff, B. (1990). *Apprenticeship in thinking: Cognitive development in social context.* New York: Oxford Press.

Rosa, A., & Montero, I. (1990). The historical context of Vygotsky's work: A sociohistorical approach. In L. Moll (Ed.), *Vygotsky and education* (pp. 59–88). Cambridge, MA: Cambridge University Press.

Santrock, J. (1985). *Adult development and aging.* Dubuque, IA: Wm. C. Brown.

Scieszka, J. (1989). *The true story of the three little pigs.* New York: Viking/Penguin.

Sell, C. (1985). *Transition: The stages of adult life.* Chicago: Moody Press.

Selman, R. (1976). Social-cognitive understanding: A guide to educational and clinical practice. In T. Lickona (Ed.), *Moral development and behavior: Theory, research and social issues* (pp. 299–316). New York: Holt, Rinehart and Winston.

Sheehy, G. (1976). *Passages: Predictable crises of adult life.* New York: Dutton.

Sherrill, L. (1954). *The struggle of the soul.* New York: Macmillan.

Shulman, V., Restiano-Baumann, L., & Butler, L. (Eds.). (1985). *The future of Piagetian theory: The neo-Piagetians.* New York: Plenum Press.

Smith, K., & Berg, D. (1987). *Paradoxes of group life.* San Francisco: Jossey-Bass.

Smith, W. (1963). *The meaning and end of religion.* New York: Macmillan.

Steele, L. (1991). *On the way: A practical theology of Christian formation.* Grand Rapids: Baker.

Stinnett, N., & Defrain, J. (1985). *The secrets of strong families.* New York: Berkley Books.

Stith, M. (1969). *Understanding children.* Nashville: Convention Press.

Stonehouse, C. (1980). *Patterns in moral development.* Waco, TX: Word.

Talbert, C. (1985). Discipleship in Luke-Acts. In F. Segovia (Ed.). *Discipleship in the New Testament* (pp. 62–75). Philadelphia: Fortress Press.

Taylor, D. (1986). *The myth of certainty: The reflective Christian and the risk of commitment.* Waco, TX: Jarrell.

Vaillant, G. (1977). *Adaptation to life.* Boston, MA: Little, Brown, and Co.

Van Wicklin, J., Burwell, R., & Butman, R. (1994). Squandered years: Identity foreclosed students and the liberal education they avoid. In J. Lee & G. Stokes (Eds.), *Assessment in Christian higher education* (pp. 75–102). Washington: University Press of America.

Vitz, P. (1990). The use of stories in moral development: New psychological reasons for an old educational method. *American Psychologist, 45*(6f), 709–720.

Vygotsky, L. (1978). *Mind in society: The development of higher psychological process.* Cambridge, MA: Harvard University Press.

———. (1962). *Thought and language.* Cambridge, MA: MIT Press.

REFERENCE LIST

Wadsworth, B. (1989). *Piaget's theory of cognitive development.* New York: David McKay.

Wangerin, W. (1986). *The Orphean passages: The drama of faith* (1st ed.). San Francisco: Harper & Row.

Wertsch, J. (1985). *Vygotsky and the social formation of mind.* Cambridge, MA: Harvard University Press.

Wertsch, J., & Rogoff, B. (1984). Editor's notes. In B. Rogoff & J. Wertsch (Eds.), *Children's learning in the "zone of proximal development": New directions for child development* (pp. 1–6). San Francisco: Jossey-Bass.

Westerhoff, J. (1976). *Will our children have faith?* New York: Seabury Press.

Westfall, J. (1991). *Coloring outside the lines: Discipleship for the undisciplined.* New York: Harper Collins.

Williams, J., & Stith, M. (1974). *Middle childhood: Behavior and development.* New York: Macmillan.

Wlodkowski, R. (1985). *Enhancing adult motivation to learn: A guide to improving instruction & increasing learner achievement.* San Francisco: Jossey-Bass.

Yancey, P. (1992). *Disappointment with God.* Grand Rapids: Zondervan.

Contributors

Dr. Frances Anderson is Professor of Christian Education and Coordinator of Youth Ministries at North Park Theological Seminary.

Dr. Richard E. Butman is Professor of Psychology at Wheaton College.

Dr. John M. Dettoni, formerly Professor of Christian Formation and Discipleship at Fuller Theological Seminary, is President of Chrysalis Ministries, an international educational ministry, based in San Clemente, California.

Dr. Perry G. Downs is Professor of Christian Education at Trinity Evangelical Divinity University.

Dr. Robert Drovdahl is Professor of Religion and Educational Ministries at Seattle Pacific University.

Dr. Julie A. Gorman is Assistant Professor and Coordinator of the Christian Formation and Discipleship Program at Fuller Theological Seminary.

Dr. Ronald T. Habermas is McGee Professor of Biblical Studies at John Brown University.

Dr. Donald M. Joy is Professor of Human Development and occupies the Ray and Mary Jo West Chair of Christian Education at Asbury Theological Seminary.

David R. Moore is in the Department of Psychology at the University of Utah.

Dr. Cynthia Jones Neal is Associate Professor of Psychology at Wheaton College.

Dr. Jim B. Parsons is a Professor in the Department of Secondary Education at the University of Alberta.

Dr. James E. Plueddemann, formerly Professor of Christian Education at Wheaton College, is General Director of SIM, based in Charlotte, North Carolina.

Dr. Les L. Steele is Professor of Religion and Educational Ministries at Seattle Pacific University.

Dr. Catherine Stonehouse is Orlean Bullard Beeson Professor of Christian Education at Asbury Theological Seminary.

Dr. Ted W. Ward is G.W. Aldeen Chair of International Studies and Missions and Professor of Christian Education at Trinity Evangelical Divinity School.

Dr. James C. Wilhoit is Professor of Christian Education at Wheaton College.

Dr. Fred Wilson was most recently chair of the Christian Education Department at Wheaton College.